ADAPT OR DIE

ADAPT OR DIE

Transforming Your Supply Chain into an Adaptive Business Network

CLAUS HEINRICH

with Bob Betts

John Wiley & Sons, Inc.

Published by John Wiley & Sons, Inc., Hoboken, New Jersey.
Published simultaneously in Canada.

For general information on our other products and services please contact our
Customer Care Department within the U.S. at (800) 762-2974, outside the United
States at (317) 572-3993 or fax (317) 572-4002.

Wiley also publishes its books in a variety of electronic formats. Some content that
appears in print may not be available in electronic books. For more information about
Wiley products, visit our web site at www.wiley.com.

Library of Congress Cataloging-in-Publication Data:

Heinrich, Claus.
  Adapt or die : transforming your supply chain into an adaptive
business network / Claus Heinrich.
      p.   cm.
Includes bibliographical references and index.
    ISBN 0-471-26543-8 (CLOTH : alk. paper)
  1. Industrial procurement.   2. Business networks.   I. Title.
  HD39.5 .B485 2002
  658.7'2—dc21
                                                    2002013140

Printed in the United States of America.

10 9 8 7 6 5 4 3 2 1

New technologies for supply chain management and flexible manufacturing imply that businesses can perceive imbalances in inventories at a very early stage—virtually in real time—and can cut production promptly in response to the developing signs of unintended inventory building.

—Alan Greenspan, in testimony to the U.S. Senate
Committee on Banking, Housing, and
Urban Affairs, February 13, 2001

ACKNOWLEDGMENTS

I would like to acknowledge and thank my collaborator, Bob Betts. Without his insight, research, and dedication, this book would not have been possible. His many years of operational experience contributed so much to the vision that is outlined in this book.

Many others at SAP contributed to this project and deserve great thanks: Ed Brice, Bob Cummings, Shoumen Datta, Albrecht Diener, J. Harris, Chuck Lawrence, Alex Renz, Wolfgang Runge, Ralph Schneider, Diane Tracy, Jim Vrieling, and Karen Zwissler.

I would also like to thank our agent Kelli Jerome and the many talented people at John Wiley & Sons, especially our editor Matthew Holt and publisher Larry Alexander. Also invaluable were Marketing Managers Laurie Harting and Michael Patterson, Production Managers Maureen Drexel and Linda Indig, and Susan Alfieri, Tamara Hummel, Joe Marchetti, Dean Karrel, George Stanley, and the Wiley salesforce.

We are also grateful to many accomplished people outside of SAP for their excellent review comments. Without them lending their collective experience and time, this book would not have the relevance to real business that was wished for. This includes David Simchi-Levi of MIT, Hubert Osterle and Elgar Fleisch of the University of St. Gallen, Ray Lane of Kleiner Perkins Caufeild & Byers, Jake Barr of Procter and Gamble, Fred Kuglin of CGE&Y, Fred Ricer Jr. of PwC Consulting, and Philip Kaminsky of UC Berkeley.

Finally, without the energy and style of our additional writing collaborators, Andrea Carlos, Bill McRae, and Corey Grice, the text would not have taken shape. Also I would like to thank Larry Heikell for his help with editing, Aaran Riddle and Anna Skinner for their help with research and resource material, and Johanna Weseman for her logistical support.

Contents

When Bad Things Happen to Good Companies

Bad is never good until worse happens.

—Danish proverb

You're the CEO of a mid-size company. Until recently, your products were making customers happy, your revenues were growing at a steady pace, and the financial community was satisfied with your performance.

But lately your widgets aren't flying off the shelves the way they used to. Revenue is falling, earnings-per-share is being squeezed, and your customers are growing increasingly dissatisfied with your products and support. You need to get to the bottom of this, and quickly, before the situation worsens.

You gather your leadership team into a conference room, and one by one you point your finger at each of your top executives.

"What's your solution?" you ask.

"We must significantly slow our rate of spending," says the chief financial officer.

"We should eliminate some of the competition by acquiring our No. 4 competitor," offers the chief operating officer.

"We need to upgrade our technology and business processes to improve efficiency," says the chief information officer.

"We should upgrade our equipment to improve our production consistency and quality," says the vice president of engineering.

"We need to discount our existing inventory to maintain our market share," the vice president of sales interjects.

"We could always just hire more customer service reps," quips the vice president of customer service.

After everyone goes back to work, you sit down, realizing the meeting was a flop. Cost cutting, acquisitions, technology and equipment upgrades, discounts—these are the same types of contradictory solutions you've heard in the past. The fact is that you've tried all of these solutions at one point or another. Your company was doing well for a stretch in the hyper-economy of the late 1990s, but here it is at the start of the twenty-first century, and once again, you're falling behind. To thrive, you know you must break the pattern of cost cutting, layoffs, and similar measures when business is bad, only to have those same measures come back to haunt you when the company is rejuvenated by an improving economy or other market variable. But what can you do?

THE STATE OF BUSINESS TODAY

If this dilemma sounds familiar, you are not alone. Despite the efforts by companies over the past two decades to prosper and maintain a competitive edge, business performance is not what it should be. Consider the following:

- *Profits are under pressure.* In 2001, the profits of U.S.-based, nonfinancial companies were at their lowest level since 1995, off $1 billion from the previous year.[1]

- *Companies continue to accumulate costly inventory.* Despite inventory-cutting initiatives in recent years, factory inventories continue to grow steadily as the economy expands. From 1997 to 2000, real inventory levels in U.S. manufacturing increased quarter on quarter from $436.8 billion to $490.3 billion—an increase of $53.5 billion, or 12 percent, in three years.[2]

- *Earnings per share are declining.* Earnings per share of S&P 500 companies fell 50 percent in the fourth quarter of 2001 compared with the previous year, the sharpest decline in over 50 years.[3]

- *The return on assets (ROA) is declining.* For mature companies, there has been a significant drop in ROA from almost 8 percent in the 1950s to only 3 percent in the 1990s.[4]

■ *Market capital values are declining.* From 2000 to 2001, the total market capitalization for the Forbes Market Value 500, composed of America's largest public companies, dropped 20.5 percent. In this 12-month period, Cisco Systems, Microsoft, Intel, Lucent Technologies, and Oracle lost more than $1 trillion in total value. The following year, the carnage continued. In 2001, the aggregate net income of the 500 most profitable U.S. firms declined 23 percent.[5]

EXPECTING THE UNEXPECTED

Past attempts to remedy these problems have provided some incremental gains, yet the problems persist. The cycle continues. Companies have spent hundreds of millions of dollars on information technology. They've followed advice from the best business leaders and consultants, and still the cycle repeats itself.

It's true for businesses large and small. Businesses today keep applying the same old solutions to their problems. And they end up repeating these up-and-down cycles rather than planning for and performing well under bad conditions—and putting themselves in a position to exploit the good times.

Today the problems facing businesses have shifted again. The rules of business have changed again. And companies globally are struggling to adapt quickly enough to exploit the new market conditions . . . again.

Waiting outside the walls of every company are the shocks of unforeseen circumstances, be they from economic, regulatory, or geopolitical impacts. Your main competitor may unveil a new technology that renders your product obsolete. A new study might be released that spurs customer demand for a different product from the one you're producing. Or the economy could go into recession, presenting you with immediate problems on both the demand and supply sides of your business.

The reality is that the predictable cycles your business may have once known will never return. It's as if a rock has been tossed into a pool of previously still water. The ripples begin to roil the waters. Then there is a second rock, and then another and another. The once calm waters churn with motion. And the rocks and shocks keep coming. Business today is in much the same state. The shocks keep coming at an ever-increasing pace. Business as usual is no longer usual. The new business reality is constant change.

To succeed in the twenty-first century economy, companies need to adapt to a new environment in which everything is in motion. Transforming your business to succeed in this rapidly accelerating environment is not optional. In short, it's adapt or die.

A New Vision for Business

Businesses today need a new way of operating that gives them the flexibility to respond quickly to unexpected changes. They need a new operating model that enables them to adapt to difficult economic conditions, while also putting them in a position to exploit a more favorable economy. And they need sustainable opportunities for increasing revenue, reducing costs, and making the most out of what their company does best.

This book is about a new method of doing business aimed at helping companies achieve these goals. Called the *adaptive business network,* this new business model joins companies into an adaptable and flexible set of business relationships (see Figure I.1). By linking companies through

FIGURE I.1   CRITICAL BUSINESS ELEMENTS OF THE ADAPTIVE BUSINESS NETWORK

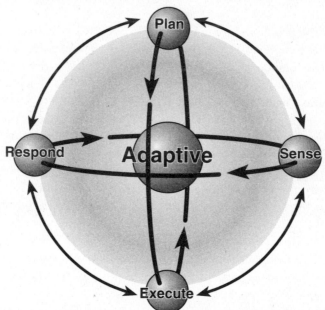

ALL BUSINESSES TODAY HAVE THESE FOUR ELEMENTS, BUT MANAGE THEM WITH VARYING DEGREES OF EFFECTIVENESS.

standard business processes and common technology, the adaptive business network allows them to work together as a loose network of partners. Working together with other businesses in the network, each company is able to respond more swiftly to changing market conditions than it could on its own. Companies within the network remain autonomous, but are able to leverage the network's cumulative ability to:

- Plan and anticipate demand and supply.
- Execute plans efficiently and effectively.
- Sense events that affect the plans as those events occur, and analyze them for impact.
- Respond to and learn from ever-changing business conditions.

The adaptive business network is designed to help businesses quickly respond to changing market conditions by capitalizing on the strengths of operating units within the company and trading partners outside the company. It is a model based on mutual goal setting—and not limited to the traditional buyer-seller relationship that exists today between most trading partners.

Companies within the adaptive business network are able to react quickly to changing customer demands by efficiently exchanging and responding to information, to the benefit of all participating companies. In addition, new partners can be added to the network quickly

WHAT IS AN ADAPTIVE BUSINESS NETWORK?

Definitions convey the fundamental character of words, phrases, or terms. By breaking the concept of the adaptive business network down to its base vocabulary construction, a clearer understanding of its capabilities and goals can be achieved.

Adaptive (*adjective*)—The ability to rapidly anticipate and/or respond to changing environmental conditions.

Business (*noun*)—Commercial, industrial, and professional dealings as well as the volume and amount of commercial trade.

Network (*noun*)—An interconnected or interrelated chain, group, or system that enables communication among all participants.

and inexpensively as market conditions change and new business opportunities arise.

Participation in an adaptive business network puts companies in a position to remain flexible, resourceful, and profitable in a constantly changing business environment. It allows businesses to meet the increasing demands of consumers who expect high-quality, personalized products designed and delivered in ever-shortening time windows, and to attract new customers and sales based on the ability to meet those changing consumer needs. The network helps reduce costs by streamlining processes to focus on what each participating company does best, and it allows all participants to collaborate dynamically with their partners to produce new and innovative products and services.

In short, the adaptive business network provides new opportunities to:

- Increase profit margins.
- Set appropriate levels for inventory.
- Accelerate cash-to-cash cycles.
- Increase earnings per share.
- Improve the effectiveness of corporate expenditures.
- Capture a greater return on assets.

A MATTER OF SURVIVAL

The adaptive business network is not intended to help companies improve their manufacturing techniques. Instead its aim is to help reduce the everyday bottlenecks of working with suppliers and customers. It greatly reduces the time delays that occur, for example, when relaying information about customer purchases to affected companies along the supply chain. In addition, it dramatically reduces the slowdowns that arise when coordinating with other companies to fill customer orders.

Nor is the adaptive business network a pricing-based scheme in which companies within a network jointly set prices. By taking a collaborative approach to managing costs in response to changing market conditions, companies that participate in an adaptive business network will achieve greater profits than they could by operating in isolation. However, each business continues to operate as an autonomous entity. Revenue sharing is possible but it is not a primary objective of the network.

Finally, the adaptive business network is not another budget-bursting IT project. Rather, its primary aim is to help companies adopt more effective business processes for working with their partners so that each participant achieves greater advantage than is possible by operating alone. Chances are good that your company already owns most of the technical infrastructure necessary to begin building an adaptive business network. In fact, adaptive business networks—based on the tried and tested fundamentals of effective business processes—will allow companies to build even more value from existing investments in IT and other business initiatives.

An adaptive business network is a strategy for entire companies and their partners, including their production, sales, operations, logistics, customer service, and purchasing teams. It is not a project that any individual company or partner can take on in isolation. Companies must undertake this effort cooperatively.

Participating in an adaptive business network requires a major shift in the way companies view their business and their trading partners. First, it requires moving from traditional supplier and customer relationships into genuine partnerships based on collaborative goal setting.

Moreover, the move to an adaptive business network enables participants to adopt standardized business processes, new measurement systems, and toolkits that ensure quality and success. An adaptive business network will enable partner companies to develop a business foundation based on measurable, sustainable, and tangible results.

For most companies, moving to an adaptive business network will become a matter of survival. Companies that quickly embrace this new operating model will be the winners well into the twenty-first century. They will quickly discover new revenue opportunities and cost cutting measures, and will ultimately become more nimble, focused, and competitive. More agile companies that can deliver products and services faster will pass businesses that are slow to respond. On the other hand, companies that do not move on the opportunity to enhance their organizational agility will watch their market share decrease and their profits fall. The inability to respond to rapidly changing market conditions will undermine their economic viability.

WHAT YOU WILL LEARN FROM READING THIS BOOK

The concepts in this book apply to multiple industries and roles within companies. For companies in mature industries, *Adapt or Die* provides the opportunity to look forward while learning from the past. For companies in new or emerging industries, this book offers a road map for success. An adaptive business network can provide real benefits for any company, whether it is in the manufacturing, retail, or service sector.

The adaptive business network must be taught, sponsored, and learned both within and among participating organizations. Such networks emphasize peer-to-peer communication, which means that everyone involved in the business processes has an important role to play. This book is essential reading material for all employees who want to contribute to making their company sustainable and competitive into the twenty-first century.

This book will help companies understand the vision of adaptive business networks and prepare businesses for the opportunities such networks will provide. The first chapters describe some of the common problems businesses face today and examine existing models for working with partners. The book then turns to the vision of the adaptive business network and how this business model can help companies solve many of those key problems. The second part of the book discusses how to prepare for an adaptive business network and describes how to move to this way of doing business in four, concrete steps. Finally, the last chapters of the book explain how the adaptive business network can work today, and offer a view for how it will work in the future.

After reading this book, you will understand how such networks operate, the strategic advantages they offer, what changes your company needs to make to move to an adaptive business network, and what technological requirements are demanded to make the transition a success. In short, you as a businessperson will learn what you can do to realign your company, your business practices, and your workforce to remain competitive in the twenty-first century economy.

CHAPTER ONE

In Search of the Holy Grail

Make voyages. Attempt them. There's nothing else.

—Tennessee Williams

It's a simple fact: The rules of business have changed.

In the New Economy, it's all about speed and service. With today's instantaneous availability of information, new cultural trends can take hold globally within weeks—and fade just as rapidly. With technological advances occurring at such a pace, new products quickly gain in popularity, only to be replaced by more advanced gadgets.

What's more, customers are unwilling to settle for mass-produced items and plain-vanilla services. They want specialized products in the size, color, and shape they prefer. They expect these products to show up at the exact time and place they need them. To keep up, companies must anticipate changing market conditions and produce a greater variety of customized products in the rapid time frames customers expect.

The challenge for business has always been to get the right products and services to the customer at the right time and at the right price. It's an ever-greater challenge with today's accelerated pace. Corporations face a whirlwind of change, highly variable demand, and shifting economic, geographic, and political influences. Businesses no longer have an option: They must adapt to survive.

What happened during the dot-com crash to Cisco Systems, the leading supplier of telecommunications equipment and Internet routing infrastructure, provides a good example of the importance of being flexible as market conditions change. When business was booming in the 1990s, Cisco signed long-term contracts with suppliers committing to inventory

SHRINKING SHELF LIVES

Over the years, everyday consumer products and services have changed to accommodate the rapidly changing nature of people and their growing expectations. Today, consumers have a broader range of wants and are less willing to wait for them. A look at children's toys and music recording media provide cases in point.

Toys Lose Their Luster

In 1959, Mattel introduced the Barbie Doll, and more than 40 years later, it is still popular. Yet, toys introduced on the market today may have a shelf life of a couple of years, if that. There are Tamagotchi games, Beanie Babies, and Cabbage Patch Kids dolls. There are Star Wars and Power Ranger action figures and Harry Potter toys spawned by movies and books. There are Spice Girl dolls generated by the rock group.

Music Technology Quickly Advances

From the 1940s to the 1980s, teenagers bought LP recordings of their favorite music. Yet, today's teenagers will likely replace their music recording collections several times to keep up with advancing technology. The 33-rpm record, first introduced in 1948, was the leading audio storage technology until the compact disc surpassed it in the late 1980s. However, today MP3 files downloadable from the Internet are already superseding the CD. If the same pattern continues, MP3 will have an even shorter life span as it's replaced by even more advanced audio recording technology.

and production capacities months in advance. This allowed Cisco to speed shipments of products to customers and maintain profitability.

The approach worked well when times were good and sales were strong. But when the economy started to slow and many of the start-up telecommunications companies and Internet businesses Cisco served went out of business, the company suddenly found its warehouses full of obsolete routers and other networking equipment, with payments due on contracted capacity commitments. Cisco suddenly became painfully aware of the need to quickly adapt to anticipate potential market shifts. Once they occurred, the company lacked the ability to respond to them in a timely fashion.

This inability to comprehend what was happening and respond quickly cost the company dearly. Cisco's revenues dropped 30 percent in the first quarter of 2001 over the previous three months, and the company announced it would lay off 8,500 workers and write off $2.5 billion in excess inventory.[1]

The situation wasn't unique to Cisco. Many high-tech companies were caught off guard by the dot-com failures. Although market changes will always be difficult to predict, companies can no longer afford to run their businesses assuming that market conditions won't change or

A HAZE OVER HAYES MODEMS*

When Dennis C. Hayes, the father of the personal computer modem, first developed the device in 1977, he had no idea his popular invention would spawn a company that would ultimately collapse due to its inability to adapt to market changes.

Hayes Corp., originally D.C. Hayes Associates Inc., was the premier maker of computer modems through the 1980s and into the 1990s. The company established an industry standard for modem commands and relished in its dominance over a market that saw most other modem makers label their products as "Hayes compatible."

Personal problems and a prior bankruptcy filing distracted the founder and his company, causing Hayes Corp. to stumble. Analysts and industry experts say Hayes was slow to capitalize on the upgrade to 56kbps modems just as overseas sales slipped due to the Asian economic crisis.

Suddenly, Hayes had trouble competing with equivalent models from U.S. Robotics, 3Com, and other modem makers. Meanwhile, modems began to be bundled with PCs, which, coupled with competition from low-cost Asian manufacturers, turned the dial-up modem into a commodity.

By then, Hayes had overproduced its modems, leading to excess inventory and the eventual halting of manufacturing shifts, worker layoffs, and a second Chapter 11 bankruptcy filing in 1998. Hayes failed to recognize the shifting market, overproduced its products, and couldn't sell its excess inventory. Hayes failed to adapt, and the company died.

---

* The Great Idea Finder, "Dennis C. Hayes" (October 30, 2001), http://www.ideafinder.com/history/inventors/hayes.htm.

will change at the same pace as yesteryear. To play by the new rules of today's fast-moving economy, businesses need mechanisms to allow them to swiftly react and change direction—even when they cannot foresee what lies ahead.

THE CURRENT BUSINESS CLIMATE

Today, businesses face a number of key challenges:

- *Globalization Demands Ever-Quicker Response Times.* For most companies, it is no longer sufficient to have an international presence with stand-alone bureaus in multiple countries. A company's operations, products, and employees must now be coordinated globally yet enable local operators to react to local market conditions on a local basis. The complexity of operating on a global scale requires that organizations have the infrastructure in place to "follow the sun" 24 hours a day, seven days a week, worldwide. Companies are doing business with new partners in unfamiliar languages and distant time zones. They are employing workers in different cultures with different work habits and legal protections. They are competing with companies, products, and ways of doing business that may be completely unfamiliar. And they are branching into new and unfamiliar markets. Meeting these challenges requires that businesses respond quickly and communicate instantaneously across all their operations worldwide.

- *Industrial Production Capacity Exceeds Demand.* Improvements to manufacturing processes have resulted in a situation where many industries now produce more goods than the economy has the capacity to consume. Moreover, the speed at which companies can add new production capacity outpaces the speed at which new markets develop. As a result, companies are increasingly finding themselves in a position where they cannot sell enough products to keep ahead of working capital, additionally, these companies look for ways to market the excess capacity through collaborative activities with companies that may require additional capacity. To thrive in this environment, companies must identify new, creative opportunities to market their products.

- *Working Capital Is Increasingly Limited.* The expectations of capital lending institutions have changed, creating a more competitive environment for access to working capital. Today, institutions are focused on earnings per share and price-and-earnings ratios (P&Es), and prefer sustained, quick-turnaround returns over long-term investments. Companies are forced first to fight for capital, and then to focus on business practices that stress short-term performance in an effort to deliver positive quarterly results, even if these actions are not in the best interest of the long-term viability and health of the company. Companies need to find ways to borrow less working capital and use it more efficiently.

■ *Consumers Have Higher Expectations Than Ever Before.* Consumers have become accustomed to getting what they want, the way they want it, right here, right now. Mass-produced goods and services no longer suffice in a climate where consumers increasingly expect customized goods and services to be tailored to their unique taste. For instance, cable TV brings in hundreds of channels 24 hours a day. But even so, consumers are increasingly turning to digital recording devices like TiVo, which allow viewers to personalize their cable programming into their own "channels." For example, the machine can be programmed to record only Star Trek reruns, Italian soccer games or all the films in a given week that star Audrey Hepburn.

But it's not just entertainment. Consumer expectations are higher than ever across a broad spectrum of industries. For example, 20 years ago travel by airplane was expensive, time-consuming to arrange and restricted mostly to well-dressed business travelers. Today, nearly everyone can afford to fly, and customers instead have turned to complaining about the food, how long it takes to reach their destination, and how crowded the planes are. Today if customers don't find the price they want, or the flexibility in layover stops and flight times, they frequently will seek out another competitor.

These factors—increasing globalization, excess capacity, reduced access to capital, and higher customer expectations—present new challenges for business. To meet these challenges, companies need to be more adaptable and flexible than ever before. They need to develop quick response times on a global basis. They need to develop new markets for their products and borrow working capital more efficiently. They need to adapt to keep up with their competitors and to respond to changes in customer demand. In the New Economy, speed and variety are key. Although some companies have made strides in meeting growing expectations, many businesses are struggling to keep up with the pace (see Figure 1.1).

FIGURE 1.1   MOORE'S LAW

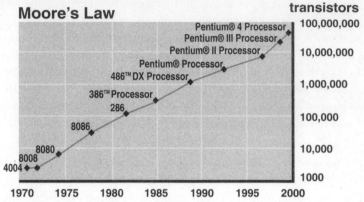

MORE THAN 25 YEARS AGO, INTEL CO-FOUNDER GORDON MOORE
PREDICTED THAT THE NUMBER OF TRANSISTORS ON A MICRO-
PROCESSOR WOULD DOUBLE APPROXIMATELY EVERY 18 MONTHS.
THAT PREDICTION, WHICH STILL HOLDS TRUE TODAY, DEMON-
STRATES THE RAPID PACE OF TECHNOLOGICAL ADVANCES THAT
HAS OCCURRED OVER THE PAST 25 YEARS. TO KEEP UP AND
AVOID BEING PASSED BY THEIR COMPETITORS, COMPANIES MUST
CREATE MORE PRODUCTS AND GET THEM TO MARKET FASTER.
REPRINTED BY PERMISSION OF INTEL CORPORATION, COPYRIGHT
INTEL CORPORATION.

THE SAME OLD RESPONSE

In response to these changing business dynamics, many organizations
have tried to either grow from within as vertically integrated companies
or assemble smaller companies into massive corporate conglomerates.
Management teams continue to focus on a variety of business efficiency
initiatives that are confined to fixing problems solely within the four walls
of their company. Some have sought mergers and acquisitions or other equity vehicles such as joint ventures as the best route for adapting to
changes in the business environment.

These attempts at reaching the Holy Grail of business most often fall
short of this goal on one account: They don't provide the flexibility that
organizations need to succeed in today's fast-moving economy. Companies
keep paving the same stretch of road again and again, hoping the new as-
phalt will make their journey more comfortable (Figure 1.2). As it turns

FIGURE 1.2   THE WINDING ROAD OF PROGRESS

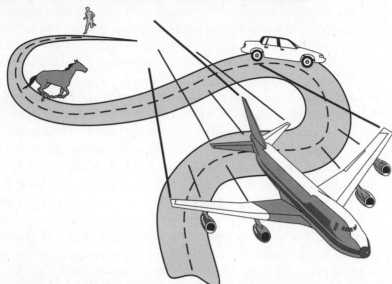

COMPANIES FREQUENTLY STRIVE TO IMPROVE THEIR BUSINESS PROCESSES BY SIMPLY DOING THEM FASTER, CHEAPER, AND BETTER. IN THE ABOVE EXAMPLE, THE SAME STRETCH OF ROAD IS FIRST COVERED ON FOOT, THEN BY HORSE, THEN BY AUTOMOBILE, WHEN, IN REALITY, THE FASTEST AND MOST DIRECT ROUTE MAY BE TO TAKE AN ENTIRELY DIFFERENT ROAD OF TRANSPORT. BUSINESSES OFTEN FOLLOW THE SAME INDIRECT PATH, COMMITTING THE SAME MISTAKES AS IN THE PAST, WHEN THERE MAY BE AN ENTIRELY DIFFERENT, FASTER AND MORE DIRECT WAY OF DOING THINGS.

out, the shortest route is often somewhere else entirely. The problems have shifted, and the old rules no longer apply.

What's needed is a new approach that provides the flexibility required to adapt to the rapid pace of today's business world, and extends beyond the company's walls. In the New Economy, a company's success no longer depends on how efficiently it operates in isolation, but rather on its ability to form flexible interdependent relationships with its partners, both customers and all suppliers.

Keeping Everything Under One Roof

The classic vertically integrated company owns and operates most or all of the elements of its supply and distribution system. It is usually a collection of smaller divisions and wholly-owned subsidiaries operated as a single company. Each of these is responsible for producing a component, a product, or a service that goes into the finished offering of the larger company. Many companies are managed as top-down hierarchical structures. Management decisions are passed down the authority ladder to the company's operation level (Figure 1.3).

A wood products company such as Weyerhaeuser Co. provides a good example of a vertically integrated company. Weyerhaeuser controls a supply chain that literally goes from dirt to consumer, and it owns almost all of the component industries in between. As of December 31, 2000, the company owned or was leasing 38 million acres of woodland in the United States and Canada.[2] From this land, timber is harvested and shipped on Weyerhaeuser-owned logging trucks to Weyerhaeuser lumber or pulp mills. The resulting lumber or paper is shipped, on Weyerhaeuser trucks, to distributors or to a Weyerhaeuser building site. Weyerhaeuser also owns and operates a real estate and land development company, which specializes, unsurprisingly, in building wooden houses.

On the other hand, a conglomerate is a centralized corporation that acts something like a holding company. It comprises independent companies managed as stand-alone entities, though the central corporation provides some direction and strategy and, in some cases, a unifying brand.

Philip Morris Cos. Inc., a multinational tobacco products company, is a conglomerate. In addition to making cigarettes, Philip Morris owns a stable of prominent food and beverage companies—including Kraft Foods, makers of Kool-Aid, Oreos, and other confections, and Miller Brewing Co., makers of Miller beer—which are managed as distinct brands. Philip Morris remains the "silent" owner, while the companies are allowed to pursue their own marketing opportunities.

A conglomerate like Philip Morris is similar to a vertical company like Weyerhaeuser in that they are both hierarchically integrated, inherently slow to respond, and normalize on the least radical thought. Companies of all types, whether they are like Weyerhaeuser or Philip Morris, need to adjust their structure so they can adapt to ever changing market conditions.

Historically, the business strategy of keeping everything under one roof was a competitive choice as companies sought to attain critical mass. In a time when access to resources and availability of distribution networks were a problem, the vertically integrated company and the conglomerate were the most efficient operating structures. The strategy allowed companies to maintain control over all facets of supply and distribution related to their products. Companies were able to increase their reach by

FIGURE 1.3 DECISION MAKING IN VERTICAL COMPANIES

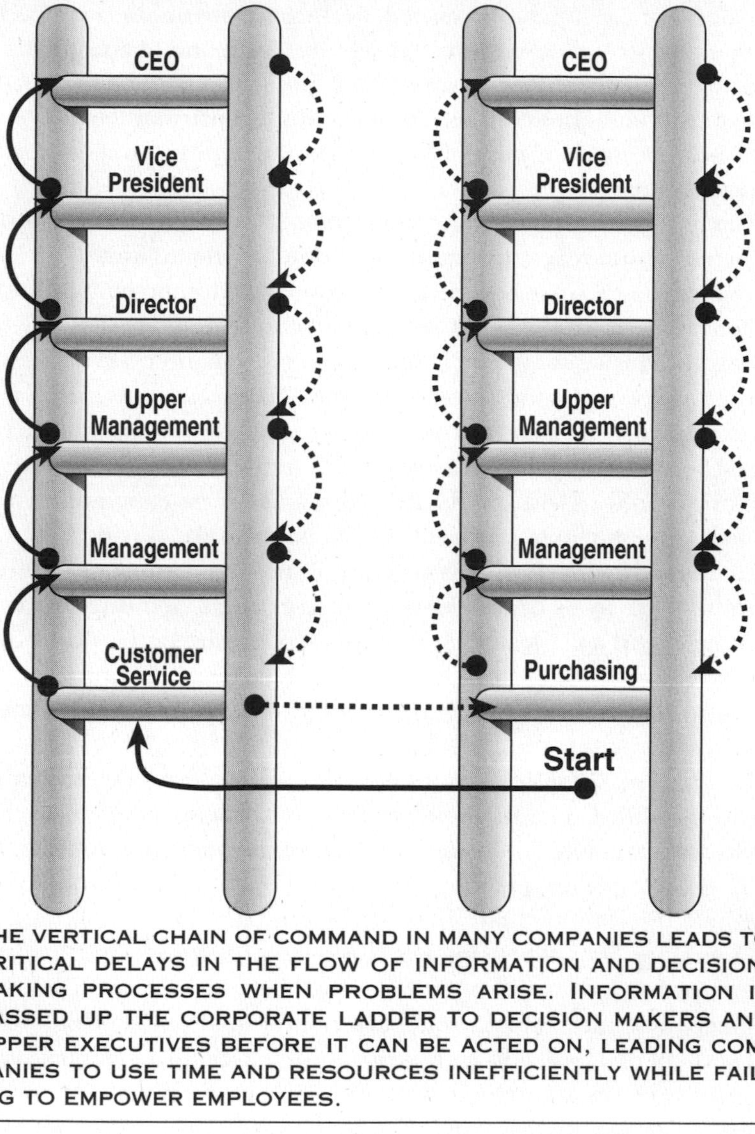

CEO	CEO
Vice President	Vice President
Director	Director
Upper Management	Upper Management
Management	Management
Customer Service	Purchasing

Start

THE VERTICAL CHAIN OF COMMAND IN MANY COMPANIES LEADS TO CRITICAL DELAYS IN THE FLOW OF INFORMATION AND DECISION-MAKING PROCESSES WHEN PROBLEMS ARISE. INFORMATION IS PASSED UP THE CORPORATE LADDER TO DECISION MAKERS AND UPPER EXECUTIVES BEFORE IT CAN BE ACTED ON, LEADING COMPANIES TO USE TIME AND RESOURCES INEFFICIENTLY WHILE FAILING TO EMPOWER EMPLOYEES.

expanding to provide an entire supply chain's worth of goods and services. Because the companies owned all the units within the supply chain, they could control where raw materials came from and how products were delivered to the consumer. Owning everything also gave them close oversight of costs and allowed them to maintain a consistent level of quality, which in turn made it possible to develop a solid reputation for their product brands.

Today, however, this is an expensive, inefficient, and risky way of attaining corporate reach. Companies tend to lose focus, and often spread themselves too thin as they attempt to do everything from within their own four walls. Even though it remains an enduringly popular way to operate, in the fast-moving electronic economy, having everything under one roof has proved cumbersome and unwieldy.

As conglomerates and vertically-oriented companies grow, they slow down. They lose the ability to move quickly and strategically because their structure is built to withstand external market pressures and has a hierarchical decision-making process. Anything that falls outside of the delegation hierarchy is dealt with as an "exception." In an effort to be diligent, committees are formed, task forces are structured, and due diligence is performed until a critical mass of managers and executives believe they have the information necessary to make a decision. This process, by its very nature, is slow and makes it difficult to adapt to rapidly changing market conditions.

In addition, these companies often duplicate many of their internal operational functions. In some cases, costly operational roles such as human resources and financials are even duplicated from division to division, greatly inflating company-wide overhead. Similarly, the management teams of individual divisions eventually become hierarchical bureaucracies, inevitably slowing the pace of business and leading to higher overhead.

Once these hierarchies form, each operational unit tends to be managed with an eye toward its own profitability. It's called *suboptimization*—the process of ensuring one's business unit or subsidiary meets its goal despite the impact on the company's best interest. It's such a part of business today that internal bonus and incentive programs often offer rewards for business divisions to achieve levels of production that, in fact, run contrary to the company's larger goals. The goals may not be sufficiently aligned to variable demand and producing more units than the business is able to absorb might bring healthy bonuses to a few individuals, but the practice can bury the rest of the company in costly inventory.

PASSING THE BUCK

Have you ever worked in a company where each division is responsible for its own fiscal health and viability? Many companies operate this way. Often, each division is referred to as a "profit center." On the surface, individual profit centers make sense especially if the company wishes to maintain the option of selling the profit center some day in the future. After all, if a division isn't profitable, why keep it around, right?

Well, it's not that simple. Creating separate profit centers within companies often motivates workers to do whatever it takes to ensure their division is profitable—even if their actions aren't in the best interests of the entire company. For example, a production plant manager may need to run the assembly lines at maximum capacity in order to be profitable, or to achieve an annual bonus. This means the plant will make as many widgets as possible 24 hours per day. However, perhaps the market for widgets has declined and sales are slowing. It might be best for the company to balance production with demand to avoid lowering its retail price for widgets. Despite the benefits to the company of curtailing production, the production plant keeps on producing widgets to meet its division goals.

Another problem with running divisions as individual profit centers is transfer pricing. Transfer pricing occurs when two or more divisions within the same company are run as individual profit centers, but work together to develop or deliver a product. Perhaps it is engineering and production, or manufacturing and transportation. These divisions often transfer money between them to pay for services rendered. While many profit centers operate this way, it often causes workers to lose sight of the real customer. Employees often believe their customer is another division within the same company.

Wrong! The only customer is the one who purchases a company's products or services, the one that pays with actual money—not theoretical currency. Until companies rectify this problem, overhead costs will continue to rise, customers will continue to feel disillusioned, and business divisions will keep passing the buck.

THE SEARCH FOR EFFICIENCY

To compensate for the major inefficiencies brought about by such growth, many companies have turned to a variety of business excellence programs to help them operate more effectively. Over the last 20 years, businesses have implemented a myriad of initiatives in an effort to achieve greater efficiency.

These initiatives read like acronym soup—TQM, BPR, TOC, ERP, MRP, and on and on. To varying degrees, they all have helped businesses improve efficiency and reduce costs. Yet each time companies have gone through the time and expense, the elusive cure-all has eluded them. Too often companies have perceived these initiatives as stand-alone solutions.

These initiatives have had mixed results. In most situations where such programs have failed, the reasons come down to cultural, organizational, and personal inhibitors. The barriers to change are too high and companies cannot or are unwilling to make the shift. Often companies institute a fragmented solution that only addresses a part of the problem. They try to find a piece of it to digest. In other situations, companies aren't willing to make the changes required to address the problem on a permanent basis. Companies also seem to use technology as a sort of penicillin, injecting it where any problem lies and trusting that the cure will follow.

The decision to pursue these business initiatives is sound—such initiatives generally represent the best thinking of the time, and often help businesses to achieve significant improvements and provide a foundation from which to build. But business-excellence initiatives do not go far enough in today's economy, because they are focused solely on making improvements within the four walls of the company. In the New Economy, the question is no longer how effectively a company operates internally, but rather, how effectively it works with its partners, where the majority of significant time delays now exist.

Following are examples of well-known excellence initiatives that have helped businesses improve in the last decade:

- *Total Quality Management (TQM).* A highly popular business initiative, TQM focused companies on the goal of delivering quality products and services to the customer while reducing manufacturing costs by eliminating useless tasks. Originally meant to help manufacturers produce consistently high-quality products, TQM preached continuous improvement of internal company processes. Quality did improve, but in most industries today quality has become a requirement and by itself

WHEN CHANGE IS GOOD*

What do local phone giant Pacific Bell and automotive insurer Progressive Insurance have in common? Both companies know that change is in their best interests.

Struggling to cut costs and boost profits, Progressive Insurance and Pacific Bell are among the hundreds of companies that have remade their corporations by embracing Business Process Reengineering (BPR), a business productivity initiative.

BPR is a process designed to increase efficiency and boost sales through structural changes and solid planning. Companies sometimes seek quick fixes by attempting to use BPR programs to cut costs. However, companies that have successfully implemented BPR have done so by improving their service to customers and by putting solid measurements in place by which to evaluate their success.

For example, Progressive Insurance improved its service to its customers, high-risk automobile drivers, by offering them 24-hour-per-day services. It also offered them mobile claims programs in which claims adjusters travel to accident sites to survey the scene and take photographs, and on-site payment and towing services.

Like Progressive Insurance, telecommunications carrier Pacific Bell undertook its own BPR program intending not merely to cut costs, but also to increase benefits for its customers. Every time it considers changing a business process, Pacific Bell weighs the costs and benefits of doing so. The company calls this "Process Value Estimation." Pacific Bell measured its BPR successes by comparing its service to customers before and after its BPR efforts. The company, which continues to remake its core processes, has seen benefits in customer satisfaction and loyalty.

In short, change can be good for corporations, provided they begin with measurable goals aimed at improving service for customers.

* Thomas J. Housel, Arthur H. Bell, and Valery Kanevsky, "Calculating the Value of Reengineering at Pacific Bell," *Planning Review* (January 11, 1994): 40.

is no longer enough to differentiate a company and its products from its competition.

■ *Business Process Reengineering (BPR).* Another popular business initiative, BPR helped fuel the economic growth of the late 1980s and 1990s. BPR enables companies to significantly reduce costs, improve organizational efficiency, and increase customer satisfaction by streamlining their organizational processes. BPR initiatives also help remove some extraneous processes within companies and improve business fundamentals. Now BPR needs to be taken to the next step as companies develop standardized business processes with their trading partners.

■ *Theory of Constraints (TOC).* TOC improves manufacturing efficiency by identifying and reducing "constraints" or bottlenecks in the production process. TOC focuses on the idea that all production processes are interdependent, and that the speed of any system is dictated by the slowest part of the process. Like BPR, TOC now needs to be extended beyond the four walls of the company to help organizations reduce bottlenecks that occur when working with their trading partners.

■ *Resource planning.* Resource planning tools, including Enterprise Resource Planning (ERP), Material Requirements Planning (MRP), Distribution Resource Planning (DRP), and similar efforts, focus on reducing inventory, transportation costs, manufacturing bottlenecks, and other processes through improved planning. All of these initiatives are capable of providing sustainable benefits, but there have also been failures. Primarily, these initiatives were taken on as information technology projects, and the process changes were never institutionalized within the companies. With the speed of the new economy, simply planning faster is no longer effective—companies must collaboratively plan with external trading partners.

MERGER AND ACQUISITION FEVER

Many companies realize that doing it all themselves doesn't provide the speed and opportunity needed to compete in today's economy. As a result, they have turned to mergers and acquisitions.

Today, mergers and acquisition activity is at a fever pitch. You can't pick up *The Wall Street Journal,* the *Financial Times,* or the Tokyo *Yomiuri*

Shimbun without reading about another deal in the works. Whether it be Time Warner Inc. merging with America Online Inc. in the communications industry to create the largest corporate merger in U.S. history, or Daimler-Benz AG and Chrysler combining two national assets in the automotive industry, mergers are taking place in sectors as diverse as media, automotive, energy, telecommunications, paper, airline, financial services, and soft drinks.

Mergers and acquisitions typically occur for one of two reasons: to gain market share or to acquire technology, intellectual capital, or other assets. Yet, they often come with a huge price tag, both monetarily and culturally.

Mergers and acquisitions are painful because businesses often view them as financial transactions and overlook the complex business-process-engineering problems they present until well after the problems start to occur. Integrating business functions such as human resources and customer service can be hugely challenging. Combining processes, data, and information systems can be both time-consuming and expensive.

Second, the cultural challenges of merging two companies are enormous. Once a merger occurs, loyalties to the old company often prevent workers from performing their best for the new one. Moreover, the management cultures of the merged companies often collide, leading to irresolvable conflicts that prevent the merged company from functioning

A MARRIAGE LOSES LUSTER

The merger of America Online, the world's leading Internet service provider, and Time Warner, a major global media conglomerate, created a powerful new corporation with potential implications for the New Economy. But like so many mergers before it, the AOL-Time Warner marriage did not gain in capital value following its completion. In January 2000, when the board of directors of both companies approved the deal, the combined market value of the companies stood at approximately $350 billion. By May 2002, however, the market capitalization of AOL Time Warner was about $78 billion. The value of the combined companies did not fall only because of the merger. All companies in this business sector have experienced significant capitalization loss. In the case of AOL and Time Warner, the merger has exacerbated an already difficult situation.

effectively. Finally, there's the problem of customer loyalty. Customers who were loyal to the old company may not be loyal to the new one, especially if the brands and procedures they are accustomed to are replaced by those of the new company.

JOINT VENTURES

On the surface, joint ventures and other equity-based alliances would seem to provide an excellent stepping-stone between a merger and a true partnership. While mergers combine two existing companies, joint ventures create a new company as an outgrowth of two otherwise separate companies. For example, telecommunications giants AT&T and British Telecom created a joint venture, dubbed Concert, to serve the worldwide communications needs of multinational corporations. Similarly, Microsoft, the world's largest software company, and U.S. television programming company NBC created the MSNBC joint venture to provide news and information and to blend the data-driven world of the Internet with the more conventional medium of television.

Companies form joint ventures to create new products or services, or to give hidden business units the opportunity to operate and innovate freely on their own. Joint ventures also allow companies to tackle new markets without the constraining regulations and other obstacles facing the parent companies.

However, joint ventures rarely provide the level of integration and cooperation that the founding companies hoped for. For one, they require an entirely new, independent management team. This new team takes time to assemble and more time to reach peak performance. Even then, few joint ventures are ever truly autonomous, instead operating in the shadow of their parent companies.

In addition, new products and services developed by the joint venture can sometimes be tainted in the marketplace by their affiliation with the parent companies. For example, MSNBC has yet to turn a profit, and the company's news operation suffers from ongoing concerns that Microsoft's involvement will harm MSNBC's objectivity with regard to technology and other news. Concert was dissolved in October 2001 after annual losses of $800 million and tepid demand.

For a variety of reasons, joint ventures offer some competitive benefits for businesses. However, they also can be problematic, and those challenges often outweigh the benefits.

M&A, JV, divestitures, and all other forms of legal arrangements will continue and are often not the root cause of the business's difficulty. However, to believe that through an essentially legal arrangement tremendous business benefits will magically materialize has been proven wrong in the past 20 years.

THE STATE OF PARTNERSHIPS TODAY

In today's fast-paced economy, keeping all business processes under one roof is too cumbersome and unwieldy. Business initiatives have helped, but don't strike at the heart of the problem. Mergers and acquisitions come with an enormous price tag, both logistically and culturally. Joint ventures and other equity-based alliances often fail to provide the level of integration and cooperation required for success.

So where is the Holy Grail that has eluded companies despite all of their efforts? It's very simple, and it comes down to this: Businesses must cooperate today to survive tomorrow. A company's success in the twenty-first century economy will be determined by the relationships it develops with its suppliers and customers.

Like mergers and acquisitions, these supply chain partnerships help companies to quickly acquire a technology, product, or market access they don't currently have. With the ability to easily add and drop trading partners as strategic needs change, companies can adapt to changing market conditions much more quickly than is possible by keeping all their operations within the four walls of the company.

Such partnerships also present a way for companies to develop the broader mix of offerings needed to meet the demand for personalized products. In addition, they allow companies to strategically bundle products and services in ways that distinguish them from their competitors.

Over the years, companies have made strides in working with partners along the supply chain. Some companies pursue linear supply chain strategies, forming strategic buyer-seller relationships with their suppliers and customers. In other cases, companies purchase materials from suppliers through hub-and-spoke systems such as the public and private exchange. Yet, as discussed in Chapter 2, neither of these partner relationships goes far enough in providing companies with the flexibility required to play by the new rules of today's fast-paced economy.

CHAPTER TWO

Seeking Partners for Greater Competitive Advantage

The problems that exist in the world today cannot be solved by the level of thinking that created them.

—Albert Einstein

Few businesses truly exist in isolation. No matter the strength, the power, and market force a company can bring to bear, it always has suppliers and customers. But not every company has partners.

To flourish in today's rapid-paced business landscape, companies need to work quickly and effectively to form partnerships with multiple customers and suppliers. Partnerships present the opportunity to quickly gain access to a technology or product, to develop a broader mix of products and services, and to achieve the nimbleness required to adapt to rapidly changing market conditions. In today's fast-moving economy, if companies don't form effective partnerships, they're not just marginalized—they're eliminated. Yet, with all the potential partnerships offer to enhance a company's competitiveness, businesses continue to either resist partnerships in general, or form partnerships that are limited in scope.

First, many companies view themselves as isolated entities. They are focused on performing better, cheaper, and faster within their own walls. Just like two divisions within a business, a company that fails to integrate its business processes and share information with its partners will not be able to work with those partners efficiently. Suppliers cannot effectively manage their inventory when they have no information about demand for the finished product. Similarly, suppliers can't respond quickly to changes in customer demand when it takes weeks or months to learn about these changes. These are just some of the issues companies could address by working more closely with their trading partners.

Second, until recently, the technology has not existed to allow companies to form flexible, low-cost relationships with partners. Over the past few decades, larger companies have begun communicating electronically through direct links with their suppliers, but these linkages remain expensive to install and maintain. In addition to its expense, this technology doesn't provide the flexibility needed to change suppliers if they are later deemed ineffective or if market conditions change.

Today, the corporate partnerships that businesses commonly form fall into two categories: point-to-point relationships, in which companies communicate with each other one at a time, and one-to-many relationships, in which a single company communicates simultaneously with many of its suppliers and customers. Examples of point-to-point partnerships include linear supply chain relationships. Examples of one-to-many partnerships include public and private exchanges. In many cases, these partnership models are pure buyer-seller relationships. There are benefits and shortcomings for each of these partnership models in a commercial landscape where competitiveness often depends on reducing the time frame from forecasting demand for a product to supplying that product to customers.

POINT-TO-POINT RELATIONSHIPS

One of the most basic ways to form partnerships with companies involves simple point-to-point communications. These relationships typically consist of a series of commands by one company and a series of responses from the second company:

Company A: Deliver the order to my main warehouse.

Company B: Yes, the order will be fulfilled tomorrow.

Communication occurs between two companies at a time, the information exchanged is limited, and the company making the purchase views the relationship as a pure buyer-seller exchange. A buyer-seller relationship in its simplest form occurs every day when people make a purchase. They know what they need, what they want, how much they want to pay

THE ROLE OF TECHNOLOGY IN POINT-TO-POINT RELATIONSHIPS

Today, many companies have formed point-to-point relationships with their suppliers and customers in the supply chain through the use of standard-based technologies such as electronic data interchange (EDI) and extensible markup language (XML).

These technologies have enabled companies to more readily communicate with partners, but too frequently merely automate manual tasks—and in some cases can even increase the cost of doing so—without improving the underlying business processes. Fundamentally, EDI and XML facilitate one-to-one relationships between partner companies, rather than fostering broader collaborative partnerships that will lead to adaptability.

Electronic Data Interchange

EDI replaces paper documents with electronic transactions. By sending standard messages, a company can communicate with its suppliers to coordinate shipments, check project status, confirm prices, or exchange other standardized information.

Although EDI saves companies time by automating simple interactions they once accomplished by phone or fax, on its own it does not provide businesses with the flexibility needed to create dynamic partnerships. EDI simply standardizes the information passing between the two companies. The unique processes of each company that uses the information remain the same. Each new EDI interface costs thousands of dollars, takes months to implement, and is difficult to maintain—making EDI the antithesis of flexibility and putting this solution out of the reach of smaller companies.

Once a company and its suppliers have invested in this technology, it is costly and time-consuming to change suppliers when they are ineffective or when market conditions change. Moreover, the tendency of companies to customize EDI makes it expensive and cumbersome for a supplier to work with more than one company at a time. For example, if a supplier serves Wal-Mart, it may need to implement completely different EDI solutions to also work with Kmart and Target. As a result, EDI has not been widely adopted.

(continued)

THE ROLE OF TECHNOLOGY IN POINT-TO-POINT RELATIONSHIPS (CONTINUED)

Extensible Markup Language

XML is a set of Internet standards that provides a common way of identifying data and makes uniform—or standardizes—the exchange of data between different computer systems and otherwise incompatible technologies.

XML should significantly reduce a portion of the cost of electronic point-to-point communications because it is based on common and widely accepted standardized Internet technologies. Some analysts predict that XML-based technologies will emerge as a more effective way to link applications between business partners than EDI because XML has been widely embedded in most current business software, making it available to more companies. Indeed, XML will likely see wider acceptance and deployment than EDI as a result of its lower cost and natural fit with the Internet.

Today, many software vendors are adding XML support to their products. This is very promising. XML holds the opportunity of future benefits provided it is not implemented by companies using EDI techniques. However, XML comes with its own set of challenges. Chief among these is the fact that numerous XML specifications, vocabulary subsets, and developer-defined variations exist, making its use fragmented. In addition, many companies have failed to tighten their business processes before implementing XML. As a result, the use of XML has simply mechanized tasks companies used to perform manually without helping them to strengthen their business processes.

and they go buy it. Companies engage in the same practice, with each transaction as a stand-alone entity.

The Linear Supply Chain

The linear supply chain is a set of point-to-point, buyer-seller relationships. Participants in the linear supply chain communicate directly with the suppliers from whom they buy and the customers to whom they sell. The relationships participants form with their suppliers focus primarily on price, the ability to deliver, and the stability of the supplier relationship.

FIGURE 2.1   THE LINEAR SUPPLY CHAIN

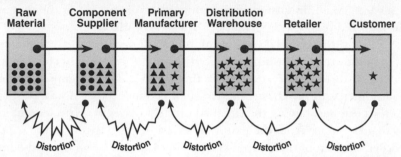

IN THE LINEAR SUPPLY CHAIN, INFORMATION ABOUT CUSTOMER DE-
MAND IS PASSED FROM ONE COMPANY TO THE NEXT IN A SEQUEN-
TIAL ASSEMBLY LINE FORMAT. INFORMATION ABOUT HOW MUCH
INVENTORY IS NEEDED BECOMES INCREASINGLY DISTORTED AS IT IS
PASSED FROM THE CUSTOMER WHO PURCHASES THE FINAL PROD-
UCT BACK THROUGH THE SUPPLY CHAIN TO THE SUPPLIER OF RAW
MATERIALS.

A classic supply chain is a sequence of companies, each passing increasingly finished materials to the next in an ordered sequence (Figure
2.1). In a linear supply chain, information passes from the retail or customer
sales point back to the raw materials suppliers as if stepping down the
rungs of a ladder. Materials flow in the opposite direction, from the process companies to the discrete companies to the consumer packaged
goods companies to the retailer who finally sells it to the consumer. Material inventories build up between supplier and customer at each rung on
the ladder.

Some linear supply chains can be extremely large and complex, with
literally thousands of companies working to deliver products to the customer. For example, the typical automaker has direct and indirect relationships with potentially 30,000 suppliers. The typical supermarket
works directly and indirectly with 10,000 to 15,000 suppliers.

Linear supply chains offer a host of benefits compared to growing
from within. By working with a wide range of suppliers, for example, companies can ensure the materials they need are available when they need
them. In addition, they can make sure they are getting these supplies at
consistent high quality and at competitive cost, and pass this quality and
low cost on to the customer who purchases the finished product or service.

Despite these benefits, the linear supply chain comes with some major
drawbacks. First, information is communicated in a point-to-point fashion
between two companies at a time along the supply chain. This leads to

significant time delays in fulfilling customer orders and in responding quickly to changes in customer demand and to distortion of the demand information due to the information "bull whip" effect.

Second, the sequential transfer of information within the linear supply chain leads to the "bullwhip effect," in which information becomes exponentially distorted the farther down the supply chain a company is from the customer who purchases the finished product. Not knowing exactly what the customer buying the finished product needs or wants, companies tend to order more from their suppliers "just in case." In turn, the suppliers order more from their suppliers, just in case, and so on down the line.

The farther back through the supply chain an order has to travel, the more the order becomes distorted, creating the uncertainty that causes companies to accumulate greater quantities of inventory. The result is that companies throughout the linear supply chain end up accumulating more inventory than they need to serve the customer, and the more inventory a company carries, the greater the working capital it needs to operate.

Third, companies within the linear supply chain have limited visibility as to what's happening elsewhere in the supply chain. Think of a string of sled dogs. For a sled dog in the middle of the team, the view never changes. All it can see is the dog right in front of it, and all it can do is

THE BULLWHIP EFFECT

Remember playing the telephone game as a child? The first child had a message, which he whispered into his neighbor's ear. The second child heard the message, and whispered it into his neighbor's ear, and on and on from child to child. By the time the message reached the last child, it was completely distorted.

Similarly, within the linear supply chain, information is communicated from supplier to supplier all the way back down the line from the customer who purchases the final product to the supplier of raw materials. Each supplier along the way makes decisions about production and supply that affect the decisions of its suppliers. By the time an order reaches the raw materials supplier, it has become increasingly inaccurate, leading the supplier to hold much more inventory than is needed. This phenomenon is known as the "bullwhip effect."

The effect is analogous to cracking a whip. When the whip is swung, the further away from the handle the wave travels, the faster the tip of the whip reacts. Supply chains operate in a similar fashion, with perhaps more painful results.

follow that dog as it moves to the right or the left, hoping that it is heading in the right direction. Similarly, in a linear supply chain, all a supplier can see is its direct customer who purchases its raw materials or components. The supplier doesn't know how many finished products customers are purchasing. In addition, it doesn't know whether customers are satisfied with the finished product. It must follow the lead of the company that sells the finished product to the customer. If that company misinterprets sales trends or fails to accurately forecast demand, all the players in the supply chain can quickly end up off track.

Take a supply chain that manufactures bread, for example (Figure 2.2). The farmer grows the wheat, which is bought by a flour mill, which then cleans it, grinds it, and turns it into flour. The flour is purchased by a distributor, which sells it to a baking company, which then combines the flour together with raw materials it has purchased from other suppliers and turns that into wheat bread. A food wholesaler purchases the wheat bread, aggregates it with other packaged foods, and sells these products in combination to the food retailer.

The process is sequential, with each supplier working in isolation from the others. It works well most of the time, but the time lags and lack of information available to participants along the chain make it difficult for them to react when forced to adapt to unexpected conditions. What

FIGURE 2.2 BAKING SUPPLY CHAIN

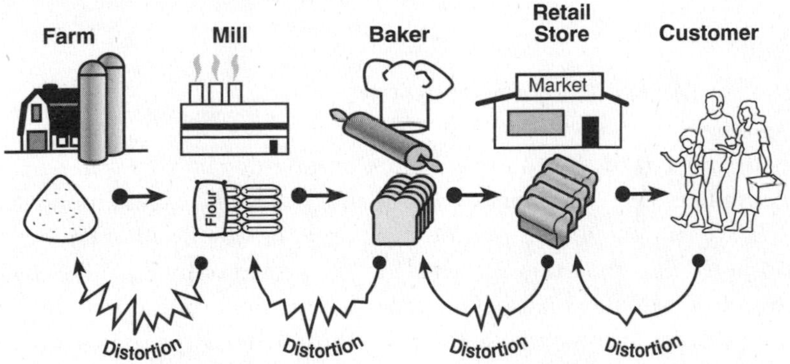

IN LINEAR SUPPLY CHAINS, SUCH AS THOSE IN THE BAKING INDUSTRY, INFORMATION ABOUT CUSTOMER DEMAND IS PASSED FROM ONE COMPANY TO THE NEXT SEQUENTIALLY, CREATING TIME DELAYS AS IT MAKES ITS WAY FROM THE CUSTOMER ALL THE WAY BACK TO THE SUPPLIERS OF RAW INGREDIENTS. THE TIME LAGS AND LIMITED VISIBILITY MAKE IT DIFFICULT FOR COMPANIES WITHIN THE SUPPLY CHAIN TO RESPOND QUICKLY WHEN FORCED TO ADAPT TO CHANGING MARKET CONDITIONS.

happens if the farmer experiences a drought? Or if the flour mill can't produce enough flour? Any glitch in the process affects on-time delivery of wheat bread to the retailer. What happens if there's a sudden market shift? Say a new study finds that millet prevents cancer, and suddenly customers are buying bread made with millet instead of wheat. By the time this information is communicated all the way through the supply chain to the farmer, inventories of wheat bread, wheat, and the packaging may have stacked up to unnecessary levels, causing everyone in the supply chain to lose revenue.

In addition, the information passed within the supply chain is limited—typically, it takes the form of an order from one company to its supplier. For example, the flour mill does not receive information regarding how well breads that use its wheat flour are selling. Nor does it know whether customers prefer breads with different types of flour over the one it is supplying. Instead, the distributor requests delivery of wheat flour by a specific date. It's a pure buyer-seller relationship. With limited information, the flour miller can only respond reactively to the baker's requests for flour and has little ability to help the baker proactively promote the products and new brands that would create more demand for both of their products.

In short, the linear supply chain is not adaptable in either the short or the long term. The nature of its relationships limits the ability of participants to react to sudden change, and the nature of the information exchanged limits their ability to plan strategically.

ONE-TO-MANY RELATIONSHIPS

With the advent of the Internet, some companies have begun working with suppliers and customers in online marketplaces. Chief among these models are the public and private exchange, in which bids, requests for proposal (RFPs), and other information are posted online. Unlike the linear supply chain, in which delays occur as information is communicated sequentially from company to company, online exchanges allow communication to reach all participants simultaneously, quickening response times and significantly reducing the bullwhip effect.

This effect is observable as companies internally collapsed multiple and disparate data and process models into an integrated model. This has been one of the key benefits of existing ERP implementations. It is anticipated that online exchanges will have a similar effect across companies.

PUBLIC EXCHANGES

Public exchanges offer a way for businesses to advertise their buying needs to the world, and for suppliers to bid on these products and services. This bid-and-respond system is touted as a way for corporations to attract new suppliers and customers by linking buyers and sellers that had never previously worked together (Figure 2.3).

FIGURE 2.3 THE ONLINE EXCHANGE

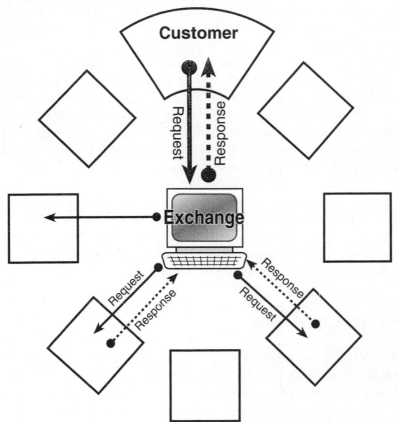

THE ONLINE EXCHANGE OPERATES LIKE A CENTRALIZED HUB THROUGH WHICH ALL INFORMATION MUST PASS. EVERY MESSAGE AND EVERY RELATIONSHIP IS LIKE A SPOKE THAT MUST BE DIRECTED THROUGH THIS HUB. IN GENERAL, THE ONLINE EXCHANGE HAS BEEN MOST USED FOR BUYING AND SELLING COMMODITY PRODUCTS. THE EMERGING EXCHANGE IMPLEMENTATIONS ARE ALLOWING FOR EVER MORE COMPLEX PRODUCTS TO BE COLLABORATIVELY DESIGNED AND DEVELOPED VIA EXCHANGES.

Public exchanges initially gained popularity by promising to stream-line industries and cut billions of dollars in costs by creating a public mar-ketplace from which to buy and sell products, jointly design products, and collaborate in real time. By the end of 2000, venture capitalists had in-vested $5 billion in more than 360 business-to-business efforts, accord-ing to Venture One, a San Francisco-based venture capital market-research firm.[1]

But after investing heavily in public exchanges, businesses now real-ize that they benefit little from opening their bids to all companies be-cause many of these companies aren't qualified as participants. Many of these companies cannot make the highly specialized products or supplies other businesses need, so in effect the pool of potential partners is not as large as anticipated.

In addition, public exchanges emphasize price, making it difficult to win bids based on other factors such as quality or speed of delivery. Be-cause of this, many companies are hesitant to participate in public ex-changes, and customers often find inconsistent quality, which leads to higher production costs and higher variability in their end products. Sell-ers also have concerns with being disintermediated from their customer and having their products become commodities.

In addition, security of information has been a concern for all par-ticipants, as well as the lack of value that public exchanges bring for the price of each transaction. As a result, although some still exist, public ex-changes have never taken off. Many marketplaces have entirely failed or have not met their business objectives, and nearly 120 of them have been shut down or acquired, according to Deloitte Consulting.[2]

PRIVATE EXCHANGES

Although public exchanges never quite delivered on their promise, a vari-ation of this medium has quickly emerged in its place: the private ex-change. Private exchanges offer companies greater control because they are owned and operated by one company, which then provides access to the exchange to selected suppliers and customers. Rather than attract new customers and suppliers, businesses use private exchanges as a way to work interactively with suppliers and customers that they select. In addition to the automation of buying and selling, private exchanges provide a way for participants to interactively manage inventory, production schedules, shipping schedules, forecasting, and sales.

Dozens of companies—including Hewlett-Packard, Dell Computer, IBM, and Wal-Mart—have formed private exchanges, and many companies have reaped benefits from doing so. For example, by linking about 60 parts suppliers through a private exchange, Dell trimmed inventory in its factories to the point where parts are held on average for just six hours before assembly, down from 15 hours the year before.[3] Manco, an Avon, Ohio-based maker of specialty adhesive products, reported saving 28 percent in distribution costs and 18 percent in freight costs by participating in a private exchange headed by Ace Hardware.[4] IBM saved $400 million in 2000 by moving its procurement processes with 20,000 suppliers to a private exchange.

However, the private exchange also has its limitations. It operates like a centralized hub through which all information must pass. Every message and every relationship is like a spoke that must be directed through this hub. This is not always the fastest way to do business. For example, if a maker of cell phones runs out of cell phone covers, is it really convenient to have to talk to the General Electric plastics exchange to get the message to suppliers? The answer is often no.

Quite often, companies have only a handful of qualified suppliers that can meet their specifications for any given product. The company usually ranks these suppliers, knowing exactly in which order and in which situations it turns to each one. Rather than communicating indirectly with these suppliers by posting the information centrally on a private exchange, it's often quicker to pick up the phone or send these partners an e-mail or fax.

Private exchanges are based on data and messages. They do nothing to change the business processes that could eliminate the order and re-order

THE RISE OF THE PRIVATE EXCHANGE*

Private exchanges are quickly gaining in popularity. According to a 2001 study by market research firm Jupiter Media Metrix, corporate spending on the infrastructure to build private trading networks will increase to more than $37 billion by 2005 from $465 million in 2001. Similarly, by 2003, AMR, a market researcher, estimates that private and public exchanges will be used by nearly 30 percent of U.S. companies.

* Nicole Harris, "Can Business-to-Business Survive?" *The Wall Street Journal Europe* (March 19, 2001):23.

processes in the first place. In general, the private exchange is most useful for commodity products. The more engineered the component a company needs, the less efficient it is to advertise this need via an online
exchange. Although not dramatic, private exchanges do increase efficiency because they mechanize certain processes, but they do little to remove human involvement.

Furthermore, a hub-and-spoke model works for large numbers of simple transactions or a relatively low volume of very complex interactions.
However, as traffic through the central hub grows by orders of magnitude, as it inevitably will, it will become increasingly difficult for this
centralized mechanism to handle the volume and complexity of the projected transactions.

Finally, companies that participate in private exchanges view them
primarily as bid-and-respond systems. They may become a collaborative
tool in the future, but today, companies have simply transferred their
buyer-seller relationship from one mechanism to another, failing to capitalize on collaborative opportunities that could provide revenue and cost
benefits to all companies involved.

Private exchanges will play a critical role in the twenty-first century
economy. However, when all the hype dies down, businesses will find that
as bid-and-respond systems, private exchanges can help them save the
most money when it comes to purchasing commodity or standard items
and in the near future highly customized configured to order items. Additionally, in the future, private exchanges will also play a critical role
for financial transactions such as processing invoices, and for posting information of importance to all suppliers and customers who work together
within a business network. The role of the private exchange will be within
the broader scope of a partnership model that gives companies greater
flexibility to respond to rapidly changing market conditions.

A BUSINESS STRUCTURE FOR TODAY'S ECONOMY

Historically, supply chain relationships have been restricted to buyer and
seller roles. This fundamental relationship has limited companies'
thought processes and kept them from moving beyond linear models. Supply chain relationships are primarily based on two functions—purchasing
and sales—with employees from other divisions within both companies
having no communication. Companies must change this mind-set to succeed in today's fast-moving economy.

In addition, companies need a more efficient communication model. Both the point-to-point and one-to-many partnership models that exist today grew out of the need for companies to gain a competitive advantage by working with their suppliers and customers. Yet, neither model provides businesses with a truly efficient form of communication. With the linear supply chain, information is communicated sequentially one company at a time down the supply chain, creating delays in responding to customer demand. With the online exchange, all information is posted through a central hub, creating an indirect, human-to-machine communication mechanism when it is often more efficient to communicate directly with a supplier or customer.

To maintain a competitive edge, companies need a more efficient way of doing business that enables them to pass pertinent information swiftly and simultaneously to only those partners that need to receive it. They need the mechanisms that enable them to learn from and respond to unexpected events. Finally, they need a business structure that allows them to work efficiently with their partners to anticipate and adapt to changes in customer demand.

CHAPTER THREE

The Adaptive Business Network Vision

Ideas won't keep. Something must be done about them.

—Alfred North Whitehead

In an effort to produce fresh breads and pastries for retailers, a group of entrepreneurs starts a bread company called Smart-and-Fresh Baking Co. However, Smart-and-Fresh isn't the average baker. It's a bread company that has a distinct edge over its competitors.

First, rather than doing everything itself, Smart-and-Fresh focuses on its core competency: developing brands for its breads and pastries, and marketing them to grocery stores. Everything else Smart-and-Fresh hands off to other businesses, and the company forms a network for these businesses to work together closely. The network includes a French pastry chef specializing in croissants, an English pastry chef specializing in scones, an Italian pastry chef specializing in biscotti, and several other pastry and bread makers, all of whom specialize in a specific baked product to ensure that each product is top quality. The network also includes flour mills that supply the flour, dairy farms that supply the milk and eggs, and a range of other suppliers that produce ingredients such as yeast, sugar, chocolate, raisins, and nuts needed to make the breads and pastries. It also includes a packaging company that provides special bags to keep the bread fresh and a trucking company to transport the bread.

Second, Smart-and-Fresh is linked together with its suppliers and the retail stores it serves via uniform business processes and top-speed technology (Figure 3.1). Linked together in this way, each retail store sends

FIGURE 3.1   THE SMART-AND-FRESH NETWORK

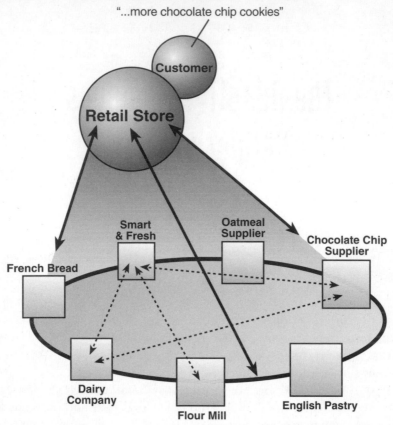

IN THE ADAPTIVE BUSINESS NETWORK, SMART-AND-FRESH IS
LINKED WITH ITS SUPPLIERS AND THE RETAIL STORE IT SERVES VIA
UNIFORM BUSINESS PROCESSES AND TOP-SPEED TECHNOLOGY. THE
RETAIL STORE SENDS SMART-AND-FRESH HOURLY UPDATES RE-
GARDING HOW MANY CHOCOLATE CHIP COOKIES ARE SELLING AT
THE SAME TIME THAT IT SENDS THIS INFORMATION TO THE CHOCO-
LATE CHIP SUPPLIER, THE FLOUR MILL, AND THE DAIRY COMPANY.
THIS ENABLES ALL SUPPLIERS IN THE NETWORK TO CONTINUOUSLY
ADJUST THEIR PRODUCTION PLANS, AND TO KEEP ON HAND ONLY
THE AMOUNT OF COOKIES OR INGREDIENTS THEY NEED.

Smart-and-Fresh and all the relevant suppliers hourly updates regarding
how much bread is selling, and which types of bread are selling fastest. So,
for example, data regarding customer purchases of Smart-and-Fresh
chocolate chip cookies is transmitted hourly to Smart-and-Fresh at the
same time it is transmitted to the chocolate chip cookie manufacturer,
the flour mill, the dairy company, and the chocolate chip supplier. Knowing

exactly how many cookies customers are buying, all the suppliers in the network continuously adjust their production plans, minimizing their need to store extra cookies or the ingredients that go into them.

Third, because Smart-and-Fresh has formed a network, both it and its suppliers can quickly anticipate and react to unexpected market shifts. A new study hits showing that oatmeal reduces cholesterol, and suddenly customers start buying oatmeal cookies while sales of chocolate chip cookies decline. The information is passed within the hour from the retail store to all affected participants in the network, who adjust their production schedules and begin producing more oatmeal cookies within a few hours after receiving the information. Then there's a truck strike in the U. S. Midwest, and the wheat producers notify Smart-and-Fresh that they won't be able to transport the wheat needed for the next wheat bread production cycle. Smart-and-Fresh responds immediately, and within 24 hours adds two Canadian flour distributors to the network who deliver the wheat flour within the time frame required.

Finally, because Smart-and-Fresh works collaboratively with its network of suppliers, it can capitalize on their strengths to increase demand for both its products and other company products in the network. For example, a market analysis conducted for the network shows that customers who buy biscotti also eat cheese and drink red wine. Upon receiving this data, the biscotti producer approaches Smart-and-Fresh and suggests packaging a new, savory biscotti with cheese and red wine and selling it as a package in grocery stores. Smart-and-Fresh agrees to the idea, adds a wine producer and a cheese distributor to the network within 24 hours, and within days begins selling biscotti-cheese-wine packages to the grocery stores, creating more demand for its products.

The network Smart-and-Fresh has created is an adaptive business network. What makes this network adaptive is that all companies have the mechanisms in place to cooperatively *plan* their activities, *execute* based on these plans, *sense* changes in customer demand as soon as they occur, and quickly *respond* to these changing conditions to adjust their plans.

The adaptive business network is a new business model that flexibly links companies into loose consortiums that collectively work together to meet the needs of customers. Companies that join these networks will remain autonomous both culturally and financially but operationally integrated and dependent on the other participants. Yet, they will work together, share information, and make decisions more collaboratively than they do today—and will have more success than they could have on their own.

The adaptive business network addresses the problems that many businesses struggle to solve on a daily basis:

- Improving forecast accuracy.

- Producing to match what customers actually buy.

- Quickly meeting demand for new products.

- Rapidly developing personalized products and delivering them to the customer.

- Maximizing profits from commodity products.

- Transforming commodity products into unique offerings by bundling them with other products and services.

- Automating mundane tasks.

The adaptive business network solves these business problems and creates new opportunities for companies along the way.

How It Works

The adaptive business network is a group of independent organizations linked by standard business processes and common technology in order to capitalize on the strengths of each organization to be more competitive than they could on their own. This business network focuses on the needs of the customer using a set of aligned measurements. It enables participants to adapt to a constantly changing business climate and thereby maximize profits.

Participants in an adaptive business network work together on everything from monitoring inventory to coordinating production schedules to sharing information about customer purchases. Each network has a lead company or "coordinating partner" that is responsible for the relationship with the customer and that coordinates the establishment of the rules that govern how the network operates. In addition, each network will have dozens to hundreds of participating companies linked to it. Some of these participating companies may provide the parts that are combined into the final product. Others may provide services such as the transportation required to deliver the goods to the customer, the technology that links participants together, or financial services for the whole group, including the customer.

Within the adaptive business network, information is communicated instantaneously and as frequently as required to make good decisions. The network can be set up to receive sales information every week, hour, minute, or even instantaneously. And the information received can be based on sales of a specific product, sales of a specific product through a specific sales channel, or sales of a product during a specific event, such as a promotion or a snowstorm. This information is communicated simultaneously—not to everyone, but only to those who need to receive it based on the processes established within the network.

Through the network, many routine decisions made by the participants are automated. Automating daily decisions enables the network to respond with speed and precision to the information that's received. It also allows companies to free up their employees to focus on more strategic goals rather than the mundane tasks that typically consume their time and add little value (Figure 3.2).

INTEGRATED BUSINESS PROCESSES AND TECHNOLOGY

Companies seeking to create an adaptive business network typically ask themselves many questions. How can we coordinate our business processes to work together faster? How can we eliminate the bottlenecks that prevent us from getting our products and services to the customer more quickly? What customer information should we share to our mutual benefit?

What links companies together in an adaptive business network are standardized business processes. By forming close procedural links, participants within a network put the mechanisms in place to flexibly respond to changing market conditions. Rather than merely placing or filling orders from their next-in-line supplier or customer, participants work collaboratively to plan for, anticipate, and respond to changes in customer demand. This change from the traditional buyer-seller relationship requires a fundamental shift in how a company's managers operate their business units and measure their success. It also requires a shift in the cultural thinking of the organization.

For example, managers of a company must change how they negotiate with their partners. They also must change how the company purchases products, how it plans its production schedules, and how it allocates its capital resources. Managers of a company must change their perspective to focus on the customer who purchases the finished goods produced by the network. They must change how they measure customer satisfaction and establish new measurements of success that are aligned to the needs of that customer.

FIGURE 3.2 THE ADAPTIVE BUSINESS NETWORK

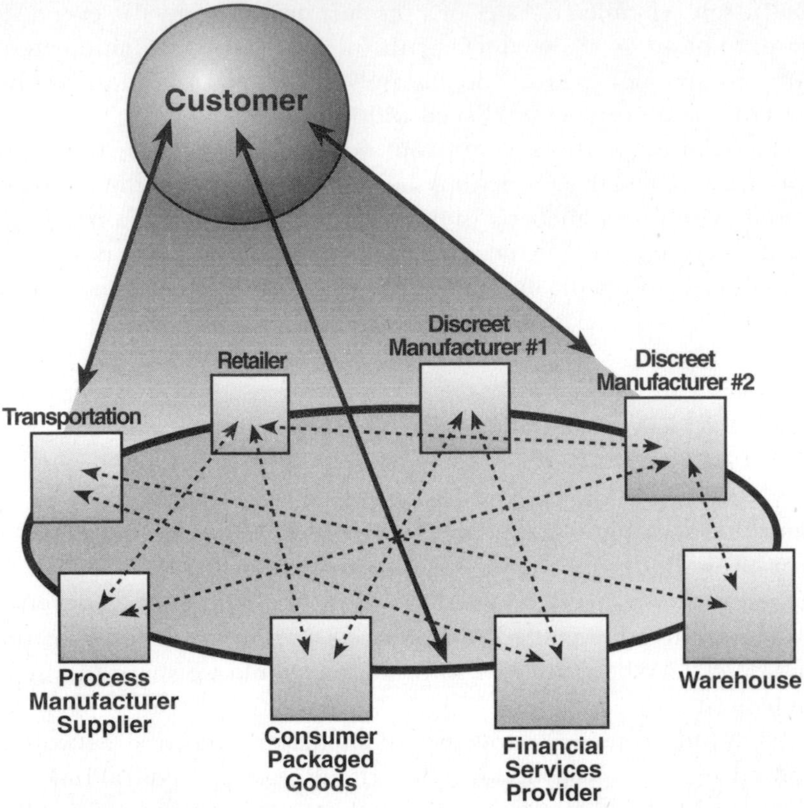

Customer

Transportation

Retailer

Discreet Manufacturer #1

Discreet Manufacturer #2

Process Manufacturer Supplier

Consumer Packaged Goods

Financial Services Provider

Warehouse

ADAPTIVE BUSINESS NETWORKS LINK COMPANIES TO SERVE THE CUSTOMER WHO PURCHASES THE FINAL PRODUCT OR SERVICE PRODUCED BY THE SUPPLY CHAIN. INFORMATION WITHIN THE NETWORK IS COMMUNICATED INSTANTANEOUSLY AND SIMULTANEOUSLY TO THE COMPANIES THAT NEED IT, ELIMINATING THE COSTLY TIME DELAYS THAT OCCUR WITHIN THE LINEAR SUPPLY CHAIN.

Finally, organizations must shift away from hierarchy toward a peer-to-peer way of operating, in which problems are resolved jointly with strategic partners outside the four walls of the company. In addition, the role of human resources within companies must change to ensure employees, managers, and executives are evaluated by their contribution to the network's measurements of success—not only those of a particular company division.

The vision of the adaptive business network is to connect companies within the network with pervasive technology that allows for distributed decision making. This technology can act autonomously, "perceive" its

TAKING COMMUNICATION TO THE NEXT LEVEL

Today, information is passed between companies with technologies and protocols such as electronic data interchange (EDI), extensible markup language (XML), and the World Wide Web. In most cases, this information consists of static, raw data that employees manually analyze and act upon within slow time frames. The adaptive business network takes communication to the next level by enabling companies to obtain information nearly instantaneously and act upon that information in near real time. This ability enables companies to operate more quickly and be far more adaptive than was possible in the past.

In an adaptive business network, simply passing accurate information between participants is not enough. Advanced technology automates decisions, enabling them to occur automatically and instantaneously based on the information that is received. When an agent in the network receives information that stocks of a key component are lower than the established limit, it will act on this information automatically. Based on information and agreements maintained by the network, the reorder takes place automatically. No time is lost while the inventory figures sit in an electronic file, awaiting human intervention. Automating decisions based on the preestablished controls agreed on by the network enables companies to quickly adapt to market changes and other unforeseen events.

Moreover, sophisticated technology within the network allows companies to analyze complex patterns so they can quickly predict and respond to future events. The network will track other kinds of information in addition to inventory counts and customer demand data. For example, it may have determined that consumption of lemonade spikes on the third day of 100-plus-degree weather. Alternatively, it may have determined that it is best to begin shipping by truck after the second day of rail traffic congestion along key routes. In each case, the network will determine a course of action based on its analysis of past events and patterns.

surroundings, and interact with other technology elements to perform basic tasks. It enables information to be exchanged instantaneously and day-to-day decisions based on that information to be automated using a framework of controls or guidelines established by the network participants. This dramatically reduces the delays that occur when working in a complex business ecosystem.

Incorporating this technology into the network enables companies to quickly add new partners as customers demand new products and services, and acquire new technologies to stay competitive without building them from the ground up or going through the demanding and painful exercise of acquiring another company. The network can simply add partners that provide the products and services it needs, while eliminating those who provide substandard or outdated products or services.

Advanced technology will track information about customer purchases, unexpected changes in customer demand, delayed parts deliveries, shop floor machine failures, and other glitches that occur within the network. It will provide information to network participants and notify the appropriate parties when problems occur, so they can react immediately. Specific elements will analyze and distill information relevant to the network. Other elements will make decisions about how to best deploy local resources to solve a problem—say, from which facility to fulfill an order for a product. And still other elements will provide the controls required to prevent chaos—for example, they will decide which production line should take the lead when several lines are vying to produce the same product.

Even without advanced technology, companies can go a long way toward reducing the inefficiencies that currently exist when working within a network of partners. Businesses can create a common portal or Web site from which they manage and share network information. And with just a spreadsheet, companies can work together more collaboratively than they do today to share information about production schedules and demand for products. Even with minimal technology, companies within an adaptive business network can significantly reduce time delays by better coordinating business processes so that they can share information efficiently and make decisions quickly.

AN EFFICIENT PARTNERSHIP MODEL

The adaptive business network shares many of the same goals as the linear supply chain and the online exchange discussed in Chapter 2. However, it has distinct advantages over both of these models.

Communications Efficiency

Unlike the point-to-point communications model of the linear supply chain and the hub-and-spoke communications model of the online exchange, information within the adaptive business network is communicated directly and instantaneously to the companies that need it. This means that companies operating within an adaptive business network have greater visibility into the activities of the entire network than they do within a linear supply chain and can quickly obtain information of relevance to their business.

Depending on the network's agreed-upon terms, participating companies may be able to see how much of a particular product sold within the past hour, whether more was sold through the retail-store sales channel than through the Internet, and whether a new promotion started this morning increased sales. Unlike the hub-and-spoke model of the online exchange, companies receive information directly and are not burdened by having to sift through extraneous data. In addition, the flow of information is truly automated, moving from machine to machine without the need for employees to post it at either end of the exchange.

In contrast to the linear supply chain, in which information is passed point-to-point from company to company, companies within the adaptive business network receive information simultaneously and instantaneously. This eliminates the bullwhip effect, in which orders become exponentially distorted the further removed the supplier is from the customer who purchases the finished product. Because all affected participants within the adaptive business network know the exact quantities of finished product that customers are purchasing, none are motivated to over-order just in case. This enables companies to plan the inventory they need with far greater precision, reducing the amount of excess inventory and the costly working capital charges that go with it (Figure 3.3).

FIGURE 3.3   CHARACTERISTICS OF THE LINEAR SUPPLY CHAIN VERSUS THE ONLINE EXCHANGE VERSUS THE ABN (ADAPTIVE BUSINESS NETWORK)

	Linear Supply Chain	Online Exchange	ABN
Communication	Point-to-Point	One-to-Many	Targeted
Relationship	Buyer-Seller	Buyer-Seller	Collaborative
Timing	Time Delays	Some time delays	Instantaneous
Bullwhip Effect	Yes	Reduced	Minimized

Collaborative Relationships with Partners

Unlike the buyer-seller models of the linear supply chain and the online exchange, customers and suppliers within the adaptive business network share much more information than simply placing and filling orders. Companies within the adaptive business network work collaboratively to understand the needs of the customer who purchases the finished product, and use that information to their mutual benefit. They share information regarding customer purchases, transportation and shipping, production schedules, the location of inventory, and other factors that affect the performance of the entire network. They work together to reduce costs by pooling resources such as transportation, warehouse space, consultant studies, and financial services. They work proactively to identify new market opportunities that take advantage of their partners' strengths to create more demand for their own products and services.

PARTNERS WHEN YOU NEED THEM

New partners can be added to the adaptive business network quickly and at low cost, opening up tremendous opportunities that aren't possible with today's linear supply chains, mechanized through electronic data interchange (EDI). No longer are companies required to invest large sums of money and time to automate interactions with their suppliers. No longer are they locked into long-term relationships with suppliers if market conditions change or the supplier is producing substandard components. The adaptive business network makes it easy to add and drop partners as needed. This gives the network the flexibility to allow for the right mix of partners to meet changing customer demands. It also offers network participants opportunities to bundle products and services in creative ways that increase demand for all their offerings. In the ABN, partners are evaluated by their peer partners on flexibility and adaptability, versus the linear supply chain where price is the primary evaluation criteria.

COMPANY BENEFITS

In Chapter 1, we discussed the challenges today's businesses face. Companies are becoming more globalized, increasing the complexity of business as well as the need for instant communication. Many companies are finding that their production capacity exceeds the market for their products. Working capital is limited. Customers have higher expectations than ever before.

The adaptive business network enables companies to succeed in the face of these challenges by providing more value to them and the customers they serve. There are three primary benefits for companies participating in an adaptive business network: reducing costs, achieving greater focus, and finding new opportunities for increasing revenue. These benefits have powerful implications for any business, regardless of whether it is a manufacturer, retailer, or a service company.

Reducing Costs

The adaptive business network enables participants to reduce costs in several ways. First, companies in the network receive real-time data about product sales, inventory levels, product shortages, and other information that affects their production, enabling them to dramatically reduce inventory. By reducing inventory, they also reduce the working capital charges. Second, the partnerships formed within the adaptive business network allow companies to better plan production capacity, making more efficient use of their investment. Third, the ability to automate mundane transactions enables companies to eliminate costly administrative processes. Finally, companies participating in an adaptive network can pool resources, reaping the economies of scale that a larger network provides.

Managing Inventory

A primary benefit of the adaptive business network is that it enables companies to align inventory with customer demand and production capacities. The only time inventory is an asset is when it exists in the right quantities, in the right place, at the right time. Other times it is a liability. Excess inventory often comes with a huge price tag—it either has to be sold at a loss or written off altogether because it becomes obsolete. Not only must a company take a significant write-off on the old inventory, it may end up cannibalizing its primary market by dumping. What's more, companies typically take out large working capital loans to pay for inventory until it is sold to the customer.

The effective management of inventory—deciding how much product is needed and where—has always posed a huge challenge for companies. In today's market of shortened product cycles, customer demand for products is even tougher to predict, making inventory quantities more difficult to manage. As discussed earlier, in the linear supply chain, the only demand suppliers can see is that of the customer who directly purchases their product, and the bullwhip effect distorts demand for a product as it is relayed back through the supply chain, making inventory difficult to manage.

The greater visibility afforded companies within the adaptive business network enables them to better manage their supply to mirror customer demand. Not only do suppliers in the network know how many units of their product the customer directly in front of them is buying, they may also know what demand is like for the finished product and can adjust their production quantities accordingly. In addition, participants know exactly how much inventory exists within the network—whether raw materials, work-in-progress, or finished goods ready to sell—and its exact physical location. Suppliers also are informed immediately when there's a product shortage. And they know what alternatives exist for getting their product to the customer.

This better access to information enables companies to work together to establish inventory levels and to dramatically reduce excess inventory—and the costs that come with it. This reduction of inventory helps reduce the cash-to-cash cycle. The ability to better manage inventory significantly improves the network's ability to address the pressures of globalization and capital market performance. Specifically, well-managed inventory improves the working capital of all participants in the network. It improves return on assets and enables the network to more flexibly respond to new competitors and enter new markets.

Managing Production Capacity

The adaptive business network helps participants to save money by providing companies with the flexibility to manage production capacity in a way that mirrors actual customer demand for products (Figure 3.4). For many companies, the adaptive business network will provide greater stability because it ensures that a percentage of their production capacity will always be used, thus allowing companies to meet their minimum financial expectations. In addition, a company that wants to expand its production capacity can do so by using the excess capacity of other network participants, increasing its market share with near zero capital investment, while preventing the other company's excess capacity from sitting idle.

FIGURE 3.4   PRODUCTION CAPACITY IN THE ABN

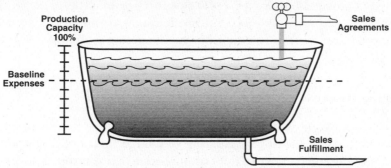

THE BATHTUB REPRESENTS THE PRODUCTION CAPACITY OF MANU-
FACTURING COMPANIES. THE ADAPTIVE BUSINESS NETWORK OFFERS
MANUFACTURERS GREATER STABILITY BECAUSE IT PROVIDES BUSI-
NESSES A BASELINE OF GUARANTEED SALES AGREEMENTS. FOR EX-
AMPLE, THE NETWORK MAY COMMIT ORDERS FOR 60 PERCENT OF A
COMPANY'S CAPACITY, THEREBY FILLING THE BATHTUB BY MORE
THAN HALF. THESE GUARANTEED ORDERS ENSURE THAT A KNOWN
PERCENTAGE OF A COMPANY'S PRODUCTION CAPACITY WILL ALWAYS
BE USED, AND THAT THE COMPANY WILL BE ABLE TO MEET ITS BASE-
LINE EXPENSES. WITH THESE EXPENSES COVERED, COMPANIES
WITHIN AN ABN CAN THEN MAXIMIZE PROFITS BY RESERVING ADDI-
TIONAL CAPACITY FOR THE MOST LUCRATIVE EFFORTS.

Similarly, if additional capacity is suddenly needed and there's not
enough within the network, a company can add another partner to the
network to meet this demand. And a company with excess capacity can
go outside the network and lease the capacity to a competitive company
to keep the plant operating within financial plan. By better using production capacity, companies can further shorten their cash-to-cash cycle,
which increases profits and overall return on assets.

Automating Mundane Tasks

Within the adaptive business network, buyer-seller transactions with suppliers are replaced with partnerships in which all participants work together to meet customer demand. This eliminates the need for many of the
administrative processes that exist today between a company and its suppliers. Through traditional methods, a single purchase order can cost a
company as much as $150 to process.[1] And since some companies work
with thousands of suppliers, these administrative costs can quickly add up.

In the adaptive business network, most purchase orders and invoices can be eliminated because prices are negotiated in advance as part of a master agreement. In addition, routine decisions are automated based on the guidelines or controls established by the network, eliminating repetitive administrative processes.

Pooling Resources

Finally, companies within an adaptive business network can reap the benefits that come with participating in a larger network. For example, participating companies can pool resources such as transportation, warehouse space, consultant studies, and financial services. And they can benefit from greater discounts from vendors based on the network's larger economy of scale.

BETTER-FOCUSED COMPANIES

The adaptive business network offers benefits for all companies—whether they are the coordinating partner or another participating company—by allowing them to focus on their core competencies and the primary tasks at hand. Many administrative tasks and attempts at new business opportunities can frequently distract companies from their primary objectives, but the adaptive network helps solve that.

By automating everyday tasks, the adaptive network enables all companies to free up employees for more strategic purposes, such as improving customer service, for example. In addition, focusing workers on strategic goals instead of mundane tasks improves employee morale.

The coordinating partner in the adaptive business network takes responsibility for marketing and promotions, and distributes the network's products to the customer. By participating in an adaptive network, the coordinating partner can focus on its core competencies while reaping all the benefits of a large, vertically integrated company or a company that acquires products and technologies through mergers and acquisitions. By forming partnerships to meet its needs, the coordinating partner has a large pool of products and services that could potentially enhance its core offerings.

The adaptive business network also brings many advantages to participating companies outside of the coordinating partner, many of whom will be small niche manufacturers who focus on a single specialty. It allows these businesses to remain small—or simply the right size—and still be competitive. For instance, a small company that focuses on the production of high-quality tires could join a network of automakers or a network of large parts machinery, or both. Because the coordinating partner will take responsibility for most marketing efforts, the tire manufacturer can retain its focus on its primary competency: making the best tires around. Based on the number of networks in which it participates and its level of participation, the tire manufacturer may not need to hire a large marketing and sales team, or spend money on a new distribution scheme.

Working within an adaptive business network, companies become better-focused and are able to much more effectively respond to today's business pressures, including consumer desire for customized products and capital market performance. A well-focused company can concentrate on what it does best while capitalizing on the specialties of other companies to meet demand for customized products and services. In addition, a better-focused company will improve its capital performance by spending working capital only on areas directly related to its core business and the offerings of the network.

EXPANDING REVENUE

Another benefit of the adaptive business network is that it enables companies to create new demand for their products and services. The ability to quickly add and drop partners opens up a large pool of resources from which companies can draw to make themselves more competitive. In addition, the efficiencies that result from instantaneous communication enable the network to be more responsive to customer demands.

Companies that participate in adaptive networks can increase revenue for their products and services in five ways:

1. By providing personalized products.
2. By bundling their products and services.
3. By using commoditization to their strategic advantage.
4. By collaboratively designing products based on specific profit goals.
5. By distinguishing themselves through speed and service.

Producing Personalized Products

The adaptive business network provides businesses with the flexibility to produce personalized products and services based on actual customer demand. Jeans manufactured to fit a customer's exact measurements. CDs that compile a consumer's favorite songs. Medication pills customized to the exact doses patients require, delivered to the patient's home. Today, all of these are considered exceptionally personalized services, but in the adaptive business world, services such as these will be far more widespread. The opportunities are endless.

The inherent delays that exist within the linear supply chain make it difficult for companies to produce customized products and services and deliver them to the customer in a timely manner, at reasonable prices. But in an adaptive network, a customer order can be communicated to all suppliers in real time, eliminating these costly inefficiencies. As a result, it's easier to build products based on actual customer orders and deliver them to customers within the short time frames they expect. Even better, these customized services will be affordable to a much wider spectrum of customers.

Bundling Products and Services

By drawing on the resources of a broad pool of companies to meet their needs, participants can reap the advantages of a larger company while remaining small and focused. The ability to add and drop partners enables companies to respond quickly to changes in customer demand, and it gives them an enormous amount of flexibility to bundle their products and services in creative ways that appeal to customers, thus providing new opportunities to increase revenue.

Companies will create new demand for their products and services by combining their primary brands or assets with those of new companies. In some cases, they will jointly create whole new products or services. For example, a brand-leading cola beverage could be combined with the No. 1 potato chip product and a well-known candy bar to create a "Picnic Pack" bundle sold at grocery stores and other food retailers. Similarly, a consumer goods company could package its shampoo with bath oil and perfume to attract more customers. Or an airline company could form a partnership with Pizza Hut to distinguish the food it offers to passengers, and form a partnership with *People* magazine or *Der Spiegel* to offer passengers more engaging reading materials.

Combinations such as this will allow companies to tap into new markets while retaining their focus on their own core competency. The additional features gained by teaming together enhance the appeal of a company's products and services. By forming partnerships with businesses in the adaptive network, companies can strategically bundle services and products in a way that enhances their core product or service.

Embracing Commoditization

Many company executives shudder at the thought of shorter product cycles. Shrinking product cycles mean that every product a company introduces has a short shelf life, which in turn means that companies need to produce a growing array of products just to maintain their profit margins.

However, companies can actually use short product cycles to their advantage within the adaptive business network. In some cases, a company can greatly shorten its product cycle to ensure its product never becomes a commodity because it's moving too quickly for its competitors to catch up. In other cases, companies can be the first to commoditize their product—then bundle the low-profit commoditized product with higher-value, higher-profit-margin items to provide an appealing package at a competitive price. The ease with which companies can form partnerships within the adaptive business network makes it an ideal framework for dominating their market by bundling a commoditized product with a set of distinguishing products and services.

Nokia Corporation understood the power of commoditization and used it to squeeze its competitors out of the cell phone market. Because the cell phone producer already had a good share of the market in the United States, it could afford a much lower price than its competitors in the European cell phone market. Armed with low-cost Nokia cell phones, European cellular carriers packaged these phones with a broad range of services at a low price, and the Nokia European cell phone market took off.

By capturing the European market with its low-end cell phones, Nokia robbed its competitors of profit on their low-end devices. This market strength bought them time to develop their high-end, more profitable cell phone/personal digital assistants. When introduced, Nokia's market reach—attained through commoditizing their basic phone line—guaranteed that the product was a success. Nokia basically used commoditization to create a barrier to entry. The strategy was sound. This type of scenario will become much more common because of the speed afforded by participating in an adaptive business network.

Optimizing Profits

The adaptive business network makes it easy for a company to collabora-tively design products with its partners based on a specific profit margin it decides upon in advance. For example, based on a market analysis, an electronics company could determine that it could sell two million units if it produces a CD player priced at $100, and capture $40 million at a profit of $20 per unit. Using advanced technology, the company could then quickly contact each supplier for options within a specific price range, and automatically narrow the options based on the response it receives.

Companies collaboratively design products based on predetermined profit margins today. However, the adaptive business network would make the process faster because it would automate the messages that get sent back and forth between a company and its suppliers, thus enabling companies to quickly design high-profit products and get them on the market.

CAPITALIZING ON SPEED AND SERVICE

With product cycles rapidly shrinking, the time it takes for a product to go from new-on-the-market to generic is becoming ever shorter. As a re-sult, it's no longer realistic in most industries for companies to differen-tiate themselves based on the uniqueness of their products alone.

In fact, even quality is no longer a very meaningful differentiator be-tween many competing products. For example, there's not much differ-ence between name-brand and store-brand aspirin. And other, more complex products—such as computers and other high-tech consumer elec-tronics—are constructed of identical commodity-level components. The components of a computer vary little from one brand to the next because a handful of manufacturers produce the disk drives, chips, and mother-boards that are used by nearly all computer makers to assemble their mod-els. Moreover, the same manufacturers in Southeast Asia make the majority of all off-the-rack casual clothing. For better or worse, it's all the same quality.

Instead, speed and service are what make a difference today. Take gasoline, for example. Gasoline is gasoline, no matter where you buy it. And at most gas stations, gasoline is priced comparably. So what are the distinguishing factors that make a customer choose one gas station over the next?

It's speed of delivery—how quickly can I fill my tank and pay for the gas? In addition, it's service—is the gas station located near my house? Do I have to pump the gas myself, or does the gas attendant pump the gas and wash my window? Can I just buy gas, or is there also a convenience store, an ATM machine, and a fast-food restaurant? The adaptive business network enables companies to capitalize on the distinguishing factors of speed and service by enabling companies to quickly bundle commodity products with other products and services, providing them with a competitive edge.

CUSTOMER BENEFITS

One of the greatest benefits for customers is that the products they expect to find on the shelves will always be there at more stable and potentially lower prices than before. No more traveling from store to store in search of a product, only to learn that there are no more left. By removing inefficiencies, the adaptive network helps customers have access to products and services when they need and expect them.

Because the adaptive business network will focus more on customers and their needs, personalized service and customized products will be a matter of course. Because the network will include a wide variety of manufacturers and service providers, consumers can expect far better, more individualized service. When shopping for a washing machine, for example, consumers will be offered more choices of color. In addition, the network could offer a suite of products and services—special racks for washing tennis shoes, an electrical-socket plug for Continental Europe, customized delivery and installation options—because the companies that provide these services are already part of the retailer's network.

The adaptive network may provide customers with lower prices. However, price and other product characteristics such as quality, customization, and service will be self-regulating based on customer priorities and purchasing decisions. Consumers will have a greater variety of products and services from which to choose, and these products and services will be more widely available—at the prices customers are willing to pay. If customers demand lower-priced goods, the network will deliver them. Similarly, if customers demand highly customized products, the network will adjust its production to address these customer demands. The objective is to make it easy for the consumer to do business with companies within the network. Networks that provide customers with what they want, when they want it, are going to be the winners.

MOVING TOWARD THE VISION

No company has yet reached the vision of the adaptive business network. But many companies are moving in this direction, and already have had success with some of the concepts. For example, some companies have tried to provide customized products that meet actual customer orders. Companies like Hewlett-Packard design similar computer printers and then wait until the last moment before shipment to build out the differentiating features of certain models. General Mills Inc. offers custom breakfast cereals for consumers who wish to design their own mix of flavors and ingredients on the Internet.

Yet, today, companies that produce customized products are forced to hold large quantities of inventory or risk delivering their customized product to the customer in an untimely manner, a choice they would not be forced to make within an adaptive business network. Because time delays within the adaptive network are reduced, companies will be able to produce customized products *and* deliver them in the short time frames customers expect, making it much more viable for companies to produce customized products.

Other companies have adopted collaborative planning, forecasting, and replenishment (CPFR), in which a company and its supplier jointly plan total inventory, forecast demand for their products, schedule shipments, develop production schedules, and perform other tasks of importance to both companies. CPFR has been credited with helping companies to significantly reduce stock-outs, decrease inventory, reduce transaction costs such as freight expenses and improve relationships between trading partners.

For example, CPFR enabled Herlitz AG, the maker of high-quality paper and office supplies, to improve its offerings to customers. Retailers like Wal-Mart, Woolworths, and METRO AG provide Herlitz with historical sales data and daily sales figures, which Herlitz analyzes and uses to produce a reliable forecast for the next day's sales. By collaborating closely with Herlitz, retail customers have reduced shelf stock-outs from 6 percent to 2 percent, lowered inventory levels, and increased inventory turns by 20 percent.[2] In this way, CPFR is a major step in the right direction because it forces companies to move from a buyer-seller relationship with their partners into a collaborative relationship in which they share information to the benefit of both companies.

However, CPFR has its limitations. First, communication is point-to-point. CPFR technology today does not enable multiple companies to

ADAPTING TO THE WIRELESS WORLD

In today's business world, many companies must respond quickly to rapidly changing business conditions. Those that remain flexible and are willing to adapt have the most success. A look at how AT&T and Deutsche Telekom responded to the rising tide of wireless communications demonstrates the importance of quickly adapting in a fast-paced business climate.

AT&T, the New Jersey-based telecommunications giant, has a rich and storied history as the largest U.S. phone company and a communications industry pioneer. But AT&T found itself quickly passed in the wireless phone market by a smaller, more nimble challenger.

Germany's leading communications company, Deutsche Telekom, capitalized on the explosive growth of the wireless industry both at home in Europe and by forming partnerships abroad. This strategy netted T-Mobile, Deutsche Telekom's wireless service, 23 million customers in Germany and a total of nearly 67 million customers worldwide as of the end of 2001. By comparison, AT&T, which has faced dire economic woes since the turn of this century, served just 18 million people by the end of 2001.

How could Ma Bell have been so easily usurped? She failed to adapt quickly, reacting too slowly to the rising tide of wireless demand, and relying too long instead on revenue from business services and consumer long-distance voice, where profits steadily plummeted. AT&T floundered, searching for a strategy in the early 2000s, finally settling on a widely criticized self-imposed, four-part breakup.

Deutsche Telekom faced many of the same hurdles, but acted and adapted faster, was willing to form partnerships with outsiders, and then remained committed to the strategy settled upon. For example, Deutsche Telekom turned to VoiceStream, a large U.S. carrier, to tap the American market. T-Mobile also offered innovative international roaming packages that helped spur growth. The ability to respond flexibly to quickly changing market conditions will become increasingly important in the fast-paced business landscape of the twenty-first century.

simultaneously collaborate on the same plan. Second, companies using CPFR work together to exchange data, but do little to alter their processes to work together more efficiently. Moreover, CPFR is narrowly focused on planning, forecasting, and replenishing products as opposed to the wider focus of the adaptive business network. CPFR takes place in a static environment in which the rules must be manually negotiated between partners, failing to provide companies with the ability to quickly sense and respond to changing market conditions.

In still other cases, companies have formed interesting partnerships, and used these partnerships as a way to co-brand their products and services. For example, Ford Motor Company formed a partnership with Eddie Bauer Inc., a major outdoor clothing retailer, to produce the Eddie Bauer Explorer sport utility vehicle that appeals to outdoor enthusiasts. It also formed a partnership with Harley-Davidson Inc. to market a Harley-Davidson logo F-150 truck to appeal to motorcycle enthusiasts. American Express Company has formed a partnership with Delta Airlines to provide customers with more Delta frequent flyer miles for using their American Express credit cards.

These examples, and many others, are excellent steps in the right direction. Yet today, many partnerships between companies are difficult to arrange and see through to fruition because each partnership is viewed as a separate and unique negotiation.

Negotiating right now is an art and a science. In the adaptive business network, it is a process. These alliances will come far more naturally and should be faster and easier to consummate because the adaptive business network mandates that companies adopt standard business processes that enable them to work together more efficiently. In addition, the network provides the structure and the common measurements of success to enable companies to work together continuously and reach common goals faster.

Moreover, the level of information and insight available in the adaptive business network is likely to generate new ideas that may not have otherwise been considered. Companies will already be working together collaboratively in the network, and the better information and insight they have into the activities of the entire network will create an environment in which companies proactively discover and pursue new opportunities to bundle their products and services.

CHAPTER FOUR

Roles and Responsibilities within the Network

A good plan executed right now is better than a perfect plan executed next week.
—General George S. Patton

Almost everybody who spends time in the outdoors has heard of Patagonia Inc., the California-based designer and distributor of outdoor clothing and sporting goods. The company began operations in the early 1970s in a tin shed next to an abandoned slaughterhouse and has since grown into a $223 million operation.[1]

However, most people probably don't know that Patagonia manufactures none of its products itself. Instead, it relies on close relationships with a steady group of suppliers that produce outdoor gear to the company's exact quality specifications.

Patagonia owns none of these companies. All remain autonomous. For example, Malden Mills Industries Inc. produces Polartec fabrics for Patagonia, and also for Patagonia competitors L.L. Bean and Lands' End Inc. according to each company's different requirements.

As lead company within its supply chain, Patagonia manages its entire network of suppliers. The company requires that manufacturers produce goods in the company's trademark colors and use the company's exclusive fabrics. The company is well known in the outdoor clothing industry for its commitment to social and environmental concerns, and expects its suppliers to live up to these same standards when producing Patagonia products.

MARKETING, NOT MANUFACTURING

Consumer brands are becoming increasingly important. In fact, brands today are perhaps more important than the actual products themselves.

Take for instance consumer apparel companies such as L.L. Bean, Lands' End, and Nike. Largely, their days of owning massive manufacturing plants to make clothing, shoes, and other goods are behind them. Instead these companies, which have powerful brand recognition and spend millions annually to ensure it, design products and create manufacturing specifications, while contracting out the manufacturing.

By turning to partner companies for help, while maintaining the perceived value of their own brands, these companies capitalize on the strengths of their partners while retaining their focus on what they do best. This is how companies will work together in the future as they join adaptive business networks.

In effect, Patagonia sets the controls or guidelines for how its partners operate. Malden Mills and other Patagonia suppliers make their own production decisions based on these controls, the information they receive from Patagonia, and the realities of the marketplace—competing orders, customer preferences, shortages of raw materials, and other supply information.

While Patagonia operates as a network, it is not yet an *adaptive business network*. Forming an adaptive business network would take Patagonia and its suppliers to the next level by enabling them to instantaneously receive information about customer demand and quickly adjust their production in response to fluctuating customer purchasing patterns.

Nevertheless, the way Patagonia works with its suppliers today provides a good example of the foundation from which companies will launch one type of adaptive business network. Like the lead company within an adaptive business network, Patagonia outsources all of its manufacturing to its suppliers, enabling it to focus on creating new products and developing brand awareness. It manages its suppliers to a set of standards and ensures all suppliers within its network are focused on customer demands and preferences. It allows companies within its network to remain autonomous and maintain responsibility for making their own production decisions within the parameters established by the network.

NETWORK ROLES

There are two roles within the adaptive business network: A company can either serve as the coordinating partner—the lead company responsible for coordinating the network—or it can serve as a participating company, often a supplier or a producer of specialty products or services. Each network is made up of multiple participating companies, but can have only one coordinating partner to lead its operations.

The Coordinating Partner

The role of the coordinating partner is to deliver the network's products and services to the customer. This lead company works with a group of autonomous partner companies that manufacture the products according to its specifications. The coordinating partner is linked to the other companies participating in the network through agreed-upon master contracts, standardized business processes, a common technology infrastructure, and a shared set of goals and measurements based on roles and relationships. Together, these factors ensure that all members of the network come together collaboratively to produce goods and services that the coordinating partner can brand and sell to its customers through retail stores, catalogs, the Internet, and multiple other sales channels.

As the lead company, the coordinating partner has many responsibilities within the network. It is the company that manages the brands to which customers respond and the sales channels through which network participants distribute those products. The coordinating partner also coordinates how the network operates, including the controls or guidelines that companies adhere to, how decisions are made, and how information is distributed among companies within the network. The coordinating partner also is responsible for establishing master agreements with its direct network partners that establish terms such as prices, the frequency with which components are delivered, and information to be shared. Once the network is initially established, the role of the coordinating partners diminishes as the network begins to adapt to new market conditions and competition.

Other responsibilities include contracting production capacity within the network, deciding on the technical infrastructure standards that link participating companies, providing the routing controls for the secure transfer of information within the network, monitoring the measurements of success for itself and network participants, adding and dropping partners as necessary, establishing prices with its direct suppliers, and focusing the network on customer demands and preferences.

The coordinating partner can take many shapes and forms. It can be a single company or a set of companies. It can be a brand and marketing-based consumer product company such as Patagonia or Nike Inc., or it can be a large manufacturing company like Procter & Gamble Co., which manufactures its own products and manages more than 250 brands. It can be a co-op, such as Fonterra Co-operative Group Ltd., the New Zealand dairy cooperative created to promote, market, and distribute the products of 14,000 New Zealand dairy farmers. There are a broad range of companies and business structures that can form adaptive business networks and serve as the coordinating partner for these networks.

Participating Companies

The role of participating companies is to meet the standards and metrics for operating within the network. Participating companies monitor information and inventory levels, and they automate as many transactions as needed to meet the established metrics. Participating companies respond to changing consumption and demand signals from the coordinating partner by adjusting their production levels and schedules accordingly.

REMAINING AUTONOMOUS

Although the adaptive business network encourages companies to form strategic alliances for their mutual benefit, participants will remain autonomous.

The adaptive business network is not a tool to encourage mergers and acquisitions, nor is it a method by which the dominant coordinating partner should excessively impose its will on smaller participating partner companies. Likewise, companies participating in an adaptive business network must not seek to jointly set prices for products. All companies will continue to remain freestanding, autonomous entities that separately report their financial results.

Despite working closely with partners in the network, each company must remain autonomous for legal, regulatory, and strategic reasons. Mergers and acquisitions will still occur. In the ABN world they might be driven by the need to get access to a network from which one of the M&A participants is excluded.

Network participants are responsible for upholding their contractual obligations and operating within the guidelines prescribed in the master agreements they establish with each other and the coordinating partner. They are also responsible for adopting technology that meets the standards of the network, maintaining their own security, adding and dropping direct suppliers to and from the network, meeting a set of key performance indicators (KPIs), and establishing prices with direct customers and suppliers.

COORDINATING PARTNER ROLES

Managing the Brands

Branding is an incredibly powerful force. The effect of brands on our consumption patterns has long been recognized—the association of vacuum cleaners with Hoover, gelatin desserts with Jell-O, and paper tissues with Kleenex are some of the most famous brand success stories in the twentieth century.

Today, most people around the world can identify numerous corporate logos, associating these logos with the appropriate brand values. Nike's swoosh is associated with youth and fitness. The Intel Inside logo is associated with quality computer components, and the golden arches of McDonald's restaurants are associated with perfectly uniform fast food. Some brand loyalties pass from generation to generation. Families in Britain remain incredibly faithful to brands of tea over multiple decades and, in some parts of the United States, families can be differentiated by the car maker they favor: Households are either Ford or Chevy families.

Because of the power and influence that such brands hold in the marketplace, one of the main roles for the coordinating partner is developing and managing customer brands, and achieving maximum value for these brands once developed by exploiting sales channels to their maximum benefit. Brand management is important in the adaptive business network because successfully maintaining and developing brands—and the sales channels through which they are marketed—is the primary avenue that a coordinating partner uses as it explores opportunities to enhance revenue.

Consumers are accustomed to paying more for a brand name, and the products of the adaptive business network have advantages when it comes to successfully establishing a premium brand. For one thing, the adaptive business network is based on dependable manufacturing, which can efficiently produce goods according to brand requirements. In addition, the network is flexible and responsive, and can be modified quickly to add new product lines or services as opportunities for new brands arise. Because the coordinating partner will often outsource some elements of the manufacturing process to participating companies, it can turn its full attention to serving the customer and concentrate its efforts on building powerful network brands that appeal to customers.

Managing the Network

In addition to managing brands, the coordinating partner is responsible for establishing the operating procedures required to ensure the network operates quickly and flexibly. To do this, the coordinating partner must consider four factors that provide the system's structure and governance:

1. *Management.* The contractual parameters that determine expectations and obligations of all participating companies. The coordinating partner is responsible for establishing these master agreements within the network.

2. *Controls.* The high-level rules and guidelines that govern how the network will operate. The coordinating partner is responsible for establishing the agreed-upon parameters that will dictate how everyday decisions are made.

3. *Decisions.* The actions taken within the adaptive network in the course of day-to-day business, as determined by the network's high-level rules and guidelines.

4. *Information.* The flow of data and information between participants within the network, including sales figures, shipping information, inventory counts, product shortages—all of the vital information on which day-to-day decisions are based. The role of the participants will determine the routing of the information.

The interplay among these four factors determines the network's ability to operate flexibly and quickly, and allows network participants to function as a single unit while at the same time remaining autonomous. As the coordinator of the network, the coordinating partner's role is to govern these four factors to protect the integrity of the individual companies and the network.

To illustrate the management, control, decision, and information functions within an adaptive network, take, for example, a fictional home décor retail chain called House Warming. As the coordinating partner of the adaptive network, House Warming establishes the commercial terms—or *controls*—that govern how its network operates, including the price of finished products, discounts, return policies, payment schedules, and so on.

As the coordinator of the network, House Warming also develops master *management* agreements with the participating companies that manufacture its home décor products. One of these companies is a candle-making company called Wax Magic. House Warming negotiates with Wax Magic to carry a selection of Wax Magic products that contribute to the retailer's brand equity, and also determines which products Wax Magic will make under the House Warming brand. While Wax Magic may also make candles for other companies based on a different set of requirements, the candles it makes for House Warming must conform to the controls or specifications set forth within the master agreement.

The master agreement also describes network policies regarding distribution models, financial arrangements, promotion patterns, co-branding agreements, sales, and consignment terms. With Wax Magic, one of the controls specifies how the candles will be stored and transported. For instance, House Warming asks Wax Magic to store some of its finished candles at its manufacturing site, some at regional distribution centers, and some at independent kitchen-products wholesale centers in major cities.

Once Wax Magic agrees to join the House Warming network, it independently passes on these specifications to its own network of business partners, including its transportation companies; raw materials vendors for wax, scent, and dye; and candle packaging companies. When this group of companies manufactures products and provides services for House Warming, the controls will be enforced to reflect the specifications of the network.

The controls also ensure that network guidelines are observed in making day-to-day *decisions*. Say a House Warming customer wants to return a candle. As the coordinating partner, House Warming has provided its customer service representatives (CSRs) with guidelines that determine whether to issue cash or credit, or require the customer to exchange the candle for another House Warming product. These controls ensure that the everyday decisions the CSRs make fall within the parameters established for the network. The objective of the controls is to make House Warming easy to do business with, and the controls enable the CSRs to use their judgment in making decisions—as long as those decisions fall within the guidelines outlined by the controls.

The role of each company within the network and its need for information determine the flow of *information* through the network, allowing the network to react quickly to shifts in customer demand. For example, according to its master agreement, Wax Magic will receive hourly data regarding the number and type of candles consumers purchase from the retail stores. The data allows Wax Magic to track the quantity and location of its candles as they flow through the network to House Warming store shelves.

Having this information enables Wax Magic to quickly respond to problems and better match production with actual customer demand. For example, Wax Magic knows immediately when demand is drying up for its floating candles and when sales of its line of tapers is increasing, and it can shift its production schedule accordingly. It also knows when a particular truck with a shipment of candles gets stuck in a snow storm, and can reroute another truck to get to the House Warming stores more quickly.

The network automatically issues information alerts to notify relevant participants of potential problems before they occur. For example, an information alert is sent warning House Warming and its suppliers that candles are selling faster than expected at House Warming stores in California, and that inventory in the San Diego store is running precariously low. If House Warming receives these alerts just before Christmas, the company will try to get more candles in stock as soon as possible. In addition to sending an information alert to Wax Magic, managers at House Warming may also send a series of queries to its other suppliers to determine the best place to order the replacement candles. Who can deliver the replacement candles most quickly? Is it Wax Magic? The regional House Warming warehouse system? A nearby kitchen-products wholesaler? Based on the data received in response to this query, House Warming will make the appropriate decision to restock its candles.

Coordinating Master Agreements

The coordinating partner also establishes network operating agreements that describe obligations, terms, and conditions for how the network will operate day to day. Upon setting up the network, the coordinating partner and its core group of suppliers negotiate the contractual structure that serves as the network's management framework. This agreement contains the basic legal requirements and specifications of the network in a template format that allows companies to quickly assent to or further negotiate the terms. The template may set out the terms of transportation and financial services within the network, commitment to brands or product, cost levels, and promotions. The agreements should also detail the participating company's obligations to the network. These include measurements such as KPIs, quality specifications required to maintain brand recognition, packaging requirements, and other terms and conditions. Establishing this template from which to build individual contracts will reduce the point-to-point negotiations that occur in business today, and allow companies to quickly join or detach from the network.

The coordinating partner uses the template as the basis for negotiating master agreements with each of its direct suppliers and customers. Each of its suppliers also uses the template as the basis for its agreements with its direct suppliers and customers. Each company that is an ongoing member of the network must sign a master agreement with its direct customers and suppliers. However, not all companies that do work with the network will be a member of the network—for example, a company may be brought in to fulfill a temporary need.

Other Responsibilities

As the lead company within the network, the coordinating partner also has a host of other responsibilities. They include the following:

■ *Planning production capacity committed within the network.* The coordinating partner is responsible for organizing the planned production capacity committed within the network and generating a master production plan for the network. The coordinating partner contracts production capacity with its network partners, who are obliged to manufacture these products according to requirements and specifications negotiated with the coordinating partner. The participating partners are also responsible for developing a production schedule based on the master production plan and report any deviations to this schedule. It is the responsibility of individual companies to decide what to do with capacity not committed to the network.

■ *Coordinating network resources.* The coordinating partner is responsible for coordinating shared resources such as transportation, financial services, warehouse space, the technological infrastructure, consultant studies, and other resources that may benefit the entire network. By pooling resources, companies within a network can obtain better rates for these services than they could by operating in isolation.

■ *Defining the standards for the technical infrastructure that allow for real-time communication across the network.* A common level of technology between network members and the coordinating partner is required for participating companies to work together within the network. One member of the network—usually the coordinating partner—must have an advanced planning system capable of developing forecasts and production plans. Alternatively, the network can hire an outside hosting company to provide the technology for the network. At its most basic level, members of the network will purchase a common technology access kit that links participants according to the needs of the network.

■ *Providing the routing controls for how information is distributed securely across the network.* Access to relevant information is important to ensure that the network responds flexibly to market conditions and opportunities. However, only the information needed to make specific decisions is shared among the appropriate network participants. As the governor of the network, the coordinating partner has access to all necessary levels of information regarding network activity. Each network member makes its own autonomous decisions based on the information it receives, within the parameters of previously agreed-upon network roles. In addition, each network member is responsible for the security and integrity of information passed between itself and other participants within the network, according to the security levels defined by the coordinating partner.

■ *Monitoring the KPIs of each partner to ensure consistent product quality and network activity.* The coordinating partner monitors the key performance indicators that must be met by specific members of the network. The KPIs are standard measurements that ensure performance, quality, and other factors of importance. Inventory position—where it is, how much there is, and how old it is—is an important measurement to most members of the network. Return on assets, production waste, and working capital also are important information to companies within the network. Furthermore, the frequency of problems, such as electricity outages, inventory shortages, or transportation obstacles, must be measured within the network. With the guidance of the coordinating partner, the network will set KPIs and manufacturing specifications that will guarantee consistent production of goods that support brand equity.

■ *Adding and dropping partners as necessary.* One of the primary advantages of the adaptive business network is how swiftly and inexpensively partners can be added or dropped. The coordinating partner is in charge of adding new partners to the network and dropping partners that produce substandard products or whose products no longer have a market. Outsourcing production to suppliers allows the coordinating partner to focus on developing brand awareness and creating new products. Moreover, the ability to easily add and drop partners enables the coordinating partner to produce customized and potentially high-profit products and services, while responding more quickly to customer preferences and branding opportunities.

- *Establishing prices with direct suppliers.* The coordinating partner establishes prices with its direct customers and suppliers, just as it does within the linear supply chain. Prices negotiated between the coordinating partner and its direct customers and suppliers are fixed within the master agreement for set periods of time. Within the network, all companies are financially autonomous. Accordingly, components purchased by the coordinating partner from its suppliers are true sales—not price transfers (as in transfer pricing between divisions of a single business).

- *Focusing the network on customers and their demands.* The coordinating partner is responsible for the relationship with the customer who purchases the finished goods and services produced within the network. This responsibility includes managing the brands and products purchased by the customer as well as the sales channels through which products are distributed. The coordinating partner focuses service on the customer, and is responsible for focusing all companies in the network on customer demands and preferences. In short, the coordinating partner and the network operate like a single integrated entity fulfilling customer demand.

Participating Company Roles

Participating companies can be any type or size. A participating company may be a manufacturer, retailer, or service provider. Its role is to bring a product, brand, or service to the network that enhances the total brand equity of the network's offerings. Within the adaptive business network, participating companies take on the following roles:

- *Negotiating contractual terms with their direct business partners and with the coordinating partner's network.* Participating companies accept the master agreement of the network, which governs how they operate based on their role within the network. A participating company will expand on the master agreement template, and negotiate terms with its own suppliers based on its relationship with each supplier.

- *Establishing and monitoring KPIs to ensure quality standards.* Participating companies are responsible for conforming to the KPIs established by the network. Participating companies may choose to establish their own set of company metrics that are independent from—but not in conflict with—the network KPIs. Each company will report its KPIs to relevant participants in the network.

▪ *Meeting the technical and security standards established by the coordinating partner.* Each participating company is responsible for adopting and conforming to a common level of technology required by the network. In some cases, this will mean purchasing a common technology access kit that links the participating company together with other members of the network. In other cases, the participant may need to make technological changes to fit into the process and meet the service levels of the network.

▪ *Maintaining security.* Each participating company is responsible for the security and integrity of information passed between itself and other participants within the network, according to the security levels established by the network.

▪ *Adding and dropping partners to the network.* Like the coordinating partner, participating companies are responsible for adding direct suppliers to the network. They are also responsible for eliminating substandard suppliers that will not enable them to meet the KPIs established by the network.

▪ *Establishing prices with direct customers and suppliers.* Like the coordinating partner, each participating company within the network is in charge of negotiating prices with the direct customer to whom it sells products or services, and with the direct suppliers from whom it purchases materials or components.

MANAGEMENT FUNCTIONS

Whether it is service- or product-based, an adaptive business network must have basic partner types in place to ensure that it is fully adaptive, and for it to be more than a group of point-to-point linear partnerships. There will be only one coordinating partner, but multiple participating partners. In any adaptive business network, there are several basic management functions that must be performed by network participants, including:

1. *Customer relationship manager,* who makes certain that the customer realizes value from the receipt of the goods or services provided by the network.

2. *Brand/channel manager,* who is responsible for maintaining and enhancing the customer's belief that the network's brands have attributable value.

3. *Product manager,* who is responsible for the customer's perception that the product conforms to its related brand or channel value.

4. *Materials manager,* who is responsible for the customer's perception that the materials in the product conform to the brand or channel value.

5. *Logistics manager,* who is responsible for the customer's perception that the product as received conforms to the brand or channel value.

6. *Financial manager,* who is responsible for the customer's perception that the value received from the products and/or services of the network were attributable to the brand or channel.

Every adaptive business network will have at least these six roles, with participants identified to fill each role. This does not mean that an adaptive network is restricted to six participants, or that each role must be defined or restricted to one participant. A single participant may perform the multiple roles of brand/channel manager, product manager, and customer relationship manager.

For example, in a retail-based consumer products network, the retail partner would perform the customer relationship manager role. The CPG company would, at minimum, perform the brand/channel manager role, but also may act as product manager to perform final assembly. Other participants may also act as product manager while making additional products available within the brand/channel. In the adaptive business network, there may be two logistics managers—one carrier for long-haul network linkages and another for "last-mile" distribution to retail sites.

The financial manager role, whenever possible, should be performed by a single participant. This will enable the network to maximize potential financial benefits. If all members of the network use a single financial institution for their working capital needs, this larger pool of clients may potentially result in a lower interest rate or more favorable repayment terms.

OVERLAPPING NETWORKS

In addition to the various roles within each network, companies may play similar or very different roles in other networks. A participating company in one network may be the coordinating partner of another network. A coordinating partner in one network may be a participating company in another. In fact, both of these situations will frequently be the case.

Take a consumer goods company like Procter & Gamble, for example. Procter & Gamble could form its own adaptive business network that includes a wide range of suppliers for its personal care products. At the same time, Procter & Gamble will likely act as a participating company in several other adaptive business networks. It could be a participating company in a retail network in which Wal-Mart was the coordinating partner, and also in networks headed by Walgreens and Target. Similarly, the suppliers from which Bristol Myers Squibb buys its fragrances for its Clairol line of hair care products may also serve as a participating company in multiple other consumer goods networks perhaps headed by Unilever and Colgate.

In reality, the business world of the future will resemble a large set of interlinked companies with connections to a constellation of networks. Networks will frequently overlap. In some cases, businesses will operate as participating companies in an array of adaptive business networks. In other cases, they will act as participating companies in some networks while serving as the coordinating partner of their own.

CHAPTER FIVE

Preparing for an Adaptive Business Network

When you cease to make a contribution, you begin to die.

—Eleanor Roosevelt

Albert Einstein is said to have defined insanity as doing the same thing over and over and expecting different results. By this definition, a lot of what takes place in business today surely rates as insanity.

Over the past two decades, companies have tried to tackle their business problems by repeatedly applying the same types of solutions, undertaking the same projects, and using the same implementation methodologies and techniques. They put a new leader in charge. They form cross-functional teams. They bring in a new consultant. They buy new technology. They keep seeking change, and each time they expect different results. This time, they think, the effort will increase efficiency, transform employee morale, and bring real, bottom-line results.

For many companies, the business initiatives of the past several years have brought substantial results. For example, between 1995 and 2000, the average annual labor productivity rate was 2.6 percent, up from 0.8 percent between 1990 and 1995.[1] No doubt, this increase is at least partially attributable to a widespread focus on improving operational efficiency.

For other companies, however, these business initiatives did not bring about the desired changes. In some cases, the business initiative itself did not fully address the problems the company set out to solve, but more often these initiatives failed because of the way businesses implemented them. They failed because companies viewed them as technology projects and neglected to make the requisite business process changes to allow the technology to work successfully. They failed because companies did not establish clear measurements of success beforehand, and were uncertain about the goals of the initiative in the first place. And they failed because companies did not have the leadership in place to take them through the significant organizational changes required to make the business initiative successful.

The adaptive business network is a revolutionary way of conducting business that requires companies to work with partners in a radically different way than they have up until now. Moving to an adaptive business network will help companies eliminate many unnecessary processes when working with customers and suppliers. Companies that succeed in making the transformation will find that the adaptive network helps them to lower operating costs, attract new business opportunities, and react more quickly and effectively to fast-moving market conditions.

However, like many previous business initiatives, the adaptive network will not bring about the desired changes if companies view this discipline solely as a technology project. In fact, the first steps to forming an adaptive business network focus almost exclusively on transforming a company's business processes. It's not until sound business processes are in place that a company can reap the benefits of technology to further increase efficiency and improve response times.

Moving toward an adaptive business network also requires that companies first have measurements of success in place. At every step of the implementation, a clear set of goals must be defined and success against these goals must be evaluated. Specific time frames for each step of the implementation must be set to ensure the move to the adaptive business network doesn't drag on and the commitment to this discipline doesn't drop off.

Finally, moving to an adaptive business network requires the willingness to change a company's core ways of doing business. Within an adaptive business network, the way managers run their company in relationship to their partners changes. The way they fulfill customer needs changes. And the way they go about much of their daily work, including counting inventory, developing production and distribution forecasts, filling customer orders, and resolving quality issues, changes.

Because of this, the move to an adaptive business network requires top managers within a company to make the proper mind shift, and display the leadership and energy to guide employees through a set of changes that some may resist or find painful. Following are some of the questions companies should consider before moving to an adaptive business network.

WHAT ARE OUR COMPANY GOALS?

Employees need to ask themselves where they want their company to be one year, three years, five years down the road. What are the company's objectives, and how will the adaptive business network help accomplish those objectives? Moving to an adaptive business network will only be a success if companies begin with the end goal in mind. They must know where they are headed, consistently chart progress, and be prepared to switch directions as market conditions dictate. In addition to establishing long-range goals, it's important to have a tactical plan that will enable the company to achieve them. To reach the objective, every step need not be planned or even fully understood, but some of the early steps must be figured out so the company is pointed in the right direction.

DO WE REALLY NEED THIS?

The adaptive business network is a growth-based strategy. If your company is highly profitable, if it is meeting or exceeding its measurements of success, and if it is not interested in expanding and responding to new opportunities, the adaptive business network may not be for you. If, on the other hand, your company is looking to expand or improve its operations, the adaptive business network provides substantial benefits. For example, if your company wants to expand its customer base, increase supplier reliability, boost revenues by forming partnerships, sell products through more sales channels, improve customer service on a global scale, overcome seasonal revenue shortfalls, or get new products on the market more quickly, the adaptive business network has a lot to offer.

The adaptive business network also helps to mitigate risks. If globalization is forcing your company to adjust its operations and respond more quickly, if it seeks new markets for its products or services, if it wants to borrow less working capital and use that capital more efficiently, or if it is struggling to meet high customer expectations, the adaptive business network can help manage these risks while helping the company remain viable.

ARE WE CAPABLE OF THIS KIND OF CHANGE?

Before undertaking this effort, senior managers need to ensure that the company's management team is capable of leading the company through this change. Issues to consider include whether the company's executives can rally the necessary employee support, and whether the company is capable of operating within the parameters of a network. Tackling this kind of challenge requires teamwork, responsiveness, and organizational will. And it requires adopting a new set of processes.

Generally speaking, if the company successfully turned off its old processes and captured measurable results from its last major business initiative, then it is probably ready for such a change. On the other hand, if the last project wasn't a success, the company's leadership at least needs to understand the reasons for the failure and make adjustments before moving to an adaptive business network. If the company's leadership cannot be honest and critical about its past mistakes, the adaptive business network could prove to be a failure as well.

In so many cases, companies have adopted new methods of working and new technology, trained everyone, and a year later found that only half of its employees were actually using the new tools. In such cases, the old way of doing business persists, with half the workforce using the new set of tools and half the old tools, because no one had the nerve to fully make the leap to the new way of working.

Moving to the adaptive network is a process, and as the company moves from step to step, it turns off the old way of doing business. There's no going back. If your company is not willing or able to turn off the old processes and systems, then you're not ready for the adaptive business network. The entire organization needs to be willing to make the change to a new way of doing business for the adaptive business network to be a success.

WHAT PROCESS SHIFTS WILL OCCUR?

Throughout the organization, some long-established practices will begin to change:

- *Ordering.* A number of significant changes will occur within the order process. Within the network itself, the traditional purchase order may cease to exist. Instead, electronic confirmations will be generated across the network. These changes will affect how departments within the company—such as purchasing and shipping—function on a daily basis.

- *Purchasing.* The centralized purchasing function will also change. It will no longer concentrate on seeking low-cost deals and chasing price reductions from suppliers, but will instead focus on forming strategic master purchase agreements that govern how partners within the network exchange products and money.

- *Customer service.* The customer service representative (CSR) role will move from extinguishing flare ups to customer advocacy. A CSR assigned to a specific product line will more proactively manage the product and related relationships by looking for ways to create new opportunities to sell the company's product line, or by anticipating problems rather than waiting for them to occur.

- *Inventory management.* Inventory accuracy is paramount in the network. For many companies formerly content to take manual inventory tallies on paper, this represents a real mind shift. Inventory methodology must be standardized across the network for it to operate effectively. Consistent network inventory management practices stabilize the operation of the network. Inaccurate or untimely inventory counts will compromise the integrity of network-based delivery comments.

- *Manufacturing to plan.* Manufacturing to plan is far more important than operating at maximum capacity within an adaptive business network. Underproduction and overproduction create inventory and customer service problems for the network. Depending on the production plan, running the machines at maximum capacity to manufacture as much product as possible may not be the desired goal of the network. In fact, one of the primary outputs of the network is a set of highly accurate plans. This enables manufacturers to reduce or expand capacity with confidence.

- *Incentives management.* Companies will begin rewarding employees for their success in meeting measurements determined by the network—and not on measurements that support the success of a single company or division. For example, there's no reward for manufacturing products just to meet output goals if there's not enough demand for those products. The effect often leads to clogging the network with unnecessary inventory.

WHAT KIND OF CHANGES CAN WE EXPECT TO SEE AS WE MOVE FORWARD?

The adaptive business network involves some high-level—and sometimes subtle—shifts in how companies operate. You may see the following changes within your company, and you will need to plan accordingly.

Common Processes Will Be Established

Common business processes will be established so that companies within the network can work together effectively. In addition, KPIs will be established, and each company within the network will be required to quantitatively measure its performance. Finally, rather than operating as isolated entities, companies will now be interdependent on each other for a certain degree of success. For example, a transportation problem that affected one company may now affect several companies, requiring them to work together in unison to identify a solution.

New Leaders Will Emerge

Jobs once consumed by repetitive tasks will become more visible and strategic. Consequently, new leaders will emerge within the company. Employees whose talents adapt quickly to the adaptive network may surprise you. Other employees, once shielded behind levels of organizational structure, will find their jobs changed or potentially eliminated. However, the adaptive business network is not an exercise in workforce reduction. The adaptive business network specifically targets many operational costs and seeks to dramatically reduce them. To make the transition a success, companies need to give workers time to adapt to their new roles and impress the company with their talents. If the personal motivations of employees do not match the company's objectives, moving to an adaptive network will create conflict. On the other hand, if employees are brought into the company's objectives, moving to an adaptive network will be a win-win for both the employees and the company as a whole.

Customer Service Will Become a Factor for Every Employee

Focusing on the needs of the customer is a critical element of the adaptive business network. Throughout the network, processes are designed to provide customers with the greatest value and service possible. In the process, the adaptive business network helps a company refocus on what the term *customer* actually means—the entity that pays for the finished products and services produced by the entire network.

In many companies, "the customer" is defined as a group of fellow employees that receive your goods, with the flow of goods through the company resembling a series of retail exchanges—"sales" and "purchases" flow from one working group to the next. In other cases, "the customer" means the operating division to whom you directly sell your part for assembly into a finished product. However, the customer is not Joe in the next assembly division. Nor is he the senior vice president who's demanding a sales report. No one from inside your company can generate a profit, and in fact, these internal buyer-seller exchanges drain value from your products and degrade your earnings per share.

One of management's primary roles within the adaptive business network is to help employees identify how their roles serve the *end* customer, and to help them focus their efforts on serving that customer. At

WILL THE REAL CUSTOMER PLEASE STAND UP?

It should be an easy answer, but ask a dozen employees who their customer is and you're likely to get a dozen answers.

Many businesses consider the next company in line in the linear supply chain—the company that they directly supply—to be their customer. They are wrong.

Other companies consider divisions within their own company to be the customer, a concept that goes hand in hand with individual profit centers and transfer pricing, where corporate departments collect revenue from one another. For example, a company's engineering department might consider its manufacturing department to which it sends manufacturing specifications and from which it receives revenue to be its customer. Wrong again.

Instead, the only customer is the final customer at the end of the line, the person or business that pays its hard-earned money for the finished good or service. It is important to keep a next-in-line company or consumer happy as supplies and services are passed along a linear supply chain; but, there is only one true customer—the final customer that pays the bills.

This can be a difficult challenge for many companies. Commodity or raw materials providers will find this especially difficult. These companies are the farthest removed from the final customer and have a long history of produce and distribute to an abstract specification, usually created by the purchaser of the material. In this case, it is all the more important to focus on the final customer, providing an identity for the company—a relationship between the company's people and the final customer. This enables the network to provide a consistent product performance.

the highest level, employees will need to understand that the purpose of the entire network is to facilitate the flow of goods and services to this customer. Everybody's job is either to provide a service to the end customer or to make sure that the goods they produce are of the highest quality possible.

How will customer service become a factor in everyone's job? Someone in accounts payable might focus on the company's invoices. Are the net payables always correct? Are they in a format that best serves the customer's purposes? Are there payment schedules that might better accommodate the needs of both companies? A personnel executive in the human resources department might focus on evaluating applicants on their ability to work creatively with customers—not just on their ability to fit into the company or division.

A Standardized Vocabulary Will Evolve

The group involved in the early stages of the adaptive business network will identify and begin to speak a common vocabulary. This is one of the most powerful outcomes from the move to an adaptive business network. Immediately, a core group of people speak the same language about key functions and goals. Everyone understands what is meant by the same term, and by extension, everyone is working to achieve it.

This creates a common work culture, which spreads as the group grows larger. For example, consider the term *order*. If you go into the same manufacturing company and ask a dozen people what an order is, chances are you'll get a dozen different answers. Is the order what the customer

A TON OF TONNES

The requirement to maintain a consistent vocabulary within the network may seem like an arbitrary or even authoritarian demand. However, consider the consequences if a buyer in Las Vegas ordered a ton of steel from Great Britain and another ton from Spain. The U.S.-based buyer will expect to take delivery of 2,000 pounds of steel—a measure that's also known as a short ton. However, the supplier in Great Britain may send a British tonne of steel, which is equal to 2,240 pounds—also known as a long ton. A metric ton, equal to 1,000 kilograms, will weigh out 2,204.62 pounds. Without a common meaning for ton/tonne, a global business could quickly loose track of inventory quantities.

service representative takes from the customer? Is it what your operations department passes on to the warehouse? Or is it what gets shipped on pallets? Is it a request or is it merchandise? To work together efficiently, companies within the network will need to agree to specific definitions for terms like these.

WHO SHOULD LEAD THE CHARGE?

The impetus to move toward an adaptive business network should always come from one of the following players within the company:

- *Purchasing,* if you are hoping to draw from a larger base of suppliers and reduce the cost of your raw materials.
- *Sales and marketing,* if you want to increase sales, improve customer service, and capture new opportunities to co-brand and co-market your product through creative partnerships with other companies.
- *Manufacturing,* if you want to make better use of your manufacturing capacity or lease extra capacity to partners.
- *Logistics,* if you want to make more strategic use of your warehouse and storage locations or your transportation system.
- *The CEO,* if he or she determines that growing through strategic partnerships is preferable to growing through mergers and acquisitions.

The company's IT department should never lead the charge for the move to an adaptive business network. The adaptive business network is not an IT project—it is a business process initiative supported by technology.

Nor should the impetus come from the company's finance department. The cost savings that result from an adaptive business network are gained from business process excellence—from speed, efficiency, and service.

WHAT MEASUREMENTS SHOULD BE IN PLACE BEFORE SETTING OUT?

Measurements are important for success in the adaptive business network, and as a company moves through the steps involved in establishing the network, the measurements become more specific and more significant. There are four basic measurements, or key performance indicators, that must be in place to measure success. Companies should set these measurement goals before embarking on each of the four steps in the adaptive business network:

■ *Inventory.* Inventory must be tracked, either as raw materials, work-in-progress inventory, or finished goods. One of the key benefits of the adaptive business network is the reduction of inventory across the network. As a measure of success, a company must be able to track inventory reduction and where it occurs.

■ *Return on assets.* Many companies measure return on assets (ROA) based on the total value of the production facilities and total revenue generated from sold units. Companies should strive for the level of ROA they decided on when creating their financial and manufacturing plan. Running a machine to maximum capacity may increase a company's ROA at a certain production facility, but it will decrease the company's overall return on assets if the company has difficulty selling the inventory it has produced.

■ *Production waste.* There are two kinds of production waste: controllable and uncontrollable. Controllable production waste is the result of faulty production, mistakes, or other errors. For example, controllable waste occurs when a brewer bottling its beer has more beer than bottles to hold it and must pour this perishable product down the drain. This waste is due to mismatched production schedules, missed deliveries, equipment failures, or employee glitches. It is called controllable because it often could have been prevented. Conversely, uncontrollable production waste is a normal part of the production process and is essential to making the finished product. For example, when a newspaper company runs its presses, a certain amount of newsprint paper is wasted to test the ink colors, optimize the press, and other factors. It is called uncontrollable because it cannot be entirely prevented. However, changes in processes, methods, and equipment may help reduce this waste. Companies will need a way to measure controllable and uncontrollable production waste, because reducing production waste is a key goal in an adaptive business network.

■ *Working capital charges.* The company must track financial measurements such as the cash-to-cash cycle. When a product is manufactured, it costs money, but it may be months before the company sells and then collects payment for that product. This ties up the company's working capital. The longer products sit in inventory, the more working capital a company needs to operate, and the costs of carrying the inventory can be substantial. The adaptive business network will reduce inventory, and as a result, the company will see a reduction in working capital charges over time.

These four measurements all move together. As inventory drops, working capital charges decrease. As production waste decreases, return on assets will increase.

Some businesses may not have, or be able to measure, all four of these KPIs. For instance, a business may not generate production waste or have meaningful working capital charges. Depending on its business, a company may not see significant improvements in each of these four categories as it moves toward the adaptive business network. However, if all four measures apply to the business, all four should be monitored. In addition, during the early steps of the adaptive business network, most businesses will only see improvement in working capital and inventory.

These four KPIs also apply to service companies. For service companies, inventory is the work-in-progress and completed projects that have not yet been paid for. Return on assets can be the amount of time employees are billing or the return on hard assets such as how many customers are staying in the company's hotels or leasing its rental cars. Production waste for service companies is the time spent on nonbillable activities, and working capital is the amount borrowed to keep the business in operation. Assets are managed differently in non-manufacturing companies, but the primary concept remains the same. In non-manufacturing companies, managers maximize their assets by selling them to as many customers as possible, as quickly as possible, while the concept or information remains fresh.

The four KPIs are important because most companies within a network should see some degree of benefit in at least three of the four indicators. However, not all businesses will see benefits in the same three KPIs, nor will they see equal benefits. As companies move closer to full network relationships with their partners, other KPI measurements will become important. Chief among these will be a metric for time compression—reducing the delays inherent in completing tasks when working with partners—which only becomes measurable at more advanced stages of the network.

WHAT'S INVOLVED IN MOVING TO AN ADAPTIVE BUSINESS NETWORK?

Companies can move to an adaptive network in four steps (Figure 5.1):

1. *Step One—Visibility.* Companies and their partners examine inventory and shipment numbers and gain agreement on the accuracy of

FIGURE 5.1   THE FOUR STEPS OF AN ADAPTIVE BUSINESS
            NETWORK

Companies can move to an adaptive business network in four steps:

Step 4—Adaptability:

- Time required for many tasks greatly decreased.
- Many tasks completely eliminated.
- Inventory and working capital dramatically reduced.
- New alliances, products, and revenue opportunities possible.

Step 3—Collaboration:

- Sharing of customer demand data with members.
- Targeted replenishment of supplies.
- Responsibility transferred to supply replenishment vendors.
- Ability to reallocate inventory to fulfill maximum number of orders.

Step 2—Community:

- Moving day-to-day transactions to the portal.
- Establishment of minimum and maximum control thresholds.
- Reduction of inventory.
- Time savings via mechanizing transactions.

Step 1—Visibility:

- Sharing of information with partner companies.
- Many routine business processes with partners standardized.
- Information posted for common view on portal.
- Greater insight into business process and data accuracy problems.

this data. The companies begin to track this information, particularly inventory levels, to a specific number of days' worth of supply. The companies also begin to share information electronically with partners via a simple portal Web site, and to make simple manual transactions via this Web site. Step One will lead to a slight reduction in inventory levels and closer ties among partner companies.

2. *Step Two—Community.* Step Two greatly improves the accuracy of inventory tracking methods by ensuring that inventory numbers are now accurate to within a few minutes, essentially making those numbers "real time." Companies will install bar code scanning or radio frequency identification (RFID) technology to accomplish this. Similarly, during Step Two, companies and their partners agree on certain predetermined threshold levels for many transactions and automate transactions that fall within these thresholds. This frees employees from mundane tasks to focus instead on the problems or "exceptions" that arise. Step Two will produce further inventory and working capital charge reductions, while redeploying employees to more strategic tasks.

3. *Step Three—Collaboration.* Partners begin to work more collaboratively. They also begin to dynamically shuffle products between facilities and orders, which can allow companies to more easily fulfill orders and further reduce inventory. In addition, Step Three enables companies to automatically replenish supplies and materials by tracking consumption from the portal Web site or directly in their respective systems, which is constantly updated. Later in this step, businesses shift to their vendors the responsibility for ordering and shipping necessary supplies. This leads to massive reductions in inventory as well as working capital. Step Three also improves the production cycle for suppliers, essentially cutting out many emergency production runs and leading to cost savings for all members of the adaptive business network. Functions eliminated in Step Three include individual purchase orders and invoicing.

4. *Step Four—Adaptability.* Partner companies begin to share information about customer demand, such as orders and sales figures, so they can respond to subtle changes as soon as they occur. Pervasive technology allows the companies to plan, execute, sense, and respond to business fluctuations with greater ease and at lower cost than before. This technology will enable partners to act in concert with existing systems, greatly reducing the time needed for many processes and eliminating others altogether. Moreover, a new web of partnerships enables the businesses to better dictate demand and pool their resources for new market and product opportunities. Most importantly, Step Four lays the foundation for companies to

remain adaptive in the face of change and adversity, ensuring they will flourish and remain viable in the long term.

These four steps put companies in a position to collaborate with their partners electronically, forecast more accurately, and generally save more time and money than 125 earlier business excellence initiatives. By starting with the basics and changing corporate attitudes along the way, these steps prepare companies for the future of business and help them establish the network partnerships that will form its backbone.

WHY NOT JUST JUMP STRAIGHT TO STEP FOUR?

This adaptive business network sounds pretty good. But why go through the time and struggle of the early steps when what you really want to do is jump ahead to the more enticing benefits of Step Four?

This same assumption of readiness is a key reason why earlier business excellence initiatives have failed. Similarly, very few companies are ready to move to the advanced steps of the adaptive business network process without first going through the basic steps.

Even if you believe your company has already accomplished the first two steps and that you are prepared for Step Three or Four, you need to validate that belief by starting with Step One. If your assumption is valid, you'll find you can move through the early steps quickly. More often, however, companies that assumed they were ready for the later steps discover, upon completing Steps One and Two, that they didn't really have the business processes in place to make the later steps a success.

The four steps chart a path that will take any business from the establishment of rudimentary business processes to adaptability by following a natural sequence of process improvements. Not only will the four steps help standardize processes between a company and its partners—increasingly necessary as they collaborate more closely—but they'll also help the company confront organizational change issues up front. Following these steps allows a company to interact with its partner companies at the beginning of this change, so that the organizational shift that companies often overlook until the last minute occurs right at the beginning of the process.

In short, it is critical to go through the four steps in sequence. Jumping ahead more often than not will lead to failure.

ARE WE READY TO BEGIN BUILDING AN ADAPTIVE BUSINESS NETWORK?

To answer this question, companies need to once again consider their objectives. If the company is already effectively collaborating with suppliers and customers, or there is no readily apparent benefit in undertaking the four steps, then the answer is no. If, on the other hand, the company's objectives could be enhanced by the opportunities that result from collaborating with customers and suppliers, then the answer is yes.

When a company is ready to move to an adaptive business network, its leadership should begin to prepare employees right away through honest and constant communication. Employees need to know there will be changes, and they need to be prepared for the fact that some of these changes will be difficult.

The hardest part of leading projects that involve change is incorporating change in the hearts and minds of people. This is why business projects often fail—it's not because of the technology, it's because people don't want to make the change. The move to an adaptive business network will go much more smoothly with consistent communications that focus on helping employees understand the company's goals and their role in achieving those goals.

If your company is willing to focus on the four KPIs discussed earlier in this chapter—and establish meaningful measurements for tracking inventory, return on assets, production waste, and working capital charges—then you are ready to begin. Your inventory accuracy may be poor, and your return on assets may be subpar. It's not necessary that these measures be accurate. What's important at this stage is that companies have established the processes and arrived at a means to make the measurements. In other words, to begin the first step of establishing an adaptive business network, companies don't have to know all the answers. They just have to know what questions to ask.

WHEN SHOULD WE STOP AND REEVALUATE?

Companies should evaluate progress toward realizing their strategy and goals every year at a minimum. Those that are not meeting their established KPIs may need to evaluate more often. A three-month trend in the wrong direction indicates that the initiative should be stopped because an adjustment may be required. Companies should also reevaluate in response to significant political, social, or economic events that may necessitate a shift in strategy—for example, if a competitor suddenly introduces a new technology that affects a company product, or if a new government regulation forces the company to adjust how it does business. Also, a company may need to evaluate its progress more often depending on the volatility of its industry.

HOW DO WE KNOW IF WE'RE SUCCEEDING?

Just like a road trip, a company knows it is succeeding if the mile markers keep flying by. Short-term, intermediate, and long-term objectives should be established, and if a company is not meeting these objectives within the agreed-upon time frames, then adjustments should be made. If, however, a company is meeting or exceeding these objectives, then it is on the right track.

CHAPTER SIX

Step One——Visibility

It is a mistake to look too far ahead. Only one link in the chain of destiny can be handled at a time.

—Winston Churchill

It's a day like any other day at the Soft-Drink Company, where Dana works as a customer service representative (CSR). Dana's primary responsibility at Soft-Drink is to take orders and represent the company to the purchasing agents of its customers. These people call Dana and tell her what products they want. She checks the inventory, and if her tallies tell her that Soft-Drink has enough of the requested product in stock, she places the order, and the goods are delivered.

Sounds easy, right? It should be easy. It's an everyday occurrence and one of the most basic processes for thousands of businesses globally. Yet, in reality Dana's job—and that of hundreds of thousands of similar workers—is a complete juggling act, and one that inevitably leaves some customers disappointed and angry.

One customer calls Dana to order 75 cases of lemonade. However, the inventory information tells her that there are only 50 cases in the warehouse. She doesn't want to lose this sale, so she puts her customer on hold and calls her friend Casper in the shipping department. He's got 25 cases of lemonade in the queue that are scheduled to be shipped to Wal-Mart, but for his friend Dana he's happy to redirect those cases to her customer. Now Dana's customer is happy. But what about Wal-Mart?

Dana's next customer wants to order 50 cases of orange soda. The inventory tallies indicate that there are exactly 50 cases of orange soda in the warehouse. That ought to be good news, but Dana knows that she'll need to verify the inventory count. It's Friday afternoon, and the count often gets overlooked with everyone trying to leave for the weekend.

Dana calls the warehouse and asks her friend Marty to do a quick count. She discovers that in fact there are only 25 cases. More phone calls reveal that Dana can get another 15 cases from the local distribution center, and Margaret, the CSR in the next cubicle, is willing to short Monday's standing order to Safeway by 10 cases so that Dana can fill her order. Again, Dana's customer is happy. But what about Safeway?

Dana's next caller says he's having a special tropical theme promotion and needs 500 cases of fruit punch next week. Dana finds that there are only 25 cases of fruit punch in the warehouse. She has been told that, rather than lose the sale, the company would make adjustments based on her commitments. So she puts the customer on hold and calls her old friend Joan who works in the bottling plant. Joan's happy to help. There's not enough time to go through the regular production planning process with this order for tropical punch, so Joan says she'll set up a special production run for Dana's order, and delay the bottling run that had been scheduled. Another of Dana's customers is satisfied. But what about the customers that were to be served by that next bottling run?

You begin to get a sense of what Dana's job is like—and what it will be like Monday when Safeway and Wal-Mart and the other customers call to angrily report their short or missing shipments. Whose orders will be raided then?

Although this story of Dana and her can-do attitude might seem exaggerated, anyone who has worked with a CSR in a manufacturing company will recognize the situation. This kind of juggling of inventory shipments and production runs goes on far more often than anyone admits.

Given this improvisational method of conducting business, it's easy to see why inventory is difficult to track at the Soft-Drink Company. Investments in automated production planning and vendor replenishment inventory software will be a waste of time until the company can fix this problem. Until companies can reach agreement and develop accurate information about basic processes like inventory and product flow, everything else is extraneous.

Dana, in her zeal to serve the customer and satisfy her management, is operating outside the processes of her company. This is not because Dana is malicious or purposely trying to harm the company; she simply has no confidence in the information provided by the systems that Soft-Drink has spent millions of dollars implementing and has instead come to

STEP ONE FAST FACTS

What's in It for My Company?

- Inventory is reduced by between 1 and 3 percent.

- Transportation costs decrease because there are fewer less-than-full truckloads.

- Companies improve basic business processes and build relationships with key trading partners.

- A single view of inventory, orders, forecasts, and plans is obtained across participating companies.

- New talent and leaders emerge from inside the company.

- The company is easier for partners to do business with.

What Work Is Involved?

- Selecting a team and product line with which to work.

- Establishing regular phone calls to discuss inventory and order commitments.

- Posting information such as inventory counts, manufacturing plans, production schedules, order schedules, distribution plans, and forecasts on a portal for participants to view and update.

- Obtaining continual management sponsorship and involvement in the Step One process.

What Technology Is Required?

- A phone system capable of conference calls.

- A simple browser or portal, or even a spreadsheet and e-mail program.

How Long Will It Take?

- Self-directed teams that are used to working together can move through Step One in three weeks. Other teams can take up to six months.

- It's important to take the time to complete this step because there's no point going any further until the teams can complete this process correctly.

rely on her informal network of contacts to fulfill the needs of her immediate customers.

There are employees like Dana in every kind of company, whether manufacturing, retail, or services. Their situations are similar. These employees try to manage a queue of services or inventory, juggling available labor, reallocating supplies at the last minute, overbooking their service, or shorting a standing order to meet the needs of a new customer. The question is whether the company rewards people for avoiding problems in the first place, or for being a hero after the problems occur.

If a company has inaccurate information regarding inventory allocation and fails to adhere to its manufacturing or distribution plan, then the company's CSRs won't know what the truth is. Once the CSRs lose confidence in their information, informal work-around processes will be established and, once that happens, chaos rules.

Some potential root causes of this phenomenon could be poorly designed or executed processes for inventory management, sales planning and forecasting, profitability planning, and managing production to plan. It could even be as fundamental as a set of misaligned incentives and objectives.

STEP ONE

The first step in forming an adaptive business network directly addresses the problems faced by employees like Dana, and helps break the patterns that make it difficult to accurately monitor inventory and fulfill orders the way customers expect. Step One improves a company's relationship with customers—and enhances the lives of the frontline employees whose jobs are to make customers happy by ordering supplies and selling products.

The goal of Step One is for companies to begin working as partners with their suppliers and customers. All companies involved will move from the traditional buyer-seller relationship in which the only information shared is the amount of orders placed, into a collaborative partnership in which a great deal of information is shared for the purpose of aligning inventory levels, distribution plans, and forecasts to the benefit of all. Step One should include a focused set of products, brands, and sales channels. Companies should not attempt to move all of their products through Step One at the same time.

The real purpose of Step One is to reorganize the company around new teams capable of performing multiple functions. These teams will focus on a new business discipline. Initially, this is a labor-intensive process. Moving toward an adaptive business network requires slowing company business processes at first, so that employees understand the significance of each process, where the processes fall short, and why they are important to the business as a whole.

Companies that undertake Step One begin to share basic information about supply and demand and post this information on a common portal, so that participants can begin to plan more effectively. Completing the step requires little investment, and commonly enables participants to reduce their inventory by 1 to 3 percent.

Step One forces participating companies to agree, on a weekly basis, to some basic facts: How much inventory is there? Where is it? How much is available to sell? How much has been ordered? What kind of products and how many of these products will key customers need in the coming week?

These questions aren't exactly the stuff of revolutions. Almost all companies have these processes operating informally. Yet, providing accurate and timely answers to these queries is surprisingly difficult for most companies. Until your company can generate this information internally with speed and precision, no amount of software is going to expedite the process of balancing supply and demand with multiple trading partners.

Step One enables companies—working together as a supply chain—to develop more accurate information about physical inventory, order positions, and production and distribution plans, schedules, and forecasts. By the time participants move on to Step Two, their data should be 80 to 90 percent accurate, and their inventory counts accurate to one day,

WHY NOT SKIP THIS STEP?

Step One may seem elementary. Confirming order position and inventory quantity, type, and location by phone between trading partners seems like a basic exercise. However, even if you are convinced that the people in your company could perform these functions in their sleep, you must validate that inventory counts are accurate and communication is effective. You may be surprised at the procedural gaps that Step One exposes. In addition, the camaraderie that builds among team members and between companies in Step One is an essential building block of the adaptive business network.

meaning that the inventory throughout the system will be accurate if updated and reconciled daily. These seemingly simple steps provide the 1 to 3 percent inventory reduction typical of Step One.

The beauty of this step is that it combines, at the beginning of the process, the demand for higher quality, more timely data, and the momentum for organizational change. Participating companies will need to engage employees strategically to achieve the cultural and behavioral shift required to make the project a success. By completing Step One, companies will gain more "visibility" into their procurement and sales activities by moving toward more accurate order, production, and inventory figures. In addition, they will begin to reduce transportation costs and production waste through better planning.

WHAT'S INVOLVED

Step One is the simplest, most basic step in the adaptive business network, yet it sets the stage for all that follows. In this step, a team of employees from different companies tackles the fundamental processes that underlie the adaptive business network, and in so doing sets in motion organizational change that will ripple across the entire supply chain.

Companies set on buying software as the first step toward revolutionizing their internal structures and external relationships will be disappointed. Step One begins with people at the most basic and fundamental levels of a company—the people who work in customer service, warehousing, purchasing, distribution, and transport. It involves changing the processes by which a company works with its suppliers and customers. The change must begin here because it's at this basic level that the most fundamental process and communication problems occur.

The key to Step One is simplicity. In this step, workers in essential jobs learn to perform their tasks on a manual level. Phone calls and human communication take the place of electronic forms and e-mail until each member of the group understands the value of accurate data. In fact, the only technology involved is a portal Web site, on which data of common interest to the company, its suppliers, and customers is posted.

Although working manually may at first seem onerous and a waste of time, it's not long before everyone involved discovers that accurate information and clear communication make their jobs easier. In subsequent steps, when the technological infrastructure is added back in, these workers carry forward a set of work patterns that promote business process excellence.

Although the people involved in Step One will be working manually, data will continue to flow as it always has in support of the other functional areas of the business, such as finance and accounting. The goal is not to shut down systems of the company, but to work around them manually in order to improve basic processes.

Getting Started

Companies should start slowly with Step One, and should not try to take all of their products or partners through the step at once. It's best to start with one product or brand, within one sales channel, using one set of suppliers and customers in that group, while establishing measurements of success. The participants should tackle a small piece of the problem first, and then expand as success is achieved.

To begin Step One, the company will need to contact and work closely with a partner company, usually a supplier or a customer. Both companies must identify the key employees who will lead the charge within their organization. In both cases, it's important to choose the team carefully.

Selecting a Team

The initial working group is the basic unit of Step One, the kernel from which the network will grow. The roles that comprise this group form the essential unit of commercial activity between two companies—a CSR from one company and a corresponding purchasing agent from another. These employees represent the basic buying and selling relationship.

In addition, the team will need a manager from the company's warehouse, plus a corresponding distribution agent from the partner company. These two represent the process of moving the actual products between the two companies. The team should also include the senior executive who initiated the project, a sponsoring senior manager from each company to provide oversight, and a consultant to focus activities.

The people chosen for this group should not be the usual overachievers or workers who blindly follow the rules and appear unmotivated to challenge existing processes. In fact, it's important to find employees with significant experience at their jobs who in the past have made no secret of their frustration with the inadequate or wrong-headed processes that currently dominate their workplace. It's important to select employees who are viewed as leaders by their peers, who are valued and trusted, and without whom daily business activities would be painful.

For example, the CSR on the team may well be a senior account person who, like Dana, has learned ways of getting around obstacles to get the job done. She may be a person who freely expresses her frustration to management about how trying and fragmented her job is. Similarly, the warehouse manager may be a seasoned employee who doesn't hesitate to let management know how frustrating his job is when orders change or are raided at the last minute.

The common characteristics of this group would be a combination of frustration with the existing situation, the ability to get the job done in spite of the limitations, and an expressed desire to remedy the situation—not just complain. These are employees who think creatively to serve the customer. What they have in common is the spirit and a desire—sometimes expressed as frustration—to have jobs that make sense so they can work effectively. Such employees also represent a valuable repository of institutional knowledge.

It is important to select employees whose involvement will lend credibility to the effort, and whose advocacy will win over the fence-sitters. Without their participation, a company may find it difficult to get the rest of the group on board.

Selecting the right senior manager also involves a couple of considerations. First, the company should choose a manager who is open to ideas, someone who has taken chances and lumps in equal measure, and is not intimidated by challenging employees. Second, the company should start with a manager who is responsible for managing a secondary product, not its major product or brand.

Choosing a Product Line

At the same time the initial working group is formed, the company also needs to select a product line on which to focus. An organization should never choose its primary product for the initial stages. In isolating a product or set of related supply functions, the company should focus on a secondary product in good standing—not one that's responsible for the company's economic viability—until it figures out the process.

For instance, the Soft-Drink Company would never initially choose the company's brand-leading cola beverage. Instead, it would choose its sparkling water or iced tea products. Once the company establishes a pattern of success with these secondary products, it can later look to apply the principles of the adaptive business network to its primary business.

Enlisting Partners

Picking partner companies is another challenge. Because several employees from the partner companies will be involved in Step One, each partner must be a trusted company that's equally willing to explore new and more effective ways of doing business.

It may be helpful to select companies with which there have been previous supply chain problems—such as a supplier or customer that just can't seem to get the numbers, products, or timing right. In such cases, there is often a problem somewhere in the processes between the companies, and subsequently the will on the part of each to make it right.

An organization should also ask its CSRs which companies seem most at home with electronic communications—which companies seem content to use e-mail or Internet attachments for communications, rather than faxes or traditional mail. A company that uses up-to-date technology will in the end make a better partner in an adaptive business network because it will already have some of the skills and technology in place as systems are automated.

This doesn't mean that technology plays a large role in Step One. The whole point of this step is to remove technology from the basic core processes of the network. Other than the telephone, the only technology recommended for this step is a simple business network portal—and if companies really want to keep it basic, they can conduct all the business they need at this step using e-mail and spreadsheets. Remember, the early steps of the adaptive business network are primarily about processes, not technology.

Establishing Basic Measurements of Success

Companies must begin taking several measurements—orders shipped on time, orders shipped according to the agreed-upon terms, finished goods inventory accuracy, products manufactured according to plan, exception handling processes, and orders committed to customers on the phone. This information will provide a picture of the effectiveness of current processes. After about 60 days, participants should feel more comfortable taking the measurements, and should see improvements in these numbers. These numbers also should be posted to the portal.

THE WEEKLY PHONE CALL

Step One begins with a regular conference call. This call should occur weekly at minimum, and may occur more often based on a company's needs and the pace at which its products flow through the supply chain. On the phone are the company's CSR, warehouse manager, the product line's senior manager, plus the senior executive, and the consultant to referee. On the conference call from each partner company will be a purchasing agent, the distribution person who will receive the goods from the company, and a senior manager.

What Happens on the Call?

Once the call has been established, the companies pass information back and forth on inventory type, location, quantity, order position—basic supply chain information. The warehouse worker tells the group what inventory he has in stock, what he has ordered and expects to arrive, and what he has sold and expects to ship. The CSR tells the group what orders she has taken, what inventory she has placed orders for, and what orders she anticipates. From the partner companies, the purchaser relays information about orders he has placed, inventory he has on hold, forecasts, and so on.

Someone within the group takes this information, compiles it into a spreadsheet and posts it onto the portal where everyone has access to it. The information becomes visible.

For example, the Soft-Drink Company may decide to pursue an adaptive business network with the companies that supply the materials for its bottled iced tea drinks. The first partner it works with supplies the glass bottles in which the tea is sold. The information exchanged on this call—and later posted on the portal—includes how many bottles are in stock at the moment, how many are on trucks in transit, how many were received on the last shipment, and how many are in production.

Although this may sound like a straightforward and amiable conversation, by the second or third week of reporting inventory counts, discrepancies usually begin to show. The amount ordered doesn't match the amount shipped, or the amount shipped doesn't match what was received, or the shipments are late on Tuesdays.

Because this is a live conversation, people start off by pointing fingers, but keeping the objective of this exercise in mind, they then step back to find out where the problem is. Over the course of several weeks, they will figure out a way to account for the number of bottles that are flowing between the two companies.

It is important during this process that someone be responsible for taking notes about how the communication takes place, as well as the problems that occur and how they are resolved. These notes become the basis for the more formal process flows that will be required.

INCORPORATING THE REST OF THE SUPPLY CHAIN

When the bumps are smoothed out and business between these two partners seems solid, it's time to add another partner. For Soft-Drink, this may be the company that makes the paper labels that are affixed to the iced tea bottles. The same process continues—the weekly phone call takes place, this time adding the people who are responsible for the labels in each of the two partner companies. Adding new people to the group will initially slow down the process, but by this time, the original group should be adept at the call, and its members will function as leaders and mentors.

This cycle continues until all companies involved in the production are incorporated. For example, Soft-Drink would add to this cast of characters a representative from the company that brews and packages its tea concentrate, plus the Soft-Drink personnel who are responsible for ordering the undiluted tea. The company would then add a representative of its partner paperboard carton company along with the corresponding Soft-Drink employee who is in charge of packaging the bottled tea.

At this point, the conversations become more heated. With everyone on the phone call, a simple: "Here's what I have on hand; here's what I need shipped" can become more complex when uttered across multiple companies. People note each other's inventory levels, and they don't hesitate to call attention to each other's miscounts and inadequate planning. "You won't have enough labels for that order!" "Next time you need that much tea concentrate, let us know sooner!"

By now there may be 20 people on the phone call. So what do they all think of this? Initial exasperation with the length of the phone calls in the early, "Don't you know how to count?!" stages eventually cedes to grudging acceptance that these processes are yielding results. Initially, the phone calls can last a couple of hours. Eventually, however, this portion of everyday business gradually becomes easier and faster for everyone to accomplish, and there's the added incentive of understanding the ins and outs of an entire product line.

Some of the same conversations will take place repeatedly, until supply chain problems for this product are resolved to the satisfaction of the group. When that happens, a customer is added—perhaps a distributor that sells the company's bottled iced tea—and the conversation, and the group of companies, move to the next level.

Working with Partners to Improve Number Accuracy

Companies moving through Step One should strive to stabilize processes and data. The stabilized processes used within the four walls of the company become the foundation of the adaptive business network. As a result, the company must have confidence in internal numbers before looking outside—it does no good to add partners to the adaptive business network until internal data is accurate.

Having stabilized processes and data, companies will be better able to respond to unforeseen circumstances when working with other companies as products are consumed, information is distributed, and assets are utilized. Without stabilized processes and qualified information, responding to these unplanned events will lead to further chaos.

At this point, accuracy of data is a relative state. Depending on the type of business, it may not be as important that the numbers used by the group are 100 percent correct. However, there should be agreement on the numbers—everyone involved in the process must agree on the reliability of data that's required to do good business. It's also important to determine what to do when the numbers are incorrect, how to resolve differences within and between companies, and how to get back on track. The companies should document how these issues are tracked and resolved.

The phone call should occur as often as necessary until everyone involved agrees that the inventory count is accurate to within a day. For Soft-Drink, the conference call occurs just once a week. Companies in a faster paced business may want to schedule these calls more often—even daily, if necessary. The goal is to agree that the inventory counts are stable.

By the end of Step One, the data posted on the portal should be at least 80 to 90 percent accurate. However, this may vary depending on the needs of the company. Accuracy of data is achieved when companies are no longer arguing about the numbers. When the group phone call grows civilized and lasts only 10 or 15 minutes—in other words, when the group has reached consensus on inventory counts, order positions, and other data, and has adopted a common set of business processes—then it's time to move to Step Two, outlined in Chapter 7.

THE PORTAL

A simple Internet portal is a technological tool that can provide greater insight into a company's operations and help businesses with the process changes they face. Any business in the group can take the lead in establishing the portal. A portal is simply an information visibility service provided to the participants.

Companies should be sure the portal includes basic security features including log-in identification, user passwords, and user ID-based profiles. User ID profiles enable companies to grant different levels of information access to different participants, depending on their role and need for information. The portal should also provide the ability for companies to enter data, such as forms and fields, and to post computer files in agreed-upon formats.

Information posted on the portal should include inventory counts by material and location; order position; and production and distribution plans, schedules, and forecasts. This information is updated manually by logging onto the portal at an agreed-on time. Plans and forecasts should be updated once a week, while inventory information should be refreshed at a minimum of once a day.

Once companies begin posting their information onto the portal, missteps, miscounts, and mistakes become obvious. By this time, the group is good at self-policing. Those partners whose processes aren't good enough show up quickly, and once it's clear that a lot is riding on getting all the numbers to match up, the pressure to do a better job becomes strong.

Posting information onto the portal enables companies to gain more insight into customer demand for their products. In turn, this better information enables suppliers to more efficiently schedule transportation, manufacturing, direct material procurement, and other activities required to fill that demand at the time it is needed. Matching these business activities more closely to actual demand results in fewer strains on the production schedule, improving the operational efficiency of all companies. It provides procurement and sales personnel with a higher degree of confidence that they have enough supply to meet demand, reducing the need to keep extra inventory on hand.

Major Process Changes of Step One

The way companies manage inventory and plan production and distribution are dramatically changed in Step One. Inventory is now counted accurately at least once per day. In addition, inventory is transformed from a financial into an operational responsibility. Now each company must know where every pallet, box, skid, and truck is located and how many units are contained in each.

Measuring the team's adherence to plans and forecast accuracy will reinforce the planning and forecasting disciplines. In subsequent adaptive business network steps, however, the system becomes less dependent on accurate forecasting. The discipline of once-a-day counting will also eventually transform to cycle counting, whereby the more important products are counted more frequently—per shift or production cycle, for example.

All processes established in Step One need to be documented and reviewed by the groups so that they're available when adding other products or teams to Step One and for future steps.

BENEFITS OF STEP ONE

Even though Step One is simple, it can produce significant cost savings. As stated previously, by completing Step One, companies should be able to see their inventory decrease by 1 to 3 percent. This comes primarily from the process of jointly tracking inventory, which almost always brings hidden stashes of goods to light. When people begin to trust that the inventory numbers posted by a company are accurate, they cease to keep their own private stores laid up for those formerly inevitable rainy days.

Achieving better inventory counts and establishing the basics for better business processes will reduce the frustration level between a company's employees and its customers, making the company easier to do business with. Transportation costs also should decrease as better communication between partners reduces the need for costly emergency and less-than-full truckload shipments.

Likewise, companies will experience fewer emergency production changeovers to accommodate unanticipated orders. This should result in better management of the production schedule, which can slightly lower production waste and improve the ability to stick to the manufacturing plan.

Opening the Lines of Communication

Another benefit of Step One is that it encourages more communication among employees both within and between companies. In today's businesses, CSRs like Dana typically are the connection between the company's customers who keep it in business and the workers in the warehouse and the manufacturing floor.

Dana also serves as the link between her company's customers and Soft-Drink's shipping and transport workers, sales, and finance employees, and the management team that oversees all of her company's operations. Company information funnels down the corporate ladder through Dana to the customer, who as the purchaser often serves as the link between that company and the outside world.

This common way of communicating, illustrated by the "Bow-Tie" diagram in Figure 6.1, is highly inefficient because it prevents companies from obtaining the information they need to operate optimally. All of the managers whose functions influence the company's profits are kept at a distance from the people who communicate with the company's

FIGURE 6.1   THE BOW-TIE EFFECT

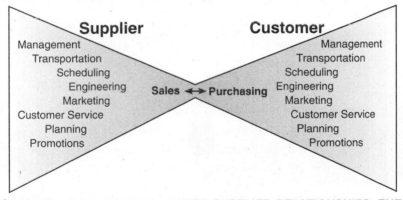

IN MANY COMPANIES WITH BUYER-SUPPLIER RELATIONSHIPS, THE ONLY POINT OF CONTACT BETWEEN TWO BUSINESSES IS VIA THE PURCHASING AND SALES OR CUSTOMER SERVICE DEPARTMENTS. THIS CREATES A BOTTLENECK IN THE FLOW OF INFORMATION AND DECISION MAKING BETWEEN TWO PARTNER COMPANIES. THIS INFORMATION CONSTRAINT, KNOWN AS THE BOW-TIE EFFECT, IS A HINDRANCE TO BUSINESS BETWEEN PARTNERS.

customers. Within one company, there is the CSR who speaks for an entire company, and within the other company, there is the purchasing agent who speaks for that company. Where is the visibility in this model? This common way of communicating constricts information rather than fostering a healthy flow of communication.

Step One improves the communication lines among companies by providing a single view of inventory, orders, plans, schedules, and forecasts, and forcing the people who are responsible for each segment of the manufacturing process to talk to each other across company boundaries. This does not remove the management accountability, rather this forces controls within the environment where today few exist.

By increasing the number of people communicating within and among companies, the bow tie is opened. Everyone within the group takes responsibility for the business function they know best. By the time companies have completed Step One, the new flow of information has given visibility to everyone along the supply-and-demand process. All members have access to the same information so they can make informed decisions (Figure 6.2).

FIGURE 6.2   THE OPEN BOW TIE

IN AN ADAPTIVE BUSINESS NETWORK, MANY DIVISIONS WITHIN TWO PARTNER COMPANIES WILL SHARE INFORMATION, THUS NEGATING THE BOTTLENECK OF INFORMATION KNOWN AS THE BOW-TIE EFFECT.

EMBRACING ORGANIZATIONAL CHANGE

Step One may appear to be rudimentary and unimportant if a company's goal is a more lofty state of intercompany integration and collaboration. However, this step is necessary to prepare for the adaptive business network. There's no point in trying to achieve greater integration through an investment such as collaboration software unless a company is first willing to move through Step One. If a company can't get its operational-level employees to agree on the phone to a common vision of reality among a handful of companies, it will not achieve success if it jumps ahead into automated vendor replenishment or other advanced business systems discussed in the later steps of the adaptive business network.

Step One is about bringing together people from different companies to understand the value of a shared set of accurate data. Notice that the primary people involved in Step One are at the basic operational level of the company. For Step One to be a success, companies must enable employees involved in the frontline trenches to participate in this organizational initiative. Not only do these employees' jobs become easier; they also develop processes that enable the entire company to work more efficiently. Management must allow these employees to spread the word to other workers. This creates a sense that participating is a reward that helps the company to operate more efficiently.

That's why the process starts slowly, one partner at a time. A company should keep it simple by limiting the phone calls to reports on inventory and orders. It should enforce progress with small wins, and it shouldn't add new partners until everyone is in agreement regarding the numbers being discussed. To use a sports analogy, at this step companies aren't looking to win the wicket. They're looking for single runs. People like to win. They like to be successful. Companies should seek quick wins and move on to the next step.

One reason Step One is so simple is that the phone calls the group makes essentially replicate the kinds of information-gathering performed by sophisticated supply chain software. De-automating these processes gives the activities back to employees to relearn and revalue, ensuring they are implemented properly before automating these processes with technology.

Removing the software from the process prevents people from hiding behind technology. The beauty of Step One is that it involves people from various companies talking about the fundamentals of business, and arriving at joint decisions about how to make business processes more effective. Step One enforces proper mind-set and behavior without letting technology get in the way. Technology isn't the reason companies don't work together efficiently—poor business processes are the reason.

In addition to establishing joint processes for factors such as counting inventory and planning production, other key processes must be established for issues such as resolving conflicts between companies. Standardized conflict resolution processes enable companies to constructively resolve problems such as misaligned delivery dates so that these issues are neither ignored nor allowed to drag down other benefits of jointly working together.

A FLEXIBLE TECHNIQUE

The exact makeup of the teams in Step One depends on what business problem they are addressing. The adaptive business network is a flexible technique, and depending on a company's needs, it might form a team centered on inventory reduction, as above, or on improved customer service levels. Such a team might include salespeople, a purchasing manager, and representatives from manufacturing. In this way, the adaptive business network can be customized to achieve different goals that address the needs of different industries.

However, there are some problems Step One of the adaptive business network cannot address. It is not an initiative intended to improve the manufacturing process. Nor is it a product quality initiative. A company can change who makes the packaging, how much inventory to keep, and how the inventory gets from point A to point B, but at this step, it should not attempt to change the product itself.

Likewise, the adaptive business network should not be used as a tool to make changes in financial reporting. Companies working together to accomplish Step One do not accrue profits or losses as a single unit. The obligation to report financial standings remains that of the individual companies within the network.

POTENTIAL OBSTACLES

Some workers may think they are too busy to take part. For example, when a company tells its CSRs that they need to participate in a two-hour phone call, it faces an uphill battle to convince them it's a good use of time.

CSRs are used to putting out fires, and anything that takes them away from fighting fires is going to appear to be a waste of time. In the short term, this step is extra work for the CSR, so expect some resistance.

Other employees, including managers, will think that Step One is overly simplistic and that the company does not need to go through this level of exercise. However, companies must validate that their basic processes are, in fact, dependable. Step One can be a hard sell to an already busy workforce, but it is absolutely crucial that these procedures are in place and that respect for accurate data is institutionalized before companies move on.

GAINING MOMENTUM

Once a company has successfully completed Step One for a selected product or brand within a specific sales channel, it is ready to move on to Step Two. It is also time to replicate Step One with a second product in the company.

The company should select another product group and a different team—again including key people from the two companies—and begin to move forward once again. To ensure these subsequent efforts are a success, it's important that the earlier teams lead the new groups so they can convey the value of the process and the benefits it provides.

Step One can be replicated from this point forward without the help of consultants or other outside people. An informal leader of any previous team should be able to lead a new one. The effect cascades, and eventually the process spreads across the entire company, with self-directed teams leading each other through the early stages of the move to an adaptive business network.

The process will quickly accelerate and, as bottlenecks are discovered, individuals in the company will work to fix systemwide problems. Step One ensures that the value of the information and processes is more clearly understood. A company can create the set of procedures to institutionalize these changes.

A company is ready to move its primary product through Step One when it has a critical mass of employees who are adept at the processes involved. For the Soft-Drink Company, that means the team working on the company's highest-selling cola product begins its transition through the adaptive business network only after there is a large contingent of experienced employees familiar with the procedures. Why? Companies need to institutionalize the goodwill and knowledge among their employees before taking on such a critical task.

MOVING TO THE NEXT STEP

One of the first indications that a company is ready to move on to Step Two is when the phone call among team members lasts only 10 to 15 minutes. That means that the group has reached agreement about the quantity of inventory flowing within and between companies, and that this group has evolved and internalized a common set of business processes. Remember that there are different groups advancing concurrently within the company. Some groups will start Step One while others are already well along, and while still others have moved ahead to Step Two.

Another measure of readiness is inventory accuracy. As a rule of thumb, accuracy within one day is usually acceptable. For others, it could need to be measured by the hour, or even in minutes. It depends on the industry, the speed at which products move through the supply chain, and the processes involved.

LOOKING BACK ON STEP ONE

At the Soft-Drink Company, Dana's world has changed roughly two months after starting Step One. Dana is conducting her weekly calls with her team. Communication among this small group of people is now smoother. Processes are now readily visible, and achievements are measured and widely recognized. When customers call Dana for the products that are part of Step One, Dana's first reaction is to go to the portal to view inventory counts and production schedules. From there, she can either confirm or provide an acceptance date for the order. Now Dana trusts the inventory; she no longer has to call around to obtain accurate numbers.

Despite these achievements, Dana and this team realize that there are still problems. Her managers are applying pressure to accelerate the results. It's time for Dana's company to advance to Step Two.

CHAPTER SEVEN

Step Two—Community

The community stagnates without the impulse of the individual. The impulse dies away without the sympathy of the community.

—William James

It's been a long, hard week at the Soft-Drink Company, and Marty, who manages the company's warehouses, has stopped by Maybe's Bar & Grill after work in search of liquid refreshment. He sees Dana across the room having a drink with friends, and she waves him over to join them.

"I understand that you're to blame for all the extra work my team is doing," Marty says to Dana with a weary smile. "We're running around taking inventory counts and spending half our time on the phone with a gaggle of people from various companies. Your new system is making more work for us."

"If it's more work now," replies Dana, "it's because you're working with a handful of companies the new way while the rest are still on the old system. We haven't finished yet. So yes, it's more work now, but just give it some time. Have you noticed any positive aspects to the new processes, or did you just come over here to gripe?"

"Well, we aren't raiding our palletized orders to fill last-minute orders any longer," Marty admits. "And the inventory does seem more stable for products that are on the new system."

"So you're seeing progress?" asks Dana.

"It seems like we keep less inventory with the new method, which made me nervous at first, but we've still been able to fill all the orders. The lemonade stock is three-quarters what it was a month ago, but we've got the same volume going out the door."

"Well, that's good news for everyone, right?"

"I'll just be glad when we aren't operating under two systems," Marty says. "I don't think we're giving very good service to customers who are on our old system. Can't we just change over all our products, and include all of our partners?"

"Be careful what you ask for, Marty," laughs Dana. "We're moving in that direction. Plus we're working on making our inventory counts and other data even more accurate so we can begin mechanizing orders."

FAST FACTS FOR STEP TWO

What's in It for My Company?

- Inventory is reduced by 1 percent to 3 percent.
- Purchase orders are reduced.
- Greater visibility is gained into the operations and dependent processes within the business partner community.
- The time required to complete processes is reduced, freeing up employees for more strategic work.

What Work Is Involved?

- Monitoring inventory in real time.
- Keeping production schedules and forecasts continuously updated.
- Mechanizing routine orders.
- Building trust in the information posted on the portal.
- Maintaining management involvement from all participants.

What Technology Investment Is Required?

- An inventory tracking system.
- A production planning tool (for some companies).

How Long Will It Take?

- A few weeks up to four months.

STEP TWO

This chapter describes the second step in building an adaptive business network. Step Two builds on the hard work of the first step by broadening the group of participants involved. In Step Two, the process changes are extended to the full community of businesses that make up the trading group, and technology is introduced to hasten the speed of communication between companies to allow for real-time informational updates systemwide.

Step Two involves mechanizing many of the day-to-day product orders that occur between a company and its partners, and using inventory-tracking systems to scan goods in and out of the warehouse. In addition, participating companies will more frequently update production and distribution plans, schedules, and forecasts that they began posting on the portal in Step One.

One of the main benefits of Step Two is that individual companies will begin to trust the inventory numbers and other data that flow increasingly quickly among community participants. By the end of Step Two, companies will have accurate tallies of their inventory in real time, and they will know what inventory has been allocated for specific orders.

By keeping this information up-to-date and accurate, and sharing it among themselves, partner companies will begin to mechanize routine transactions, saving time and money. They will see more small reductions in inventory and working capital. They will be one step closer to fully collaborating with their business partners for everyone's gain. By the end of Step Two, trading partners will be ready to act on this information to automate routine orders and other business transactions.

EXTENDING THE COMMUNITY

By the end of Step One, a core group of companies is working together to verbally communicate fundamental business information and to manually perform basic business functions. In Step Two, the focus moves from a company's direct suppliers and customers to concentric rings of companies that form a trading community. Now the group may include companies involved in the production and delivery of a specific product, from secondary suppliers to service providers down to the retailer. This extended group participates in the phone call and begins to post and monitor information on

INVENTORY TRACKING SYSTEMS

The adaptive business network requires that information be communicated rapidly and accurately. Inventory tracking systems are capable of reading, tracking, and tracing inventory using a number of innovative technologies. These allow direct entry of data into computer systems without using a keypad, making data entry virtually cost and labor free. With inventory tracking technology:

- Data entry is streamlined, automated, and inexpensive.
- The information is rapidly available in electronic form.
- Information is more accurate than manual methods of data entry.

the portal. The community that will eventually become the adaptive business network is assembled.

It's important to note that this community will be built around standardized business operations and processes. Business is setting the rules, rather than taking its lead from the information technology (IT) department. The people who are going to live with the rules establish them. The people who manage the processes design them.

WHAT'S INVOLVED

In Step Two, more use is made of the portal to post inventory quantities, share up-to-date schedules, plans, and forecasts, and mechanize day-to-day orders and other transactions. After adding the new participants to the community, the portal can provide visibility from one end of the supply chain to the other on order positions, and inventory quantities and locations in each of the participating companies. Sharing this information via the portal reduces the time required to complete basic business processes when working with other companies. The time it takes from when a need is discovered to the time it is filled is significantly shortened.

Achieving Greater Inventory Accuracy

One of the goals of Step Two is getting inventory accuracy to "real time"—that is, having inventory counts that reflect what a company actually has on hand moment to moment, as close to instantaneously as possible.

Depending on a company's technology and order volumes, real time may correspond to systemwide inventory updates every 60 seconds or every two minutes. Once-an-hour updates are not acceptable as real time in Step Two. Knowing how much inventory exists and where it is located is paramount for companies to begin automating day-to-day orders.

Clearly, it's not possible for company employees to dash around every warehouse and distribution center, constantly counting inventory. As a result, most companies will need to invest in an inventory tracking system such as a bar code scanner or radio frequency identification (RFID) technology, both of which register and track the movement of goods during the manufacturing process, at and between warehouses, and off production lines.

The bar code system is perhaps the easiest and most cost-effective choice for inventory tracking. An RFID system is similar in principle with the bar code scanner, but uses wireless technology to accomplish the same goals. When a unit of materials is transported from the warehouse, it is scanned before being loaded onto the delivery truck. This reading is sent to the inventory system, and it almost instantly deletes a unit from the inventory totals. When the material arrives at its destination, another device receives the shipment by scanning the material into inventory.

Some companies will be able to use existing technology tools and adapt them to the new procedures. The systems in use at this point in Step Two

BAR CODES

Since their invention in the early 1950s, bar codes have greatly accelerated the flow of products and information in business and commerce. In fact, there are over 225 bar code languages, called "symbologies," which have their own characters, features, and printing and decoding requirements.

The bar code pattern represents numbers or alphabetic characters, typically made up of lines, spaces, and areas of light and dark. These images are read by electro-optical systems that use reflected light to illuminate the image and translate dark and light areas into data. The host system matches this data with information stored in a database and puts the information to use for inventory control, shipping and receiving, quality control, automated reordering, or electronic commerce.

RFID

Radio frequency identification (RFID) is a small electronic communication system that consists of an antenna or coil, a receiver with decoder, and a transponder, commonly called an RF tag, that is electronically coded with information.

When an RF tag passes through the system's electromagnetic zone, it detects the antenna's signal. The antenna passes information between the tag and the receiver. The information is decoded and the data is passed to the host computer for processing.

RFID systems come in a wide variety of shapes and sizes. Antennas can be built into a car door or into a personal digital assistant (PDA). They can be mounted on an interstate toll booth to monitor freeway traffic. They can be placed in a 12-pack of soft drinks or in a jacket lapel. RF tags can be screwed into pallets or added to credit cards for use in security applications.

RFID systems are extremely useful because they can operate accurately even when tags are covered with paint, fog, snow, ice, or crusted grime. In these visually and environmentally challenging conditions, bar codes would be useless. Moreover, RFID tags are fast—they can accurately pass data between antenna and receiver with response times of less than 100 milliseconds with no human intervention.

aren't intended to replicate the functions of a full-scale inventory system. All that is needed in Step Two is basic track-and-trace features that are capable of updating inventory numbers in real time and of sharing information within and between companies.

The capability to share information is important. It does no good for each warehouse to know independently what inventory it has if that information is not shared. In a community setting, information is of limited utility if it is not shared among partners. Lack of information-sharing quickly leads to overbooked inventory.

Posting Schedules, Plans, and Forecasts

In Step Two, participating companies must also begin to keep their production and distribution schedules, plans, and forecasts that they began posting in Step One more frequently updated. No longer is it sufficient to revise these schedules, plans, and forecasts weekly; they must be updated at least once a day, or more frequently, depending on the complexity of the product line and the speed at which inventory is used. To accomplish this, participating companies need to agree on common planning standards including the length of time covered by each production and distribution plan, and what information should be included in it.

Companies with a small number of production and distribution sites can simply draw up their plans on a spreadsheet and post them onto the portal. Companies with multiple production and distribution sites will need to invest in a more sophisticated planning and scheduling tool to help them track production schedule information as changes occur and to keep forecasts frequently updated.

Mechanizing Orders

By the end of Step One, the working group will notice during its phone calls that many items are consistently ordered in the same quantities. For companies with a regular production schedule, the type and number of products ordered varies only slightly under normal conditions.

Everyone on the phone call will be able to anticipate what the order quantities will be as ordering and reordering these standard products becomes almost a rote activity. The only situations that actually require discussion are the "exceptions"—special requests for rarely ordered products, larger than normal orders needed for promotions, smaller orders than the norm, and so on.

In Step Two, the working group begins to communicate the need for mundane, day-to-day orders via the portal, although the actual placement of orders remains manual until the end of this step, when automatically generated electronic notifications are considered sufficient to authorize an order. At this point, the traditional purchase order will be eliminated from the ordering process, excising time and money from standard business operations.

Expanding Use of the Portal

As more partners are added and the weekly phone call grows in complexity, the role of the portal becomes more important. In Step Two, the portal goes from being a fairly accurate data repository to serving as the definitive information source for all participants in the trading community. By generating user profiles based on a company's information needs, the portal also begins to organize the participating community members by role and responsibility.

The first responsibility is that of managing the portal itself. As the business community takes shape, one company will structure and deploy the portal, not only at the site of its own operations but also at those of its partners. Because it initiates the use of the portal, this company will establish and maintain many of the standards and processes that define business activity within the trading community. These include time horizons or agreed-upon grace periods that determine the point at which production plans and orders between companies become commitments.

For instance, if a company reserves production capacity from another member of the community, at what point is it committed to paying for the capacity it has reserved? One month before production? One week? The same time horizons exist with materials. If a company has provisional orders from a partner company that require a raw material source time of two weeks, when is the commit date that obliges the raw materials supplier to fulfill the order, and the company purchasing the raw material to accept the order and pay for it?

As companies within the community work increasingly close together, under-using production capacity or carrying excess inventory becomes a burden to all. Therefore, in a closely integrated group of companies, establishing time horizons for operations is strategically important. The company that manages the portal must work with all partners in the trading community to establish when production capacity, materials, and orders are committed among participants in the network.

Establishment of these time horizons and commit points simplifies the process of adding new partners to the trading community. If new companies agree to these terms, they can be added to the community quickly and easily because the business process infrastructure has already been determined.

As the portal evolves, it also helps to formulate other roles and responsibilities in the trading community. Because the quantity of data that flows between community members is so vast, the portal can be used to partition and organize this information so that it is easily accessed and monitored. The portal organizes each participant's view of the data so that only the information needed for specific processes is delivered to the people responsible for those processes.

GETTING STARTED

By the end of Step One, participants are still conferring by regularly scheduled phone calls to establish inventory accuracy, coordinate orders, and share information regarding scheduling, planning, and forecasting. All parties use the portal to view data and enter new information pertinent to each company.

In Step Two, the group involved on the weekly phone call increases to include more members of the supply chain community. In addition to the core team of buyers and suppliers that came together in Step One, Step Two may bring brand managers, representatives of discrete and process manufacturing, warehouse coordinators, transportation providers, and retailers into the phone call.

Companies will be added to the phone call one or two at a time, with each passing through the stages of Step One. After each addition, the community waits until communication and processes have stabilized, and then adds more members. The whole community has been assembled when the entire supply chain for a single product within a specific sales channel is represented on the call.

At this point, the actual business transactions among companies are still performed manually. Some participants on the call will actively exchange information—placing orders, querying inventory levels, planning and scheduling shipments—while others will participate to better understand the interactions between partners and how the process works.

Some participants on the phone call will interact for the first time, even though their responsibilities in their respective companies overlap. For instance, a product company's brand manager may directly communicate with the retailer at the end of the sales channel, with the conversation focusing on how each manages and plans promotions. Brand managers from both companies can then use this information to fine-tune their revenue plans and plan more effectively. The brand manager at the retail company can schedule promotions more effectively and better coordinate the delivery of products for these promotions. The brand manager at the product company can better coordinate its promotions with retailers, reducing costs and improving the effectiveness of its promotions.

All participants keep their inventory totals updated in real time on the portal, which aggregates the information onto spreadsheets. Each company also posts its production and distribution schedules, plans, and forecasts onto the portal and keeps this information updated as circumstances change.

The working group references this information as it discusses inventory levels and order positions. As with Step One, the goal is to create a common set of business processes so that participating companies can better plan and allocate inventory based on a greater understanding of what inventory exists, where it is located, and its condition throughout the supply chain.

Sharing this information enables companies to begin mechanizing their order processes by establishing the minimum and maximum range of inventory quantities for the products discussed during each phone call. From its group experience, the team should be able to agree on certain minimum and maximum tolerable threshold levels for these items.

Once these minimum and maximum—or "min-max"—controls are established, they are entered as formulas onto the spreadsheet. The min-max controls on the portal mechanize part of the ordering process. At the beginning of Step Two, orders are generated when participants of the phone call determine the need for more goods. Once the acceptable minimum and maximum inventory levels are in place within the portal, the appropriate people in the trading community receive electronic notification when inventory levels fall below the preestablished thresholds.

For example, the Soft-Drink Company usually orders between 40,000 and 90,000 gallons of high-fructose corn syrup in each month. To make the purchase, Soft-Drink's purchasing department phones and faxes documents to its high-fructose syrup supplier requesting the order. The appropriate purchase orders are drawn up, invoices are cut, accounts payable and receivable move into action. With each order, the paper changes hands again and again—needless time and money spent. Since the Soft-Drink Company almost always buys the same amount of corn syrup every month, handling the same manual purchase process is an inefficient way to do business.

During Step Two, the Soft-Drink Company and its supplier agree on minimum and maximum thresholds for orders—in this case, perhaps 40,000 to 90,000 gallons. These orders will be set as min-max thresholds on the portal. The portal will monitor these orders against that item's minimum and maximum threshold. If the order entered falls within the parameters of the min-max, no alert is generated. However, if Soft-Drink places an order for high-fructose corn syrup of below 40,000 gallons or above 90,000 gallons, an alert is automatically sent to both Soft-Drink and the syrup supplier so they can determine why the order fell outside of the norm.

This small step has the potential to produce big changes in how the team operates. The amount of data that the team discusses by phone is greatly reduced. Once standard ranges of inventory are established and automated, monitoring inventory no longer requires the daily attention of the team. Rather, the team only focuses on those inventory situations that are the exceptions.

At this point, the appropriate person still determines whether to place an order. That is, the need for an order is mechanized via e-mail, but it is still validated by the purchasing agent, who files a paper purchase order. Later in the process, e-mail or other electronic notification becomes the trigger for all parties to place their orders—the customer service representative doesn't wait for the purchase order to authorize the shipment. By the end of Step Two, participants will operate under standardized master agreements that eliminate the need for individual purchase orders to be created.

CREATING MASTER AGREEMENTS

After a company has determined min-max levels with its key suppliers, it should establish master agreements with each of these companies. Master agreements are standing contracts that define how companies within the community will work together. The master agreements are revisited at each step toward the move to an adaptive business network, as companies work together more closely. In Step Two, they primarily serve as purchasing agreements, authorizing the purchase of specific goods or services among the companies involved, as long as the companies conform to rules of the agreement.

By creating master agreements, companies in the community separate the operational aspects of purchasing from the financial transaction, allowing employees to order the goods or materials that are needed without worrying about the monetary aspects of the sale. As long as the order falls within the min-max threshold or other pre-negotiated rules, the order goes forward, a purchase order is in place and an authorization against the agreement is created. The companies involved already know when and how they will be paid for the transaction.

BENEFITS OF STEP TWO

As day-to-day orders are mechanized in Step Two, the time required to process these orders is reduced. A worker at Soft-Drink can enter the desired order onto the portal Web site—which only takes a few minutes—and be free for other tasks.

With more time for the projects that really matter, workers will accomplish more. Employees, freed from their previous, routine tasks, can perform more strategic work. For example, rather than wasting hours completing tedious paperwork for routine purchases, the purchasing department could spend that time searching for a more reliable supplier or negotiating increased service levels with a preferred vendor.

THE ADAPTIVE BUSINESS NETWORK AND THE WORKFORCE

Unlike many other business initiatives, cost savings in the adaptive business network are not built on employee layoffs. In fact, many companies have already realized gains through major workforce downsizing in the 1980s and 1990s. This is not the goal of the adaptive business network.

The adaptive network starts from the assumption that the workforce in participating companies is the right size for the work flow. This doesn't mean when a company moves to an adaptive business network that everyone will maintain his or her previous positions. The network requires change. It structures jobs differently than the traditional workplace. It also requires workers to learn new skills.

These changes will energize some employees, who will find their jobs are more strategic and less routine. Others will be alienated. In every company, there will be workers who don't want change. There will be others who cannot change due to lack of skills, and given the speed and complexity of the adaptive network, cannot be brought up to speed in time.

Because the adaptive business network increases revenue opportunities, reducing the size of the workforce is not usually the result of moving to this new model. However, those workers unable or unwilling to learn new skills or work methods may be displaced.

In addition, by coordinating more closely with suppliers and other partners, the community will gain a clearer understanding of its needs. The community can better match production and distribution schedules to ensure it produces the correct quantity of materials and ships them when and where these materials are needed. Managers will have better tools to improve planning, scheduling, and forecasting.

Furthermore, inventory levels will drop—typically by another 1 to 3 percent over that achieved in Step One. In Step Two, insufficient levels of inventory are automatically reported to the community so that adjustments can be made. Because existing inventory and planned production are constantly monitored, excess inventory and stock-outs can be avoided.

By automatically notifying the business community of inventory needs, the portal helps participants to significantly reduce the number of hours spent performing rote ordering functions. As a result, processes run more smoothly, and customers are better served. By getting an accurate tally out in the open, managers and executives can further reduce inventory by identifying and eliminating hidden or misplaced items.

POTENTIAL OBSTACLES

Two business divisions within companies may have difficulty adjusting to Step Two—the IT department and the purchasing department.

IT departments have certain ingrained instincts—noble in other environments—that need to be managed during the move to an adaptive business network. Specifically, the IT department may want to turn the technology investments needed for Step Two into a larger IT opportunity. For example, IT may want to expand the use of the new technology across multiple divisions, spreading the technology farther and faster than is necessary.

Another potential IT department concern may include the accuracy of the inventory numbers and other data. At this stage in the move to the adaptive business network, it's important not to become sidetracked by projects designed to cleanse data throughout the company. Data integrity projects need to be limited to the information necessary to achieve Step Two. If companies are not careful, technology—or at least IT departments—can slow down the process. Keep the technology focused.

Similarly, the purchasing department may claim that it is losing control of the company's purchasing power, as many of its previous daily tasks are eliminated. However, the purchasing department may retain control over the minimum and maximum standard thresholds. It will monitor purchases for compliance with the master agreements.

Releasing daily control of purchasing, whether it involves creating purchase orders for high fructose corn syrup or legal envelopes, requires a mind-set adjustment. Similarly, allowing suppliers and other partners to view information that companies once viewed as proprietary may be difficult to accept at first. An organization must be willing to hand off designated tasks to the community.

Working to change an organizational mind-set is another challenge. Many employees may feel uneasy about mechanizing part of their daily routine and fear layoffs. They may be concerned about taking on new, more important strategic roles within the company. However, once employees see that they rarely have to scramble to solve unexpected problems, they will begin to embrace the adaptive business network. Many employees will begin to feel more empowered by their greater strategic roles.

MOVING TO THE NEXT STEP

As with Step One, if your company already monitors inventory in real time, and continuously updates its plans, schedules, and forecasts, Step Two will only be a validation, and you will be ready to move to Step Three within weeks. However, if your company struggles to fill orders in a timely fashion, and your plans are inaccurate or are not updated properly, Step Two could take as long as four months to complete.

By the end of Step Two, the community will be managed by a logic— a set of procedures that governs its actions and that is measurable and sustainable. Before leaving Step Two, a trust level must exist in the community that is based on confidence in each participant resulting from their performance against standardized measurements.

This isn't to say that all companies within the community blindly lay aside their previous rivalries or privacy measures. Rather, while individual companies may not trust each other in the abstract, they must trust that all members of the community follow the same rules, and that these rules protect the integrity of each company while enhancing their mutual benefit.

A company is ready to move on to Step Three when:

■   *The procedures are standardized.* The community must establish and self-administer a standardized set of agreements that describe roles and responsibilities and that delineate the level of service that will exist between participants.

- *The technology is stable.* A company may move on once it is confident that its systems—including the portal, the inventory tracking system, and the planning and scheduling tools—are stable and work reliably.

- *The data is accurate.* All companies trust that data flowing across the community is accurate, and agree to commit to automatically generated orders and other requests for activity.

The community is ready to move on to Step Three, for example, when the level of trust among participants reaches the point where an electronic notification is sufficient to act as an authorized order against a standing master agreement. Likewise, they are ready to move on when a CSR such as Dana is confident enough to process customer orders based solely on the figures presented on the portal. At that point, trust in the system is complete.

LOOKING BACK ON STEP TWO

At their last meeting, Dana and Marty agreed to rendezvous again after a couple of months to check in with each other. They meet for coffee on Friday afternoon.

"Okay, Marty," says Dana, "Are you going to complain some more about this process, or have you found that it's beginning to solve some of the problems down in the warehouse?"

"Well, it's been painful," replies Marty. "But I have to admit that it's making my job easier. I'm able to plan my personnel in the warehouse to match the shipments. And here's what's really great—since the inventory numbers on the portal are reliable, I don't have half my team counting inventory just to make sure we can fill standard orders. Everybody trusts what they see on the portal, and that makes everything go much more quickly."

"Yes, it's a relief to be able to trust those numbers on the portal," says Dana. "I know I can commit to an order on the phone. If the portal says the inventory is there, I can sell it there and then. It saves so much time and bother."

"What's surprising to me," adds Marty, "is that we are able to do all this at the same time that we hold less inventory—I have open rack space in the warehouse. That used to scare me, because it meant that we were looking at stock-outs in the near future. Now, I'm not afraid of that open rack space. I trust that we have the inventory we need to serve our customers.

"I like the new way of doing business, but I wonder if we can reduce inventory even further. I'm anxious to move on to the next step."

CHAPTER EIGHT

Step Three—Collaboration

If you fail to plan, you plan to fail.

—Old saying

Dana is pleased with her job by the end of Step Two. The most routine and repetitive aspects of her day-to-day responsibilities—handling orders for the most stable and predictable products—are now reduced. As long as inventory accuracy is maintained and orders remain within the standard range, she can look beyond the immediate needs of supply and demand to watch for greater opportunities for her customers, recognizing trends or shifts in business that she didn't previously have time to notice.

Dana sometimes has to handle an emergency order, untangle a messy situation with a supplier, or resolve a predicament where inventory counts have gone awry, but the new systems have made her job more manageable and meaningful. Because she is not constantly distracted with the need to extinguish brushfires, her long experience in the company makes her a strategic asset for both Soft-Drink and its customers.

Nevertheless, Dana still has to perform some routine tasks such as processing orders and manually monitoring data that is posted on the portal. Because much of this activity involves processing the same information with the same suppliers month after month, it makes sense to turn those responsibilities over to the suppliers themselves.

STEP THREE FAST FACTS

What's in It for My Company?

- A 10 percent to 50 percent reduction in inventory.

- Less working capital and a greater return on assets.

- Smoother production cycles, less production waste, and fewer emergency production runs.

- Elimination of the order process for repetitive products or volumes.

- Employees increasingly freed of routine, repetitive tasks.

What Work Is Involved?

- Moving to global available-to-promise (ATP) software.

- Implementing vendor replenishment (VR).

- Adopting vendor managed inventory (VMI).

- Broadening master agreements with partner companies at each stage.

What Technology Is Required?

- An Enterprise Resource Planning (ERP) system (at least one company in the community).

- A collaborative Advanced Planning System (APS) (at least one company in the community).

- An inventory tracking system (also required for Step Two).

- A portal (also required for Steps One and Two).

How Long Will It Take?

- Up to one year.

STEP THREE

In Step Three, the speed of change increases, and the disciplines that companies established by working with their partners truly begin to produce results. The boundaries between companies start to shift as trading partners begin to collaborate more fully, and responsibilities once handled by companies become visible and are handed over to their suppliers, saving time and reducing costs for both companies. By automating or eliminating steps from processes such as managing inventory and processing orders, both companies begin to enjoy major cost reductions. Employees are increasingly freed of routine, repetitive tasks and can focus more fully on strategic activities.

During Step Three, companies adopt processes and technology that enable them to dramatically reduce inventory while maintaining or improving sales and service levels. Companies may be able to reduce their inventory levels—whether it be raw materials, work-in-progress products or finished goods—by as much as 50 percent.

Consider the ramifications for the Soft-Drink Company if it could reduce its brand-leading cola beverage inventory by half. Fewer forklifts. Smaller warehouses. Lower overhead for lighting and air conditioning in these facilities. The list goes on and on. Regardless of the industry, this enormous inventory reduction will result in significant interest payment savings on a company's working capital. The cost savings a company can recognize are substantial, especially once its primary products are ready for this step.

New Responsibilities

Step Three requires a shift in responsibility and accountability. In Step Three, the interaction between companies shifts from a buyer-seller relationship into a supplier-consumer relationship. For the first time, the supplier not only sees the orders its direct customers place, but also has information about how much its direct customers are actually consuming. Service levels, negotiated as part of the master agreement, define how suppliers and customers work together to replenish products and the quality of products the customer will receive. Both the consumption company

A SIZEABLE INVENTORY REDUCTION

An average company maintains between 6 and 10 weeks of finished goods inventory. Using techniques like vendor replenishment (VR), vendor managed inventory (VMI), and global available-to-promise (ATP) software has allowed many companies to reduce the finished goods inventory they carry to between two and five weeks plus transportation time—a 50 percent reduction for most companies.

and the supplier company have a responsibility for monitoring compliance with the agreement.

The supplier in Step Three is now responsible for ensuring materials are on hand when needed, meaning that the high-fructose corn syrup company that Soft-Drink buys from is responsible for resupplying Soft-Drink when notified. The consumption company must be capable of notifying its supplier of its needs in advance, through order information, production plans, sales forecasts, and so on. It also provides existing inventory quantities that must be updated in real time. This enables both companies to eliminate the cyclical relationship of requesting and responding to orders. Later in Step Three comes another modification to the master agreement, calling for the supplier to be responsible for ensuring that the consumption company has enough materials on hand based on its production plan and sales forecasts. This shifts the responsibility for replenishing products from the consumption company to the supplier company. This is a significant process shift that eliminates the sales order/PO process therefore providing both companies labor cost savings, in short, lead time to supply with lower inventories.

WHAT'S INVOLVED

By the end of Step Two, companies have accurate tallies of their inventory in real time and share this information with their partners via the portal Web site. Companies also post their production and distribution plans, schedules, and forecasts on the portal and keep these documents frequently updated. In addition, businesses have mechanized orders that fall within the minimum-maximum threshold and are electronically notified when inventory levels are dropping and need to be replenished.

These advances have put the participants in a position to collaborate more effectively with their partners, thus saving time and money for all involved. Step Three builds on the disciplines that participating companies established in Steps One and Two, using the increased flow of information to arrive at accurate decisions regarding inventory levels and order replenishment.

Step Three consists of two phases. First, participants will begin to operate under vendor replenishment (VR) agreements, in which companies authorize suppliers to replenish inventory based on shared consumption data.

After this piece is in place, companies should consider moving some of their products to vendor managed inventory (VMI). With VMI, the entire ordering process is transformed. Responsibility for inventory replenishment is completely handed over to suppliers. Each of these steps requires greater levels of collaboration, as companies increasingly entrust the responsibilities of placing orders and managing inventory to their partners.

Global available-to-promise (ATP) software is used in conjunction with the vendor replenishment and vendor managed inventory phases of Step Three. This software allows companies to reallocate inventory to other customers even after it has been placed on order.

Companies should perform an analysis to determine which products should be managed by the supplier company. The effort of moving to a VMI arrangement may outweigh the benefits for small-size shipments, less critical materials, and intermittently used products. The priority of the customer, the value of the material, the speed at which it is consumed, profits, the willingness of the supplier, and other factors will determine whether each product should be moved to VMI.

The Technology of Step Three

With a shared respect for data accuracy and process excellence in place, it's time to enhance the technological capability of the community. In addition to global ATP software, an enterprise resource planning (ERP) system and an advanced planning system (APS) must exist within the community. Typically, these will reside with the company that hosts the portal or the company responsible for delivering the finished products to the customer.

Other companies in the community will need specific business hardware and software capabilities—such as the inventory-tracking systems discussed in Step Two—but not every company will necessarily need to invest in an ERP and APS system to complete Step Three. Based on the complexity of their operations and their technical infrastructure, these companies may opt to use an ERP or APS system, but doing so is not required to participate in the community.

GETTING STARTED

Step Three involves automatically aligning the production and distribution plans of the consumption company with that of the supplier company. Based on these plans, the two companies agree on replenishment quantities and time frames. This helps match the supply to the projected need and forms a new contractual relationship between the supplier and its direct customers. The consumption company is responsible for notifying the supplier company when it has used its supplies, almost as soon as the supplies are used.

It is important to compare actual consumption against forecasted consumption for deviations. This must be performed continually throughout the day. If a company has multiple days worth of inventory on hand, there's more of a buffer to absorb deviations. However, the greater a company's success at reducing inventory, the more sensitive it becomes to errors, and mistakes are magnified. As inventory is reduced, companies must monitor actual and forecasted consumption more frequently, with the goal of matching inventory more closely to consumption.

VENDOR REPLENISHMENT

There is little value in having Dana order the same products and quantities at the same locations week after week. Such repetitious processes can be automated, and whether a company is the supplier or the customer, it stands to benefit. Therefore, a key concept in Step Three is the automatic replenishment of certain regularly consumed items.

In Step Two, Dana and her team laid the groundwork for the automated replenishment of supplies by setting rules such as the minimum-maximum threshold controls that trigger electronic purchase orders and automatic alerts when orders need to be placed. When this process is working smoothly, the day-to-day ordering process requires less attention, allowing Dana's team to focus on the exceptions to the norm. In Step Three, companies completely automate routine orders, further reducing the time it takes to fulfill them.

Vendor replenishment is a set of agreements and procedures that enables suppliers to continually restock their customers' inventory based on the actual quantity of products or materials consumed. The master agreements established in Step Two are broadened to ensure product specifications, proper payment, and other terms negotiated between the supplier and its direct customer.

Vendor replenishment is defined in terms of responsibilities. The supplier is responsible for ensuring materials are on hand based on either consumption notifications or an agreed-upon plan. The consumption company is responsible for sending consumption notifications to its supplier and for managing its inventory on site. With VR, if there is a stock out, the responsibility lies with the consumption company.

The customer continuously monitors its consumption and electronically notifies the supplier the quantity of products it has consumed. The supplier then automatically replenishes supplies to the level consumed based on the master agreement between the companies. No traditional order is placed—effectively removing a step from the inventory replenishment process—and the consumption company never has more or less inventory on hand than is required to meet its production plans.

To take a simple example, the Soft-Drink Company had 40,000 12-pack beverage cartons and used 20,000 of them last week. Throughout the week, the paper products supplier that prints and assembles the 12-pack cartons for Soft-Drink received continuous consumption notifications totaling the 20,000 cartons used. According to the standing master agreement between the two companies, the paperboard supplier is responsible for ensuring that Soft-Drink always has between 15,000 and 40,000 12-pack cartons on hand. The supplier, therefore, will automatically deliver thousands of new cartons this week before Soft-Drink's inventory falls below the 15,000 threshold.

Unless unforeseen problems arise—perhaps a snowstorm blocks major highways and prevents the truck delivery—the customer's stock is always replenished when needed. VR is especially useful in manufacturing situations where quantities are mathematically predictable from period to period, and where standard materials are used. Because orders for these products are calculable, it's a waste of time to involve people in the order process.

To ensure VR works successfully, it is important that the consumption company provide its suppliers with accurate information. Failing to provide the supplier with accurate data regarding inventory levels or its condition could lead to stock-outs. For example, an overnight forklift driver in Marty's warehouse at Soft-Drink might accidentally back into a pallet of bottles, crushing them. Fearing discipline, the driver might just stash the damaged goods behind other boxes in the back of the warehouse. Until other coworkers notice the problem weeks later, the bottle supplier will not realize that Soft-Drink has far fewer bottles than needed, which could result in a costly halt to Soft-Drink's production line.

In Step Two, companies began to post inventory information on the portal in real time and update plans frequently, ensuring companies have better information with which to work. VR uses this increased level of information to further eliminate inventory. With VR, the supplier and its direct customer effectively create one pool of inventory to work from, where before each company maintained its own, separate pool of the same inventory. Creating one pool of inventory from which to work reduces inventory for both companies.

VENDOR MANAGED INVENTORY

Vendor managed inventory optimizes the consumption company's inventory levels even further by shifting responsibility for inventory replenishment to the supplier. VMI is different from the standard buyer-supplier relationship in which the customer places an order with its supplier when goods or services are needed. Under that scenario, the consumption company is in complete control of the size of the order and when it is placed. The consumption company also maintains information about how much inventory is needed and how much product needs to be produced.

With VMI, the supplier has access to the consumption company's inventory count, consumption rate, and production plans—and is responsible for ensuring that supplies are on hand when needed. As with VR, the master agreement stipulates the financial terms of the relationship and ensures that the right products are on hand at the right time.

Shifting Responsibilities with VMI

As with vendor replenishment, vendor managed inventory is defined based on the relationships between consumer and supplier. The supplier company is responsible for having inventory or material on hand based on the master agreement, at the core of which are production schedules, distribution schedules, and production plans of the consumption company. The consumption company is accountable for delivering accurate data to the supplier, and the supplier is accountable for analyzing that data and fulfilling the requirements.

The supplier company is also responsible for managing the inventory on hand and determining the quantities needed for regular use, expected variances, and unforeseen events. If there is a stock-out under a VMI arrangement, the responsibility lies with the supplier. With VMI, the ultimate measure of success is if the customer never runs out of supplies.

VMI is more than simply responding to a consumption notification or a long-range plan. Instead, companies use statistical analysis on a daily

MANAGING INVENTORY AT THE CUSTOMER'S SITE

Most vendor managed inventory (VMI) programs require that the supplier maintain inventory at the consumption company's site to guarantee that the company always has adequate supply on hand. This inventory is placed on consignment or is kept in a locked area or "cage" in a warehouse or storage area. The supplier still owns and manages the inventory even though it is stored on the consumption company's premises.

When workers remove inventory from the cage or consignment area, it is scanned as a sales transaction. This represents the moment at which inventory changes hands and the purchase is complete. The customer only pays for the inventory upon consumption.

Using automated transaction systems, the supplier can view the entire inventory stored at the consumption company site. The supplier uses this information, as well as consumption data, production plans, and sales forecasts from the consumption company, to statistically determine proper inventory levels and shipping times.

Determining the most cost-effective way to replenish the consumption company is one of the primary challenges of VMI, and is the test of good VMI technology. The software must be able to track consumption rates, supply levels, orders, forecasts, sales, and transportation costs to determine how much inventory is needed at the customer site to protect against disruptions from stock-outs. It must also determine what rules should be applied to provide the most cost-effective service level. To arrive at an optimal replenishment plan, the software must weigh several factors simultaneously because the best solution is often a combination of several factors.

basis. VMI requires the supplier to do the materials requirement planning (MRP) and detailed scheduling for the consumption company based on that company's detailed production plans and distribution schedules. VMI requires the consumption company to confirm the plan developed by the supplier company.

This shift in responsibility requires a much greater degree of collaboration between partner companies. With VR, the customer must simply send its supplier a message indicating it needs more supplies. However, with VMI, the consumption company must rely on the supplier who determines the timing and quantity of materials to be replenished. The consumption company measures the success of the relationship based on compliance to previously agreed-on plans.

Why Move from VR to VMI?

Moving from VR to VMI is beneficial because it removes more steps out of the order process. In so doing, the consumption company receives the correct level of inventory, wastes less time notifying the supplier of its consumption, and can assign fewer people to the order process.

The supplier is able to keep only as much inventory on hand as is necessary to meet the inventory stipulations in the master agreement. Because the supplier knows the consumption company's production schedule, the production capacity of the plant becomes apparent. Once the supplier establishes the amount of inventory necessary to operate the consumption company's plant at capacity, it can reduce on-hand inventory to the amount necessary to serve the plant between shipments. The supplier has less money tied up in its finished product inventory and therefore a stronger cash flow. At the same time, the consumption company has sufficient materials on hand to operate at capacity.

As inventory is consumed, the supplier tracks it electronically using a bar code scanning or RFID system, which constantly updates this information. Under a VMI model, the forklift crash would have been noticed more quickly due to the change in the availability of the pallet. Suppliers track the ID numbers on pallets, boxes, and crates for usage, freshness, and other factors and would have checked up on an ID number that was not being consumed. A few supplier-initiated phone calls could have uncovered the damaged goods more quickly, potentially preventing a stock-out.

Companies should move one or more of their products to VMI if they agree that doing so would further reduce inventory and enable them to capture a greater return on their assets. Before undertaking the effort, however, they need to agree on who will own the inventory, and at what point ownership will shift from customer to supplier. Who owns the inventory that's waiting to be used at the customer's site? Does the transfer of ownership occur upon consumption or at an earlier point? If these differences can be resolved, and if VMI processes are properly implemented, inventory can be reduced by 50 percent, and both the consumption company and the supplier company can substantially reduce costs.

GLOBAL ATP

In Step One, Dana resorted to borrowing inventory to fill her orders. She knew that she could borrow inventory that was on order and held for shipment to fill her quick-turnaround requests, and that no one would be the wiser if she replaced the borrowed inventory from new production or other sources before the original order shipped. By replacing the borrowed inventory, Dana was able to halt the ripple effects she created before they caused any problems for customers. Global ATP software works in much the same way.

Global ATP is a software application that automates the search for available products, but does so across multiple warehouses and companies in order to maximize the availability of a limited amount of inventory. Global ATP allows a company to reallocate its inventory systemwide, based on changing customer needs or market dynamics. This flexibility is an important step toward adaptability. Global ATP helps companies match supply with demand while maintaining a reduced inventory. On a single screen, companies can view what inventory currently exists, what products are in progress, and whether there are alternative products that they may be able to substitute to fill an order, giving them multiple options for filling orders (Figure 8.1).

For example, the Soft-Drink Company has earmarked 100,000 cases of soda for a large grocery store customer, slated for shipment in a week. In the meantime, a substantial convenience store chain is selling the same soda faster than expected due to the summer heat, and places a larger-than-anticipated order for 50,000 cases. The convenience store chain needs the soda in two days, but Soft-Drink only has 20,000 cases on hand, and its bottling subsidiaries can't produce enough in the next two days to fill the rest of the order. It would be a shame to turn away business and risk disappointing the convenience store chain.

Because the initial order of 100,000 cases of soda is reserved for shipment a week in advance, those cases are "soft-pegged" for shipment. In other words, they can still be considered sellable inventory as long as they can be replaced before the shipment takes place. The Soft-Drink company's global ATP system shows that enough soda can be produced in four days, and so suggests a "reallocation scheme" whereby 30,000 cases of soda from the pallets waiting to be shipped are transferred to the new order. As a result, both orders are filled, and Soft-Drink still has time to recoup the cases of soda it borrowed from the batch earmarked for the grocery stores before that order ships in seven days.

FIGURE 8.1 FULFILLING ORDERS WITH GLOBAL AVAILABLE-TO-PROCESS TECHNOLOGY

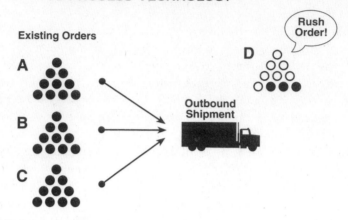

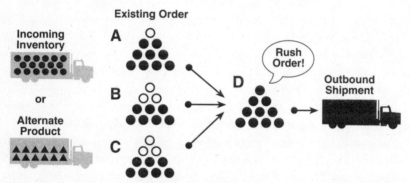

GLOBAL AVAILABLE-TO-PROMISE (ATP) TECHNOLOGY ALLOWS COMPANIES TO REDUCE THEIR INVENTORY BY PROVIDING THEM WITH MORE FLEXIBILITY TO FULFILL ORDERS. IN THE FIRST EXAMPLE, THE COMPANY DOES NOT HAVE ENOUGH INVENTORY TO ACCOMMODATE RUSH ORDER D. IN THE SECOND EXAMPLE, THE COMPANY IS USING GLOBAL ATP AND IS THEREFORE ABLE TO REALLOCATE INVENTORY TO WHERE IT IS NEEDED MOST URGENTLY. INVENTORY IS BORROWED FROM EXISTING ORDERS A, B, AND C AND FROM SIMILAR BUT SLIGHTLY DIFFERENT ALTERNATIVE PRODUCTS TO FILL RUSH ORDER D. INCOMING INVENTORY, WHEN IT ARRIVES, WILL REPLACE THOSE PRODUCTS EARMARKED FOR THE ORIGINAL ORDERS A, B, AND C SO THESE ORDERS CAN BE SHIPPED ON TIME.

Had the grocery store shipment been slated for delivery the next morning, before more soda could be produced, the global ATP system would have identified those 100,000 cases as "hard-pegged," and therefore unavailable for reallocation.

Global ATP also allows Soft-Drink to make the reallocation decision based on other factors, such as the importance of the customer, potential profits from the opportunity, and shipping cost and time. Because global ATP can shuffle products in this way, the company has more options to fill orders from lower levels of inventory, and can accommodate unexpected orders or reallocate them based on customer profiles and sales priorities.

Using global ATP software, the company can also tell the customer when it will be able to fill the order, perhaps with multiple shipments, or that it can fill the request by offering alternative products to satisfy the

ONE COMPANY'S SUCCESS WITH GLOBAL ATP

Netherlands-based Computer Service Solutions (CSS), a reseller of information technology products, used global available-to-promise (ATP) to reduce inventory and improve service to its customers.

The company, which boasts 24 offices, 2,200 employees, and more than 30,000 customers, streamlined its supply chain and improved service by eliminating its own warehouse operations—effectively reducing its owned inventory to zero. CSS was able to shift its previous inventory to available-to-promise stock at its distributors' warehouses, greatly reducing inventory in the overall supply chain. By closing its warehouse, CSS wiped out the expense of operating the facility and of packing and shipping goods. Total back-office personnel requirements were reduced by 40 percent.

CSS also improved its customer service with global ATP. For instance, CSS can now obtain information about product availability in one minute, as compared with one hour before it adopted global ATP. Delivery commitments can be made in two hours as opposed to three days, and the average order cycle time has been reduced from four to two days. On-time and complete order fulfillment rates have been improved by 50 percent, and the ability to draw inventory from a larger number of distributors has reduced back orders by 30 percent.

demand. In the end, the company may still have to turn away a surprise order on occasion, but it will do so based on the most solid and current information.

ATP software can also be used to accommodate a larger number of orders because it allows products and materials to flow through the pipeline more quickly. In such an environment, products are not assigned to customers until the last moment before shipment, meaning companies make exactly what they need and move the older goods first. Products move faster through the system rather than sitting as inventory for extended periods. The faster a company can deliver products to the customer, the greater the return on its investment.

Absolute inventory accuracy is essential for global ATP. If the global ATP system starts reallocating inventory that doesn't exist, or isn't where it's supposed to be, companies will immediately experience problems. Real-time inventory accuracy and electronic inventory track-and-trace systems such as a bar code scanner or RFID technology are mandatory. Also, global ATP software is a tool intended to help companies with multiple warehouses, distribution sites, and sales channels. If companies have just one site, ATP is not necessary.

BENEFITS OF STEP THREE

Reduced Inventory

By more precisely monitoring consumption rates and automating the replenishment process, customers, and suppliers that complete Step Three more closely match supply to demand, reducing the amount of inventory for both companies. In addition, by eliminating time-consuming order processes and by replenishing supplies exactly when the customer needs them, inventory within the system drops.

Moreover, instead of the supplier and its customer each maintaining separate inventories of the same product, the supplier maintains a single inventory for both companies and replenishes products based on consumption. When the supplier is responsible for maintaining inventory, there are simply fewer places for inventory to build up. Finally, global ATP allows companies to use lower levels of inventory to serve the same number of orders.

Combined, these factors enable companies that complete Step Three to see dramatic inventory reductions, ranging from 10 percent to 50 percent.

Smaller Working Capital

By reducing inventory, businesses will trim operational cash requirements or working capital charges, which reduces the recurring monthly interest payments that companies pay on revolving lines of credit. Depending on the size of the business and its revolving debt, these savings can total hundreds of thousands or even millions of dollars.

The VR and VMI models may allow reduce working capital for suppliers by enabling them to negotiate more favorable payment terms with their customers. Because the supplier typically increases its number of inventory "turns" per year, it gets paid more frequently. Each payment will be smaller, but will come more rapidly and regularly. Getting paid more frequently, in turn, reduces the supplier's working capital charges and interest payments.

SIGNIFICANT COST REDUCTIONS FOR COMPANIES

Companies moving to an adaptive business network can significantly reduce their costs by shortening their payment cycles and reducing the total amount of inventory they carry. Take a company with $1.2 billion in sales per year, for example, or an average of $100 million per month. If the company has to wait an average of 60 days to be paid for its products, it has $200 million in outstanding accounts receivables at any given time. If the company's monthly working capital carrying costs for these outstanding payments are 2 percent of their overall value, the cost to the company is $4 million per month or $48 million per year.

Similarly, if the same company carries $100 million in inventory and turns over its inventory monthly, and the monthly cost of carrying that inventory amounts to 3 percent of its overall value, the cost to the company is $3 million per month or $36 million per year.

By reducing their payment cycles and the amount of inventory they need to operate, companies can save millions of dollars annually. For example, this company would save $42 million annually by shortening its payment cycle to 30 days and cutting its inventory in half.

More Strategic Flexibility

By eliminating the need for ordering and moving the responsibility of inventory management to the supplier, the consumption company frees its workers from mundane chores to handle more strategic and analytical tasks.

From the supplier's perspective, Step Three provides more production stability, freeing production capacity for more innovative or profitable efforts. When a supplier can form ongoing VR supplier relationships with a sufficient number of companies, production levels become much more stable. If the supplier can reach a level, for example, where 50 percent to 60 percent of its production capacity is on VR, the company has essentially covered its expenses, and the rest of its capacity can be used to create more innovative, higher profit products or leased at a profit to other manufacturers. Of course, the levels of committed production capacity required for a company to cover its expenses vary.

Smoother Production Cycles

The smoother production cycles that result from implementing VMI help keep costs lower for both suppliers and customers. Suppliers have greater insight into the needs of their customers and can plan accordingly, reducing the need to make emergency production runs for unforeseen orders. Emergency production runs can dramatically harm a company's profit margin because paying workers overtime and recalibrating manufacturing processes for short runs is costly.

For example, due to increased summer demand, the Soft-Drink Company needs another 500,000 paperboard 12-pack cartons this week to fill an unexpected order. However, the primary company that prints, assembles, and delivers these cartons can only recoup its costs and turn a profit for a production run of at least one million cartons. This is the minimum amount the firm can produce and still charge the standard rate. Anything smaller results in a loss for the carton supplier, or higher prices for the customer.

The printing company has three choices, none of which are ideal. First, it can produce the 500,000 cartons at a loss. However, that hurts its business and makes the paperboard company less willing to work with Soft-Drink in the future. Second, it can print the 500,000 cartons, but charge Soft-Drink a premium rate to do so. But that hurts the soft drink company's business and makes it less willing to work with the carton supplier in the future.

As a third option, the paperboard company can make one million cartons and force Soft-Drink to keep the overrun as extra inventory. But this solution may be unacceptable to Soft-Drink, which would be required to hold double the number of cartons it needs—inventory that it may or may not use.

Had these partners been operating under a VMI scenario, the paperboard printing company would have had better insight into the greater-than-expected consumption of cartons by its customer and planned accordingly. Under a VMI arrangement, the paperboard supplier would have known by monitoring the portal Web site routinely that reserves of 12-pack cartons were quickly dropping at Soft-Drink's primary bottling facility. Because the high consumption rate was outside the norm, managers at the printing company would have called their counterparts at Soft-Drink to verify the production plan, collaborate on revised forecasts, and negotiate a way to handle the increased need for boxes before the problem occurred.

This level of proactive planning helps prevent surprises and short production runs, ensuring a smoother production cycle. Rather than paying premium prices for raw materials and other supplies on a short time frame basis, suppliers will be able to forecast demand more accurately and therefore provide customers with the materials they need, when they need them, at a price that is acceptable to both. In the interdependent business networks of tomorrow, it will be in all parties' interest to work together in this fashion.

POTENTIAL OBSTACLES

The biggest obstacle to Step Three is the shift of control. The suppliers may not want to take responsibility or be held accountable for replenishing supplies, and employees at the consumption company may fear a reduction in workforce due to the elimination of the order process. Labor unions may view this as an outsourcing deal that threatens their workers.

In addition, sharing confidential information such as inventory levels, production capacity, and customer consumption with suppliers can be a scary prospect for executives at the consumption company, especially because a supplier may also be working with the company's competitors. It is important that confidentiality terms be spelled out in detail in the master agreement to ensure confidential information remains private. Once company executives begin to see the cost benefits of Step Three, they will embrace them and be more willing to assume the risk.

Finally, there may also be an increase in production and transportation costs due to an increased number of production runs and deliveries if VMI is not focused on long-term planning, but only on short-term schedules. By sequencing production schedules appropriately, transportation costs also will be reduced.

MOVING TO THE NEXT STEP

Once a company has had success with a first partner, it's time to add others. Businesses need to recognize that Step Three can be a lengthy process, depending on the complexity of a company and the technology and systems it already has in place. Standardized processes for replenishment will propel companies through Step Three, but there is no set timeline for adopting any of these processes. However, it is recommended that companies adopt a cumulative timeline of no more than one year for this step.

Companies should not attempt to put 100 percent of their business on a global ATP, VR, or VMI model. Rather, they should be satisfied with the new cost savings they receive from transforming 80 percent of their business to global ATP, VR, and VMI. Once they have successfully adapted 80 percent of their business to Step Three, it is time to consider moving on to Step Four, the final step of the adaptive business network.

A company and its partners are ready to advance to Step Four when:

- Their global ATP, VR, and VMI systems are stable and operate reliably.

- They have met the objectives established for inventory and working capital reductions.

- The core dependent elements of the business are participating in this community.

- The procedures and technology are in place to quickly add new partners to the community.

LOOKING BACK ON STEP THREE

A half-year into Step Three, Dana agrees to have a talk with Joan from the bottling plant and Marty from the warehouse at Maybe's Bar & Grill. Dana gets there first and finds a table. She reflects on the past six months, how far Soft-Drink has come, and how much her company's operations have changed. Her own personal growth has been significant. Starting as a CSR and order taker, she's now working with a team to plan 20 percent of her company's business. Dana thinks to herself: "We've made a lot of changes quickly, but I feel like we've really accomplished something. I've personally learned a lot and have developed some valuable skills."

Soon, Joan and Marty show up. They shake hands and seem happy.

"How are things going?" Dana asks.

"Well, we still haven't smoothed out our processes entirely," says Joan. "But we can see the improvements. We're getting the inventory when we need it, and the schedule jams that occur each month can be counted on one hand."

"I'm sorry to be a wet blanket," says Marty, "but things from my perspective aren't all that great."

"What's the problem?" Dana asks.

"We used to send 50 shipments per day and now we're doing more than 100. I've got drivers running everywhere. I can't even give my guys breaks. I live in constant fear that we're going to run out of stuff, because we don't store as much."

"Well, have we run out of stuff yet?"

"I don't know if it's luck or skill, but we haven't run into any problems in the last 60 days."

"So it's better?"

"Things are somewhat better," Marty says, "but I wonder if there's a way to stabilize transportation costs and operate even more efficiently than we are right now."

"Buck up, Marty," says Dana as the waiter delivers three frosty mugs to the table. "We're almost there."

CHAPTER NINE

Step Four—Adaptability

Whenever you see a successful business, someone once made a courageous decision.

—Peter Drucker

The need to be adaptive isn't new. Businesses have always faced challenges from competition and vicissitudes of the market. What's new today is the speed and flexibility with which companies must respond to their business environments and, given these challenges, the difficulty of effectively linking production to demand.

The Soft-Drink Company has just completed Step Three, and Dana is noticing some significant changes. Dana herself realizes she is less harried than she used to be, because she no longer needs to log onto her computer to address inventory problems early in the morning before heading to work. She arrives at work in the morning, and flips on her computer. Finding no problems that require her attention, she walks into the cafeteria to get coffee.

In the cafeteria, she sees Cathy, another former customer service representative, who also now works as a planner. "How are things going with your customers?" Dana asks. "Is this working well?"

"Yes, it's working pretty well, for the most part," Cathy says. "But I'm having some problems with the planning. The amount of information I need to sift through is overwhelming, and some of our costs are inconsistent."

"You're right, we're still running into logjams with production schedules, and it's still taking us longer than necessary to get things done," says Dana. "We're planning to discuss these issues at a management meeting

STEP FOUR FAST FACTS

What's in It for My Company?

■ Improved across-the-board business performance of between 15 percent to 25 percent.

■ Increased sales due to improved customer service and faster response to sales opportunities.

■ Significant cost savings that result from carrying lower inventory, borrowing less working capital, reducing production waste, capturing a greater return on assets, and reducing the time required to complete processes.

What Work Is Involved?

■ Standardizing services across the network, such as transportation and financial services.

■ Developing common business processes and standardizing them in master agreements and automated controls that govern the operations of the network.

■ Adopting pervasive technology to automate decision making and share information throughout the network in near real time.

What Technology Is Required?

■ Pervasive software, such as software agents or Web services, is required to handle the immense flow of data exchanged within an adaptive business network.

■ This software will operate within the technological infrastructure that most companies have already implemented. However, some upgrades may be necessary.

How Long Will It Take?

■ Adaptability is an ongoing discipline.

■ As with any strategic business plan, companies should establish one-, two-, and five-year goals, and develop a road map for achieving these goals.

■ Companies should keep each goal simple and focused, get it done, and move on to the next goal.

later this afternoon. Our three leading customers and our prime supplier will also be there."

STEP FOUR

Like the Soft-Drink Company, organizations will be motivated to move to Step Four to capture even more efficiency than they were able to accomplish by completing Step Three. By the end of Step Three, companies have more visibility into the replenishment cycle. They are informed when supplies are running low, and take steps to prevent stock-outs before they occur. In some cases, doing so will lead to cost swings. For example, the cost of production may increase as companies produce in smaller lot sizes. In addition, the cost of transportation may rise as companies deliver materials in smaller quantities.

At this point, the company in charge of the product brands will begin to search for ways to operate even more efficiently, and will move to the next level of collaboration by pooling transportation, warehouse, financial, and other resources to keeps costs down for all the participants. Pooling these resources is the first step toward moving from the loose community of assembled participants in Step Three into a network of partners that results by the end of Step Four.

At the end of Step Four, companies are linked as a network with customers and suppliers throughout the supply chain. Companies within the network are connected by standard business processes and technology. Being connected in this manner enables companies to obtain information about consumer demand almost instantaneously and respond quickly to changing market conditions.

Companies can adapt by working together to develop new products and services and by adding and dropping partners rapidly as market conditions change. Information about customer demand is communicated instantaneously to all companies that need to receive it, and many routine decisions, once handled manually, are automated based on a set of predetermined rules agreed on by companies within the network.

Motivated by the opportunity to further lower logistics costs by working even more collaboratively with partners, the company responsible for the finished products generally emerges as the coordinating partner responsible for managing the network and negotiating the terms by which the trading community operates. Companies that join the community operate by a set of core rules outlined in the master agreement, which is again expanded. And companies within the network begin to pool resources such as transportation, warehouse space, and financial services to achieve greater economies of scale and reduce costs for all participants.

Moving to an adaptive business network results in two major shifts: First, companies have access to a wealth of accurate information in real time, allowing them to operate more effectively and respond quickly to market changes. Most notably, they will be able to track information about actual consumer purchases and unexpected changes in customer demand as soon as they occur. Second, many of the costly delays that exist when working with customers and suppliers are greatly reduced or eliminated as companies use technology to automate a wider range of routine decisions.

Tracking Customer Purchases in Real Time

A key difference between Step Three and Step Four is the emphasis on consumer demand for products versus consumption of supplies by a company's direct customer. By the end of Step Three, businesses begin employing vendor managed inventory (VMI) to monitor how much their direct customer is consuming in order to replenish the necessary materials when needed. In Step Four, participants share data about the finished products and services purchased by the consumer, not just information about what their next-in-line customer is buying.

The ability to track customer purchases in real time is fueled by pervasive technology such as software agents or Web services. When added to the network, this technology operates much the same way as colonies of ants or worker bees. Individually, each piece of software performs a simple task and cannot accomplish much. However, as a swarm of thousands working cooperatively, their pervasive presence and collective power is dramatic. Imagine a world in which thousands of software applications quickly and quietly perform routine business tasks, saving companies time and money and automatically alerting executives to trends never before noticeable with previous business tools or the simple human eye.

Through the use of such software, information about customer purchases is transmitted instantaneously as the sale is made to all relevant members of the network, along with other pertinent information such as other products purchased by the customer at the same time and available demographic information about the purchaser. Companies within the network also use this kind of advanced technology to analyze information about consumer purchase patterns, enabling them to predict future demand with far greater precision.

The ability to monitor and analyze what customers are purchasing in real time gives companies throughout the network a far better understanding of demand and what products each company needs to manufacture. It also gives companies more time to change course before they're locked into production schedules and unwanted runs of inventory.

Companies within the network also begin to exchange a wealth of other information related to the success of their business—information that is both more timely and more accurate than what they've previously had access to. The companies track everything from inventory levels at different points along the supply chain to where shipments are in transit to shop-floor machine failures and other glitches. This information will be passed to all appropriate parties, and when problems occur, the network can react immediately.

Automating Routine Decisions

A second big shift that results from the adaptive business network is that decisions are made in response to information as it is received, and many of these decisions are automated based on a set of predetermined rules or controls agreed on by the network. Using advanced technology to automate decisions greatly reduces many of the costly delays that exist today as companies work with their suppliers and customers to serve the consumer. It enables companies to respond far more swiftly to changing market conditions.

For example, the Soft-Drink Company, in an adaptive network with its suppliers, distributors, and retailers, might employ information agents to continuously monitor inventory levels by counting the amount of soft drinks sold in each store. These information agents—very small, specialized software applications—are linked with the point of sales system that rings up purchases at each store cash register.

The information agents are also linked to decision agents that contain preset inventory limits. Each information agent indicates when a certain beverage has sold and sends the decision agent a current inventory total for that product. As long as the inventory remains above the decision agent's threshold, nothing happens. But if it's hot outside and cold drinks are selling fast, the amount of inventory might fall below the decision agent's threshold. The decision agent then sends alerts to both the distributor and to Soft-Drink.

This alert notifies the distributor to deliver more of the beverage that is selling quickly so that the store always has on hand the drink that customers are buying. The alert is first sent in the form of an electronic purchase order to the distributor closest to the store. In response to the order, the distributor's automated system checks its inventory and instantaneoulsy responds. If this distributor responds that it cannot fulfill the request, the decision agent sends an electronic request for replenishment to its backup distributor and so forth until the order is filled. These exchanges occur nearly instantaneously and automatically, without human involvement. Consumption information is rapidly made available to those who need it, enabling companies to quickly make adjustments when customers are purchasing products slower or faster than expected.

Once a distributor agrees to fill the order, an information agent notifies a decision agent at the transportation company when the shipment is ready. Other software provides information on weather and traffic before trucks are routed and dispatched. Geographic positioning systems (GPS) track the movement of the trucks, relating that information to software agents at the warehouse, which schedule workers to unload and receive the shipment. The shipment is electronically scanned into the inventory system using software in handheld devices, and the system instantaneously alerts other systems throughout the network that the new shipment has arrived.

All activity across the entire network of companies—manufacturing, warehousing, shipping, delivery, and consumption—is monitored by management agents. These high-level software applications ensure that activity throughout the network conforms to the master agreements established by the coordinating partner and the participating companies. Spread in this manner across the entire network, pervasive technology such as agents can handle routine decisions around the clock—quickly, quietly, in the background. This frees employees from routine activities and operational chores, allowing them to focus solely on the exceptions to the norm.

WHY MOVE TO STEP FOUR?

The ability to track consumer purchases as they occur, exchange information nearly instantaneously, and automate routine decisions provides a wealth of benefits for companies participating in an adaptive business network. Companies that move to Step Four will be able to:

- Take advantage of greater sales opportunities while significantly reducing costs to realize an additional 15 percent to 25 percent improvement in company performance.

■ More precisely link production to customer demand, reducing the risk of stock-outs or excess inventory, while increasing the likelihood that the inventory on hand matches what customers are actually buying.

■ Reduce the amount of working capital needed to maintain large stores of inventory, as well as the interest payments that accompany this debt.

■ Capture a higher rate of return on their assets. By receiving timely information about customer demand, for example, companies participating in an adaptive business network have the flexibility to alter production, design, transportation, and other factors as close to the sale as possible. They can also more successfully delay differentiation on core products, broadening the market for the products they manufacture.

■ Reduce production waste by scheduling longer production runs, minimizing the downtime and changeover waste that occurs when a manufacturing system is reformulated to accommodate a new order.

■ Save money by pooling resources such as transportation and financial services with other companies in the network.

■ Increase sales by quickly realigning distribution of their products in response to unexpected swings in customer demand.

■ Borrow production capacity from other companies within the network to meet demand for hot-selling products.

■ Create more demand for their products and services by bundling them with those of other companies in the network.

What's Involved

Step Four involves the adoption of an even greater number of standardized business processes. Support roles such as transportation and financial services are standardized throughout the network. Common business processes are institutionalized as automated controls that form the rules for how the network functions. Companies take the business process changes implemented in the previous three steps and extend them further by incorporating them into the master agreement that governs the day-to-day operations of the network.

In addition to these standard business processes, companies will adopt pervasive software, such as software agents and Web services, to respond to business fluctuations with greater ease and flexibility than ever before. This new technology will allow companies to share data through the network almost instantaneously. It will also act in concert with existing systems to reduce the time needed for many processes, while eliminating others entirely.

Business Process Changes

Rather than operating in isolation, companies in Step Four begin to achieve greater economies of scale by pooling resources such as transportation, financial services, warehouse space, technology, and consultant studies. The coordinating partner negotiates these services, which are incorporated into a master agreement template.

The master agreement is similar to those established in previous steps, but will be expanded to delineate the roles and relationships of the network. The master agreement also outlines the exact key performance indicators (KPIs) that companies must meet as well as the specifications for goods produced by the network. Each company within the network uses the master agreement template as the basis of its negotiations with its next-in-line suppliers and customers, adding to the master agreement based on its individual needs with each of these partners.

The roles and relationships outlined in the master agreement form the basis for how the network functions on a day-to-day basis. Many of the rules outlined in the master agreement are incorporated as automated controls that manage the way decisions are made throughout the network. For example, the master agreement may specify replenishment quantities, the specific materials to be shipped to specific locations, the commitment point on an order, customer service levels, and how to handle situations that fall outside the norm.

Pervasive Technology

In an adaptive business network, businesses are likely to have multiple suppliers and partners, allowing them to tap the innovation and alternatives offered by many niche companies. In the past, companies could not avail themselves of these options because it was difficult and expensive to create the linkages between entities. To coordinate with dozens of network partners and monitor the vast amount of information across the network, companies must turn to new software tools for help.

By Step Four, it will no longer be feasible for organizations to manually monitor and maintain this complex web of partnerships, information, and contractual relationships. Instead, software will tirelessly perform these tasks 24 hours per day, such as monitoring the delivery and receipt of inventory shipments, tracking sales and transactions, tallying critical data, and alerting workers to events and circumstances across the network.

Companies within the community will need to adopt a new genre of software that is pervasive throughout the adaptive business network, and that will serve as the glue that bonds the network together. This software will serve as a company's eyes and ears, keeping track of transactions, sales and supply events, monitoring external demand signals, and other factors. It will act and make decisions accordingly. This software will effectively allow a business within a network to sense and adapt to its changing surroundings.

Pervasive technology can come in many forms. Software agents are small, simple software applications that perform a single task and then securely communicate information to other agents via the Internet. These applications will be inexpensive and easy to install, operate, and customize. Agents will provide the quickest and least expensive option for forming the linkages necessary in an adaptive business network.

Because these software elements are small, they use minimal computer processing power. This speeds their ability to process tasks, while keeping the cost low and installation easy. Each element performs one task and one task only. Like a socket wrench that fits one nut or bolt, each agent is not complex but does its single job perfectly.

Software agents, Web services, and other pervasive technologies are capable of interacting with large numbers of computer systems, software applications, databases, and legacy systems because they translate their messages into a common language using industry standards, such as eXtensible Markup Language (XML) or Java, before relaying the information elsewhere in a suitable format. As a result, this technology will be capable of working with almost any existing computer system, allowing companies to take advantage of the technology investments they've already made. This also means that companies can link to the network quickly and inexpensively and communicate information between partners without all the participants sharing a common computing platform.

Is My Company Ready?

Step Four requires another large mind-set change. First, it involves adopting an expanded set of standard procedures required to work efficiently with customers and suppliers within the network. Second, it requires

WHAT IS PERVASIVE COMPUTING?

Pervasive computing within the context of the adaptive business network is more than the ability to access information virtually anywhere and at any time. It provides businesses with the ability to sense and respond to changing market conditions more quickly than was possible in the past.

Computing will become pervasive when a sufficiently powerful and omnipresent infrastructure is in place that links together many of the incompatible technologies that exist today. Some of the technologies that will likely contribute to pervasive computing in the future are software agents, Web services, smart devices, and standardized wireless protocols.

Software agents: Agents are very small software programs built to perform tightly defined tasks within automated systems. The most common form of agents are simple Web crawlers that seek out information on the Internet. Other agents can perform simple tasks and make basic decisions. The amount of information that an agent is able to generate or monitor is small, but in a network with other agents, the sum is greater than the parts. A network of agents can form responses and generate actions that will seem "natural" or serendipitous, providing recipients with services that are both personalized and valuable.

Web services: Web services refers to flexible, Internet-based applications that can interact with each other based on the exchange of data in standardized protocols, usually XML. Web services allow people to create new Web-based applications that are dynamically assembled from components distributed across the Internet. Unlike server-based, fixed applications and operations that resist change and are slow to respond to their environment, Web services adapt themselves to information and updates as fast as they are reflected on the Internet. In essence, applications that interact based on rules and within preestablished controls will themselves navigate the Internet, interacting with each other using Web standards and protocols, much like humans use Web browsers today. Used together with software agents—which can act as the senses for Web services systems—these applications can generate services that rely on the context and opportunities specific to times, places, and individuals.

WHAT IS PERVASIVE COMPUTING? *(CONTINUED)*

Smart devices: For software agents, Web services, and adaptable business networks to interact with each other and deliver services to the consumer, an infrastructure of compatible devices and pervasive communication systems must be in place. As computing devices grow smaller and more powerful, and find their way into cars, cell phones, credit cards and "smart tags" affixed to merchandize, these devices will become the conduit between interlinked networks and the services they offer consumers.

The pervasiveness and usefulness of smart devices will also increase as hardware improves. In the near future, the batteries that power these tools will cease to be energy storage cells and will become energy generating devices. Once handheld devices are capable of power generation, these gadgets will become significantly more omnipresent.

Wireless protocols: A standardized wireless protocol will be required to realize the vision of a fully pervasive computing future. Today, three different broadcast protocols are in use across the United States to deliver digital information to handsets. This means that a cell phone that works fine in California may not operate in Oklahoma, and that signal coverage can vary greatly across the country—or across the city—depending on the kind of device and the existing business arrangements between carriers.

All of Europe and much of Asia operate with a single wireless protocol, the Global System for Mobile communications, or GSM. It's no surprise that both Asia and Europe have far more advanced wireless networks than North America, and that so-called 3G or Third Generation features like wireless e-mail and Internet are much more common there than in the United States and Canada. Development of these services—and features that tie banking and commercial transactions to handheld devices or cell phones—are economically feasible when large numbers of people concentrate their usage on a common wireless protocol. Standardization of protocols and broadcast networks must take place before the benefits of a connected environment can be realized.

automating a larger number of processes once completed manually, which can be a large change for employees used to handling those processes. Third, the move to greater automation increases the level of technological complexity of the company. Finally, the company faces increased exposure as it joins with other customers and suppliers to work together to jointly solve problems.

Before moving on to Step Four, business managers need to think again about the company's goals and what they want their company to be in the future. The move to full adaptability provides great benefits to many businesses. It also will profoundly change how a company conducts business. Before moving to Step Four, a company's leaders need to ask if the company is fully ready for the following:

- *A higher level of coordination with network members.* To move to adaptability, companies will adopt a set of processes and procedures that become the standards for the network. Ordering and purchasing decisions, inventory management, supervision of logistics and transportation, responsibility for establishing quality control specifications—the authority for all these functions will be coordinated at the level of the network.

While individual companies will remain independent in Step Four, the network will make exacting decisions regarding how goods are produced and handled at these autonomous companies. Company managers will need to ask themselves if they are prepared to work closely with their partners and coordinate certain decisions with other members of the network. Each company must also ask itself if its internal corporate culture can support these changes.

- *The increased complexity.* Step Four is much more difficult than the previous steps, but the benefits are also significantly greater. In Step Four, companies begin to automate many more business processes than in Step Three. In addition, the move from Step Three to Step Four involves increased technological complexity and a heightened degree of automation among an expanding number of network partners.

The complexity involved in Step Four increases depending on several factors. Individual networks may face inconsistent transportation schedules, supply mix problems, highly variable customer demand, the need to quickly develop new products on an ongoing basis, or frequent and rapid change of trading partners. These factors can add to the complexity of Step Four. Companies need to consider from both a technological and cultural perspective whether they are ready for this move to greater automation.

- *The magnitude of change.* Before moving to Step Four, companies need to step back and honestly evaluate if they can maintain the pace of change. Steps One and Two are fairly simple, and the impact on the company and its culture is comparatively small. Step Three is a big jump, with a lot of changes and new technology all at once. The move to Step Four is equally significant.

Every company is different, and each has a finite rate at which it can absorb change. After Step Three, it may take a while for the company to stabilize. If a company moves too quickly into Step Four, it can paralyze the organization. Watch for signs of change fatigue. If employees are making simple mistakes, if there is an increase of people calling in sick, or if attrition rates start to rise, don't try to force more change. It's okay to pause between Steps Three and Four.

Other companies will develop a hunger for change, and will want to charge forward into Step Four. These differences in corporate culture are neither good nor bad, but before moving on to full adaptability, every company needs to evaluate its ability to sustain an increased level of process and technological change.

GETTING STARTED

After corporate executives and managers have decided they are ready for Step Four, they must develop a road map for their companies to move to an adaptive business network.

Preparing Employees

The previous steps have established organizational change at the grass roots of the company. Operational-level employees have been among the leaders of change management as processes become increasingly automated. In Step Four, the pace of change in the workplace accelerates as software tools further automate decision processes in network trading relationships. At this point, the network operates at such speed and with such a vast array of information that only advanced software can perform the interactions among companies in the network.

As a company moves to Step Four, management must communicate to employees, speaking honestly about the changes that will take place. It is important that employees not be afraid of the change. While many jobs will change, this is not a head-count reduction exercise. Job changes will take place, but new opportunities will also arise. Management must communicate the extent of the change and the benefits and opportunities that arise because of it. The adaptive business network provides companies with the opportunity for expansion of their market, and is not an occasion for downsizing. Employees should have the opportunity to prepare for new job challenges with targeted training and educational programs.

Preparing the Company

The management of each company will need to evaluate key factors within the business itself. They must identify the company's key differentiators. In other words, as each company moves toward the final goal of adaptability, each company needs to determine what unique capability or characteristic it offers the network, and how it can strengthen that ability or make it more useful for its partner companies. A company must also determine what weaknesses it brings to the network.

Business managers will need to evaluate the company's strengths and weaknesses and establish programs and policies to improve both. These might include training and educational programs, technology upgrades, and improvements to internal processes. If the company has gone through the three previous steps, it is likely that a new set of leaders has emerged in the process. Before moving on to Step Four, a company must be sure these new leaders have the training and support they need to be effective in their roles.

Preparing the Managers

Managers need to learn new ways of running their business. For example, many managers who are used to making decisions based on month-old reports will now operate with near real-time data. This may seem overwhelming at first, and could lure corporate executives to micromanage their organizations by managing for the moment rather than seeing their organization in the big picture. This could effectively lead to oversteering of a business based on the instant nature of the information. It's important that managers avoid overreacting and analyze trends in such a way that it helps employees adjust to the changes taking place.

Putting Time Measurements in Place

Companies that set out to complete Step Four should continue to measure their progress in meeting the four key KPIs described in

Chapter Five: inventory levels, working capital charges, return on assets, and production waste. These measurements are defined in each company's master agreement. In addition, each company should continue to post its progress meeting these KPIs on the network portal for all participants to view.

In Step Four, companies should also begin to measure the amount of time it takes to complete key processes. The adaptive business network reduces the time required to complete three key processes:

1. *Consumer order to fulfillment.* Largely a measurement for retail and consumer product companies, this is the time that elapses between a consumer's order for a finished product and the fulfillment of that order.

2. *Time to supply.* This is the time that elapses after an order is placed from a customer in the supply chain to the time the customer receives that product. The supply frequency of necessary parts for production is measured in cycles—from supply to use may be a two-, three-, or four-hour cycle. For effective just-in-time manufacturing, a manufacturer should carry no more than half a day's supply at any one time.

3. *Time to produce and assemble.* This is a measurement for how fast a company can manufacture the components, get them to the assembly center, and produce a finished product. The elapsed time can be measured by adding the time required to manufacture all components, plus the time required to get these components to the assembly center, plus the wait time before the components are assembled, plus the time required to assemble the components into a finished product. In today's high-tech industry, for example, this is usually between 8 and 12 weeks.

The more success companies have in reducing the time it takes to complete these processes, the greater their success will be in meeting the other four KPIs.

Rise of the Coordinating Partner

In Steps One, Two, and Three, companies establish closer trading and communication relationships with their primary business partners. Moving to full adaptability in Step Four will draw these partners even closer, and enlarge the trading network to include an even larger web of partners, suppliers, and service providers. However, there's more to adaptability than more collaborative and expanded business relationships. In Step Four, the business relationships between network participants become strategic.

By the end of Step Three, companies are delivering materials to their customers more frequently and in smaller quantities. At this point, the brand company may see some costs start to swing, motivating it to find ways to save money by pooling transportation, warehouse, financial, and other resources. Pooling these resources is the first step toward moving from the loose community of assembled participants in Step Three into the network of partners that results by the end of Step Four.

At this point, the brand company starts to emerge as the coordinating partner, evaluating itself and its prospective partners tactically. After evaluating its own strengths and weaknesses, the brand company will weigh these advantages and disadvantages when choosing companies with which to form partnerships. Certain partners—or even former competitors— could help shore up weaknesses. Other companies may share too many overlapping competencies to make an effective network partner.

Sharing Services throughout the Network

By the end of Step Three, the coordinating partner realizes that it has reduced costs as much as possible through the point-to-point relationships that exist between itself and its suppliers. Inventory reductions have reached a plateau and costs of services such as transportation may be inconsistent.

In an effort to save costs by pooling resources, the coordinating partner brings together its core group of partners—including a key retailer, its primary discreet manufacturer, and its primary process manufacturer. The companies realize they can jointly benefit by forming a network. They realize they can capture greater profits on the same products sold. They also realize they can sell their products in greater volumes if they reduce costs and improve service to the customer.

The first opportunity is to pool resources by jointly shopping for improved services. Generally, the coordinating partner emerges as the leader of these negotiations. For example, the coordinating partner might form a relationship with a financial services company, which will act as the primary bank and lending institution for all the members of the network. The coordinating partner will work with the financial services company to establish rates and services that will be consistent for network participants, depending on their role within the network.

The coordinating partner will also establish logistics and transportation services for the network. The lead company will work out network agreements with multiple warehousing and trucking companies, each of which offers the network increased flexibility for storage and movement of goods at prenegotiated rates.

Linking Partners

In Step Four, the coordinating partner helps determine which software agents should be downloaded and installed by the partner companies. The coordinating partner works with an information technology provider or creates software kits that link network participants by role and responsibility.

For example, each warehouse may receive one type of technology kit, each retail company may receive another type of kit, and each transportation provider may receive yet another. Each kit will include the agents and other network components necessary for that type of participant to take part in the network. The IT provider assembles the technology kits for each type of participant and makes them available for download from the network portal.

In the initial stages of the adaptive business network, the software linking together companies within the community should include four elements that correspond to how the network will be managed, what information is exchanged, and how decisions will be made based on the controls or rules established. These four types of software elements interact with one another to seamlessly handle transactions, manage information, and other operational duties within the network (Figure 9.1).

The four types of software elements are as follows:

1. *Management software agents* maintain the contractual terms and obligations between partner companies and apply these high-level guidelines to the activities of other agents.

2. *Control agents* govern other agents based on input from management agents. They are the muscle of the management software level. Control agents set the parameters for other agents to make decisions or react to information.

3. *Information agents* generally collect data such as inventory totals, sales data, and goods movement. Although the other agents must interact with each other, information agents can themselves offer utility for simple informational tasks. Information is the fuel of the adaptive business network, and information agents are the workhorses that power all the others.

FIGURE 9.1   THE Z DIAGRAM

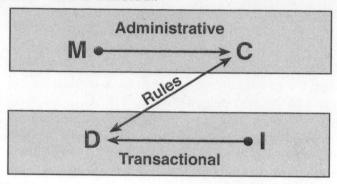

M = Management Elements
C = Control Elements
D = Decision Elements
I = Information Elements

EVERY BUSINESS HAS AT LEAST FOUR KEY ELEMENTS: MANAGE-
MENT, CONTROLS, DECISIONS, AND INFORMATION. THE CORRELA-
TION BETWEEN THESE ELEMENTS FORMS A Z. MANAGEMENT SETS
THE CONTROLS WITHIN WHICH DECISIONS ARE MADE BASED ON IN-
COMING INFORMATION.

4. *Decision agents* are powerful tools capable of automatically authorizing purchases, reallocating inventory, and other tasks. Decision
agents interpret data supplied by information agents and react to it
within the parameters set by control agents.

The agents in each software kit reflect the terms agreed on in the
master agreement. For example, the master agreement may specify that
materials must be received by a customer one to two hours before production, that they will always be received at Door No. 18 and that they
should arrive on 36″ by 36″ pallets. The four software elements will work
together to track compliance to these standards, informing the customer
and supplier immediately when an order does not meet these standards.

Linking Processes

Companies within a network should start simply, by linking one process at
a time all the way through the network. For example, an adaptive business
network could be set up to track the movement of goods all the way from

HOW MANY AGENTS WILL THERE BE?

More than 80 different types of agents have been defined to date. These will continually evolve for use in adaptive business networks, and open standards and software development kits will eventually lead to hundreds of unique agent applications.

the providers of raw materials to the suppliers of components to the finished goods at a retail store. By monitoring customer demand for products and components all the way through the network, companies can test their technical infrastructures to see how well they track information before they begin acting on this information through automated decision making.

Once they are satisfied with their tracking system for the movement of goods throughout the network, companies may want to use agents or other software to predict inventory stock-outs before they occur. The next step would be to automate supply orders when they fall below a minimum threshold, and so on.

The network should also link companies to solve the common market challenges each faces. For example, the coordinating partner may form a network to be adaptive to price fluctuations. In this case, to be fully adaptive, a coordinating partner will need to establish multiple trading and service partners for each of its primary supplies. The network would need to include participants that could provide supplies at various price points to meet different pricing scenarios.

For instance, for a set of key components, the coordinating partner may establish network partnerships with a premium supplier, a midpriced supplier, and a commodity-level supplier, each of which can provide equivalent components within their price range. Even though these companies may be traditional competitors, each of them will be integrated into the network. Depending on order specifications and economic factors, the coordinating partner will determine which of the suppliers to use.

If the coordinating partner forms a network to provide greater adaptability in creating and bundling new goods and services, it will pursue network agreements with those companies and service providers that offer it the broadest opportunities for new product development.

Once a network removes its primary bottleneck, it will add new partners to reduce other constraints in the network and to create new advantages for the participating companies. As networks mature, the breadth of the companies involved will grow, and the network will become increasingly adaptive as it grows to include a broadening array of companies.

BENEFITS OF STEP FOUR

Each of the previous steps produced cost savings. Steps One and Two each deliver 1 to 3 percent reductions, primarily in inventory. Step Three provides an additional savings of between 10 percent and 50 percent, mostly by streamlining and automating processes between major trading partners.

Step Four produces even more savings while for the first time offering revenue opportunities, providing companies an additional 15 percent to 25 percent improvement in overall business performance. Companies capture additional sales as the result of improved customer service and faster response to sales opportunities. At the same time, companies reduce costs by capturing a better return on assets, lowering inventory, and borrowing less working capital. The mix of benefits will vary based on a company's role within the supply chain as well as the baseline from which it is starting.

Reducing Inventory and Working Capital

Even the best forecasting and planning software can only extrapolate from previous sales patterns to divine what customer demand will be in the future. As a result, companies create products and push them out to the market, often uncertain of consumer demand. In today's fast-changing economy, demand can shift quickly. Linking demand directly to production closes the loop, reducing the risk of creating unwanted inventory.

In Step Four, the network begins to share real-time, technology-generated customer demand data among relevant partner companies. Network participants use this information to make joint decisions with their partners regarding inventory levels, order positions, and production schedules. Sharing this information enables companies to reduce the risk of creating unwanted inventory and borrowing large amounts of working capital to cover these costs.

Delaying Differentiation

Another major benefit of forming an adaptive business network is that it enables companies to more successfully delay differentiation of products.

Global available-to-promise (ATP) software installed in Step Three allows businesses to reallocate inventory that has already been earmarked for sale, as long as that inventory can be replaced from other sources or from production before shipment. When used in conjunction with consumer demand information supplied by pervasive software, global ATP can reduce the amount of finished goods inventory carried by participants within the network. Unsold finished goods can kill a company if the whims of customers or economic factors fluctuate.

The integration of agent software with ATP systems can help delay the ordering of supplies and the production of finished goods until the last possible moment, buying companies additional time to assess data regarding customer demand, negotiate lower priced purchases, or adapt to other changing environmental factors. The use of this combination of advanced software also provides businesses with more time to alter production, design, transportation, or other factors as close to the actual sale as possible, ensuring maximum adaptability.

For example, a cell phone maker has 10,000 liquid crystal display (LCD) screens in stock that it plans to incorporate into a specific model of cell phones. Before it assembles the phones, however, the cell phone maker realizes that demand for that specific model has fallen sharply. The cell phone company is able to react by simply installing the LCD screens in a more desirable cell phone model.

Had the phones already been made, the 10,000 LCD screens would already have been installed, packaged, and shipped to a warehouse as unsold finished goods, and could not have been incorporated into another model. At a certain point, a product can no longer be changed or differentiated to meet customer demand. The longer a company can delay differentiation, the greater the market for its products.

Within an adaptive business network, software agents link back to the global ATP system to provide information about customer preferences. Final production of the products can be delayed until information about actual customer purchases arrives via software technology. The components used to make the product can remain unassembled until the products can be customized to consumer taste.

Reducing Production Waste

One of the measures of efficiency established in the early steps of the adaptive business network was production waste—the amount of waste generated by the manufacturing process.

In an adaptive business network, production waste can be greatly curtailed. Changeover waste, created when manufacturing systems must be reformulated to accommodate new and different orders, can be significantly reduced if companies include sufficient numbers of manufacturers in the network, with whom they can collaborate to carefully plan production capacity.

For example, the Soft-Drink Company could contract with a high-run manufacturer for its primary paperboard cartons and a secondary producer of short-run specialty cartons for uses such as promotions and lower volume brands. Within a network, individual companies don't have to make everything. They don't have to overdilute their product mix. Companies can focus on what they do best and use production capacity more efficiently, which leads individual companies in the network to achieve higher returns on assets.

Pooling Goods and Services

By Step Four, businesses will likely have dozens of companies as partners in their network. This allows all participants to draw from a greater pool of resources when providing their service, manufacturing their product, or bundling these goods and services together. As a result, companies can be more adaptive in both the good times and the bad.

When business is brisk, companies within a network can act on business opportunities quickly and strategically. Because companies are in a network, they have a greater pool of resources from which to make and market new and appealing products. By relying on valued partners and their assets, companies can deliver to customers something more than the sum of the parts. Companies can offer their customers new and innovative bundles of products and services that satisfy multiple needs in a single package. Having more resources in the pool also enables companies to quickly add production capacity. It enables them to tap additional sales channels for their products and services.

In an economic downturn, a company's exposure is diminished. Instantaneous consumer demand information provided by the network and inventory flexibility provided by programs such as global ATP enable each company in the network to carry less inventory while maintaining the adaptability to respond to changing market conditions. Even in bad economic times, there are always sales channels that perform well, and a greater pool of resources gives companies more sales channels through which to market their products.

The size and scope of the adaptive business network and its partner companies gives all the participants more options in marketing their goods and services. In short, the greater pool of resources created by the network provides all participants with more flexibility and additional options for adapting in the face of change. Each company in the adaptive business network focuses on its core strengths and uses partnerships to gain access to a larger pool of goods and services. The network provides a larger pool of resources than any single company can feasibly maintain on its own.

Consider computer printers, for example. A printer manufacturer makes a midpriced, multipurpose color inkjet printer for the home and small office. In an adaptive business network, this manufacturer could differentiate its products from the competition by turning to its partners. The printer manufacturer takes advantage of its partners in the paper products industry by bundling the printer with standard white paper, plus cardstock for printing business cards, and photographic paper for printing digital photos. A plastics manufacturer in the network helps differentiate the printer by molding plastic covers for the printer in popular colors. Another network partner designs software that integrates photo memory for print photos. Another partner company designs a program that creates printable photo albums from digital photos. Yet another partner includes an offer for discounts on wireless Ethernet connections for the printer. All of these features are bundled with the original printer to add to its value in the market. All of these features are combined quickly and cost-effectively, in response to customer demand to increase profits for all participants.

Managing Customer Demand

By involving its partners, a coordinating partner can manage demand for network products more creatively, helping members throughout the network to capture additional sales. For example, if a product is not selling in a certain sales channel, the coordinating partner can divert the product to a different sales channel where customer demand is higher. Let's say customer demand data shows 15-inch LCD screens packaged with computers with Pentium III chips priced at $499 are selling faster than the same LCD screens packaged with Pentium IV computers selling at $699. By working with its LCD screen supplier, a computer manufacturer can quickly realign the distribution of LCD panels to the factory that produces Pentium III computers, increasing sales for itself, the LCD screen supplier, and other suppliers involved in manufacturing the Pentium III computers.

In addition, an adaptive business network enables participants to react more quickly to promotional opportunities. The coordinating partner is responsible for managing customer demand for finished products within each sales channel. However, this company can achieve better results by drawing on partners in the network when undertaking a promotion or discount pricing program.

For example, a consumer goods company would learn faster of the need for a promotion by forming a network with the retail companies to whom it sells its products, and would be able to react more quickly to these opportunities by linking to its suppliers. By involving the network's financial services company, it could identify the most effective financial incentives. By involving its transportation company, it could quickly deliver its promotional products to retail stores. Tighter coordination among partners enables all companies within the network to respond swiftly to promotional opportunities.

POTENTIAL OBSTACLES

There are three potential hurdles to overcome in Step Four. As discussed earlier in this chapter, the influx of data and the information generated by automated agents could cause corporate executives to oversteer their organizations. It is important that they keep in mind the larger trends and avoid overreacting to the immediacy and wealth of information available to them.

Second, pervasive technology has great potential. However, depending on its use, software such as agents could become an annoyance for consumers—and in some cases an invasion of privacy. By monitoring personal preferences and tracking consumption and spending habits, agent technology walks a fine line between help and hindrance. To make this software beneficial, companies must be careful to never use agents in a way that is invasive or that enables them to become a nuisance. Consumers must be allowed to retain control, so they can turn the software off.

Finally, companies setting out to complete Step Four can easily become technically overloaded by the overwhelming amount of data as well as culturally overloaded by the amount of change involved. It's important that companies understand their goals before embarking on this effort, and develop an achievable road map for success that enables them to absorb these changes at a pace they can handle.

SECURITY IS PARAMOUNT

Pervasive technology, such as software agents and Web services, requires strict levels of security. Multiple security mechanisms ensure the sanctity of private corporate information within the network, and in the larger Internet business environment. Each software application will be encoded with a specific and unique identification tag. This precise ID scheme will enable rules-based security, which ensures that each application knows precisely with which other applications it is communicating.

Kerberos is a powerful industry-standard security protocol that bolsters the protection of data. A security system that authenticates users when they log in and renews their key at each new session, Kerberos will be used with many upcoming agent applications. Together, the unique ID system and powerful Kerberos security systems will assure businesses that all their important information is safe, secure, and private.

WHEN IS STEP FOUR COMPLETED?

Adaptability is not a goal. It is nature's way of responding to environmental changes in order to survive. When companies begin Step Four, they establish a set of baseline KPIs on which to measure their success, and set time frames for achieving these goals. As with any strategic business plan, companies should establish one-year, two-year, and five-year measurements, and outline a road map for achieving each milestone.

If by Step Four a company has reached the goals it set out to achieve, it should enjoy its success but not become complacent. Adaptability is an ongoing discipline. Beware of the potential for innovations from competitors, a dwindling market, or unforeseen changes to the political, regulatory, or economic climates that could affect business. The larger business environment will continue to change, and companies must respond intelligently and resourcefully to these changes in order to prosper. The ability to adapt as reflected in the adaptive business network is the only path to long-term survival.

CHAPTER TEN

The Adaptive Business Network in Practice

People can have the Model T in any color—so long as it's black.

—Henry Ford

No fully developed adaptive business networks yet exist. Nevertheless, companies as varied as Southwest Airlines, Wal-Mart, and Dell Computer have pursued strategies to make themselves more flexible and responsive to new business opportunities.

Take Dell Computer, for example. Dell has grown to be the world's largest PC maker by building tailor-made computers based on actual customer orders.[1] The company responds to customers quickly while maintaining very low inventory levels.

Unlike traditional computer companies, which build computers based on estimates of how many will sell, Dell assembles computers based on the components and quantities customers order by phone or from the company's Web site. Once a customer places an order, the company's response time is fast.

For example, Dell can transfer a customer order to the factory within 24 hours after receiving it, and typically delivers its custom-made computers to customers within a few days. Dell achieves these quick response times by drawing from a small inventory of components at a local warehouse, while working with a myriad of suppliers to obtain the components it needs when it needs them. By shifting the liability of inventory to its suppliers, Dell is able to turn its inventory every 10 days.

Dell is an example of a manufacturing company that has incorporated aspects of the adaptive business network. Like a manufacturing company within an adaptive business network, Dell produces its computers based on actual customer orders—not on forecasts predicting what customers will buy in the future. Dell gives its customers a broad selection from which to choose, and then delivers these customized products quickly. The company works with a large network of suppliers, and it keeps the inventory it carries to a minimum.

However, an adaptive business network would offer companies like Dell even more benefits. Rather than merely shifting the liability for inventory to other companies within the supply chain, all companies within an adaptive business network reduce the stock they carry by taking a joint approach to inventory and tracking it throughout the network. Moreover, an adaptive business network enables companies to sense changes in customer demand in near real time, and quickly make adjustments. Finally, an adaptive business network allows companies to more fully delay differentiation of their products by assembling more components after customers place their orders, and get their products to customers quickly by offering alternative components when the requested components will take more time to obtain.

The benefits of an adaptive network extend far beyond traditional manufacturing or assembly-based industries. Even though their products and processes vary, companies in various industry segments can benefit from participating in an adaptive network. Whether in the manufacturing, retail, or service sector, companies today face many similar challenges:

- Managing inventory, both physical and intellectual.
- Balancing supply with demand to capture the greatest return on assets.
- Managing a wide array of roles and responsibilities across company boundaries.
- Reducing costs while expanding revenue.

This chapter explores the challenges faced by the manufacturing, service, and retail sectors, and the benefits the adaptive business network provides to companies within each of these three broad industry segments.

MANUFACTURING COMPANIES

Challenges

For a manufacturing company, success boils down to four factors—product quality, manufacturing costs, product innovation, and return on assets.

■ *Quality.* Today, manufacturing companies are focused on measuring and improving quality. For instance, the ISO 9000 certification is an international family of standards and guidelines for certifying company quality. Total quality management (TQM) advocates continuous improvement of internal company processes as a means of improving product quality while cutting costs. The Malcolm Baldrige National Quality Award, established by the U.S. Congress in 1987, encourages American companies to continually improve their operations. Six Sigma is a measurement-based strategy that focuses on process improvement and the elimination of manufacturing defects.

All of these standards and programs have sprung up over the years to focus companies on quality, inducing companies worldwide to spend billions of dollars to improve their products. However, quality issues remain: Is quality consistently good? Are quality goods produced without becoming damaged in the process?

■ *Cost.* Another constant challenge for manufacturing companies is producing goods at the lowest possible cost. Companies constantly work on eliminating waste, running their production lines more efficiently, and designing products that are inexpensive to produce. Companies worldwide have spent billions on factory automation to reduce their production costs. However, manufacturers face many different types of costs—the cost of manufacturing, warehouse costs, packaging costs, promotional costs, transportation costs, the cost of handling returned products, and so on.

Because many of these costs are difficult to trace, often companies don't have an accurate picture of their true expenses. Companies need to look at total costs for the organization, including their overhead costs and the cost of getting their products on the market, not just production costs. Additionally, companies have difficulty in getting to the root cause of some costs because it lies outside of the company.

■ *Innovation.* To remain innovative and consistently produce new products is a third challenge for manufacturing companies. How can the company take products to the next level and differentiate them from those of the competition? Is there a way to revolutionize an established product—what Intel cofounder Andy Grove calls "creative destruction"—and take it far beyond what competitors offer? Manufacturing companies must always think of ways to try to improve their products before their competitors beat them to it.

■ *Return on assets.* A fourth challenge for manufacturing companies is capturing the greatest possible return on their assets. Is there a way to build the baseline components now and delay differentiation of the product until after receiving the actual order from the customer? Is the company effectively managing its plants, inventory, and warehouses? Is it distributing its products as widely as possible? Maximizing the return on assets is a primary responsibility of management within manufacturing companies.

MEETING TODAY'S CHALLENGE

Most manufacturing companies work with their suppliers as part of a linear supply chain. These relationships usually consist of pure buyer-seller interactions, with all of the accompanying limitations.

For example, a pure buyer-seller relationship within the auto manufacturing industry works like this: Car dealers send the automaker volume sales figures for the cars they sell on a weekly basis. In addition, the dealers send sales projection forecasts to the auto maker quarterly, which it then uses to develop a detailed forecast and production plan. The automaker then produces cars based on these sales volumes and forecasts. Suppliers send parts to the automaker, which assembles the finished cars and ships them to the car dealers. Once at the dealer, cars have 30 days to move off the lot before the interest payments begin. The dealer typically pays these interest rates on loans borrowed from the automaker's financial services company.

The automotive industry has reduced inventory to a great degree by adopting just-in-time (JIT) manufacturing, which requires suppliers to deliver their parts to the auto manufacturer exactly when the assembly line needs them. Just-in-time delivery has vastly helped to reduce inventory costs for automakers by eliminating the need for expensive warehouse space and the systems needed to manage them. However, inventory still accumulates in the parking lots of auto dealerships and in supply warehouses. Automakers continue to sign long-term contracts with their suppliers to provide parts, committing them to supply levels that may not mirror demand.

Companies in the automotive supply chain operate as independent entities, typically managing their transportation, warehouse, and financial needs separately from one another. For example, the supplier of brakes will have a separate transportation provider from the seat supplier and the electronics manufacturer, even if all three are located in the same area and could reduce costs by coordinating their shipments to the auto manufacturer through a common trucking company.

BENEFITS OF THE ADAPTIVE BUSINESS NETWORK

The ABN offers manufacturing companies many ways to address their key challenges. It provides them with ways to build their products more consistently by focusing on the base product and delaying assembly of the final product until later in the process.

Today, automakers assemble the entire car before it leaves the factory door. In an adaptive network, software tools such as agents would instantaneously exchange information among car dealers, automakers, and suppliers to remove the time delays that currently exist in the supply network and enable them to build cars based on actual customer orders. The automaker can then focus the production process, producing a relatively large number of standard base vehicles with a small number of feature choices, such as body style, engine size, color, and transmission type.

Skilled factory workers would assemble the chassis and key systems according to manufacturing plans, thereby ensuring the quality control of the base vehicle. But rather than ship finished cars directly to the car dealers, the automaker would then ship these base-vehicle frames to a regional delayed differentiation center, where components such as the seats, specialty wheels and tires, stereo systems, and other accessories will be added based on the actual customer request transmitted at the car dealership (Figure 10.1).

Agents would send customer orders to the automaker, its suppliers, and the delayed differentiation center, enabling customers to get the exact car they want when they want it. Using software agents, the network would track inventory, orders, and the movement of goods from company to company throughout the network. When a customer places his order at the car dealer, the network would engage the delayed differentiation centers to locate a base vehicle in the requested color and with other built-in features. It would then arrange for the installation of accessories that match the customer's order, in the time frame

FIGURE 10.1   DELAYED DIFFERENTIATION

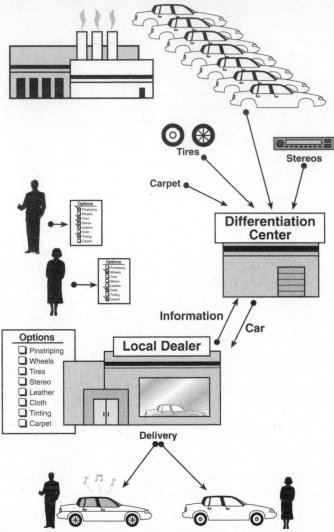

DELAYED DIFFERENTIATION EXPANDS THE MARKET FOR A COM-
PANY'S PRODUCTS BY ENABLING BUSINESSES TO PRODUCE A SMALL
NUMBER OF BASIC MODELS AND CUSTOMIZE THEM CLOSER TO THE
TIME WHEN THE CONSUMER ACTUALLY PURCHASES THE FINAL PROD-
UCT. THIS ENABLES COMPANIES TO SMOOTH THEIR PRODUCTION
CYCLE AND BETTER SATISFY CUSTOMER DEMAND. IN THIS EXAMPLE,
THE FACTORY MAKES HUNDREDS OF BASIC AUTOS. CONSUMERS SE-
LECT THEIR OPTIONS AT THE LOCAL DEALER, WHICH RELAYS THE IN-
FORMATION TO A REGIONAL DELAYED DIFFERENTIATION CENTER
CHARGED WITH INSTALLING THE CUSTOM OPTIONS. CONSUMERS RE-
CEIVE WHAT APPEARS TO BE A COMPLETELY CUSTOM AUTOMOBILE.

requested. Using global available-to-promise (ATP) systems, the car dealer would determine the options for delivering the accessorized car from any one of the delayed differentiation centers, and send back a list of options to the customer.

One option may be to deliver the car the customer ordered within 24 hours, with the exception of one component—say a CD player and speaker set that are less powerful than what the customer initially requested. A second option might be to deliver the exact car the customer wants within 72 hours at a set price. A third option might be to deliver the car in one week at a lower price. This setup would enable car manufacturers to customize their cars to a far greater degree than is possible today—and still deliver a tailor-made car within the short time frames car buyers expect.

Imagine how this scenario would change the way inventory is managed in the automobile industry. Car dealers would no longer need acres of parking lots for all of their cars. In fact, they would hold virtually no inventory at all, except for a few showroom cars with different engine sizes and transmissions for customers who want to test-drive them. They would walk customers through their showrooms, showing them door panels with different paint colors, seats with different fabric, stereo systems with different components—all of which customers could choose from when ordering their cars. Customers will still experience the positive aspects of buying a car—listening to the stereo, smelling that new car scent—without requiring the car dealer to stock the exact car they will buy.

Within this distribution model, there is less overall inventory in the system, because the same standard car chassis can be customized to fulfill the demands of a broader customer base closer to the time of delivery. Compare this to today, when a car dealer must have on hand a wide range of models, colors, and styles to address the individual needs of buyers, sometimes creating customer satisfaction problems by requiring the customer to buy options they don't want.

By delaying final differentiation on a standard car chassis with a standard engine and transmission, for example, the automaker could use the same chassis to suit the needs of both a customer who wants the car with a high-end stereo system, chrome alloy wheels, and racing tires *and* a customer who wants a basic, stripped down model to commute to work. The network can use the same car body to fill the needs of a variety of customers, instead of just one if it had produced the finished car and then sent it to a car dealership.

By waiting to assemble the finished car until after they receive the customer order, auto manufacturers also broaden the market for their cars, ensuring that more are sold at full price. With cars produced to match customer demand, car dealers could greatly reduce the need for rebates and other discounts to promote slow-selling models. In fact, car dealers may be able to demand more money for these customized automobiles because these vehicles will be more fully personalized and therefore will have more value to consumers.

The beauty of all of this is that it's accomplished without increasing costs. In fact, the adaptive network enables the car manufacturing and selling network to lower its cost per unit and capture a greater return on assets by enabling companies to get their products to market faster, while more closely matching production to actual customer demand.

In addition, carmakers would reduce inventory by entering into fewer volume contracts with their suppliers, minimizing their commitment to purchase inventory that may be obsolete by the time it's needed. Because it is easy and inexpensive to add suppliers to the network, automakers would likely buy in smaller volumes from a broader range of suppliers, eliminating their need to sign long-term contracts.

The adaptive business network also provides the automobile network with opportunities to become more innovative by developing creative partnerships. The differentiation centers could offer a host of after-market parts and accessories, such as specialty painting and installation of bicycle racks, trailer hitches, or built-in mobile communication units.

Like the auto manufacturer, auto parts suppliers would be able to make products that more closely match actual customer demand. With more accurate information about customer demand from the automaker, suppliers could also delay differentiation on key auto parts until a few days before the car is produced. For example, the auto manufacturer may enter into an agreement with its bumper manufacturer to build 500,000 front bumpers over three months, but require the bumper manufacturer to hold off on painting each bumper until just before a car is assembled— and after an order has been received specifying the car's color.

Some traditional suppliers such as the seat and electronics manufacturers would no longer ship to the automaker. Instead, they would ship to the delayed differentiation center or directly to the car dealer based on information received via agents from both locations.

For example, if none of the delayed differentiation centers can deliver a car with the desired CD player within the time frame the customer has requested, the electronics manufacturer may ship the CD player directly to the dealer, who would then be responsible for installing it when the car arrives. In turn, these direct links would enable component manufacturers to reduce inventory by matching their production more closely to demand.

In contrast to the linear supply chain in which suppliers only receive orders from the customer directly in front of them, suppliers within the network may receive information from market analyzes performed for the entire network—such as why consumers are buying specific types of cars and problems that occur after the cars are sold.

With greater access to information about customer buying habits, suppliers within the adaptive business network can be more innovative and find creative ways to improve their own products while bolstering the quality of the finished cars to which their products contribute. For example, the bumper manufacturer may realize that the plastic on the bumpers it produces oxidizes over time, and proactively approach the paint supplier within the network to create a new coating to prevent bumpers on both new and old car models from oxidizing.

In other cases, suppliers may be able to broaden their reach by turning their product into a service. For example, the paint supplier could expand its market by setting up shop next to car assembly plants, and actually painting the cars in custom colors in addition to supplying the paint.

Finally, the adaptive business network will enable all participants to reduce costs by sharing services they currently manage independently. For example, participants within the network may share transportation and warehouse space. They may share market reports analyzing trends in customer demand. Network participants may jointly work with financial companies to obtain lower interest rates on working capital. Pooling resources such as these opens a wide range of opportunities for everyone in the network to reduce costs.

Today, the technology does not exist to continuously monitor all the data required for automakers to cost-effectively work in this manner and offer many of these services. Just imagine the inventory jumble an automotive company would have if it tried to maintain the quantities of inventory needed to use delayed differentiation to this extent, develop these partnerships, or provide some of these services. The cost would be astronomical. Pervasive software such as agents make all of these processes possible. Because agents are designed to work with each other as well as with existing systems, they can be implemented quickly and cost-effectively. This provides automotive companies with a much greater degree of flexibility than they have today.

RETAIL COMPANIES

Challenges

Retail companies struggle with three major issues: capturing the greatest return on their assets, keeping the cost of inventory low, and attracting customers:

- *Return on assets.* The biggest asset for retail companies is size, in square footage, in their retail stores, while their struggle is to make the most profit from each of these square feet. This means attracting customers and stocking their shelves with the right mix of products so that products will move off the shelves quickly.
- *Inventory and stock-outs.* Another problem retail companies face is managing inventory. Knowing how much inventory to carry, when to purchase it, and where to store it are huge challenges. The inability to anticipate and respond quickly to changes in customer purchasing habits means that retailers often compromise their profits by carrying too much or too little inventory.

  If retailers carry too much inventory, they may be forced to discount their products and lose revenue. Stock-outs are even worse because the entire sale is lost. In addition, the retail relationship with the customer is jeopardized, for this person will go elsewhere to purchase the product she seeks, and potentially change her shopping patterns.

  Complicating the problem is the fact that customers increasingly expect more variety of products. Consider the typical grocery store, which 20 years ago carried a standard selection of products. Today, that same grocery store may also be expected to carry fresh-baked products, low-fat food, low-cholesterol food, health food products, and ethnic food. Customer expectations for greater variety make it more complicated for retailers to store and distribute inventory.
- *Attracting and retaining customers.* A third challenge retailers face is attracting consumers to their stores and turning them into loyal, repeat customers. In developed parts of the world, population growth is slowing and the population base is aging, which means retail companies are

competing for shrinking dollars. This means that attracting and retaining customers is a bigger challenge than ever.

MEETING THE CHALLENGE TODAY

Retail companies employ a variety of techniques to meet these challenges today. To manage their inventory and capture a greater return on assets, retailers sometimes require suppliers to sell on consignment and take responsibility for the inventory until consumers actually purchase it off of store shelves. In addition, retailers sometimes rent shelf space to their suppliers, charging more for the middle shelf that sits at eye level than for space on the bottom or top shelves. Techniques like these only serve to increase costs for suppliers, who in turn must compensate by raising prices to consumers. There's no cost taken out of the supply chain. The costs simply are shifted from Point A to Point B.

In other cases, retail companies have tried to reduce costs by turning their storefronts into warehouses. They eliminate the need for stocking clerks to unpack boxes and stack items on shelves by simply stocking and selling straight out of the box. In fact, some retailers now require manufacturers to package for presentation—that is, design and package the shipment box so it looks nice without being unpacked. The box can be placed directly on the shelf as a presentable, promotional item.

Retailers have also tried to capture a greater return on assets by building large superstore centers in a few strategic locations, accompanied by smaller stores that primarily stock the items consumed by the demographic mix of that area. Since retailers know exactly what products are moving off of store shelves in specific stores, they can design an inventory to fit the consumption habits of individual demographic areas.

For example, a grocery store in a high-income, upscale neighborhood may carry a greater share of fancy breads, health food, and low-fat food, whereas a grocery store in a middle-class Chinese neighborhood may carry a greater share of Asian products such as Hoisin sauce, Chinese vegetables, and noodles. However, stocking each store to serve the demographic mix of that neighborhood raises costs by requiring grocery stores to purchase products in smaller volumes and hold more inventory in their warehouses. It also raises transportation costs by forcing them and their suppliers to ship products in smaller units.

Retailers have implemented a laundry list of incentives to attract and retain customers. Today, the catch phrase is "shopping as an experience"—

the idea of making shopping convenient and enjoyable for customers. Retailers try to attract customers through partnerships with coffeehouses, banks, jewelers, and fast-food companies so that customers can drink a double latté, withdraw money, and eat at McDonald's while buying tools or shopping for groceries. They display coupons on store shelves and at checkout counters to turn shoppers into loyal customers. They set up tables with free samples to make the shopping experience pleasant and encourage shoppers to try new products. The list of incentives goes on and on.

All of this is intended to attract customers and keep them coming back. Although many of these incentives enable retailers to increase their customer base, they can also increase costs and compromise overall profit margins.

BENEFITS OF THE ADAPTIVE BUSINESS NETWORK

Within the adaptive network, information about customer purchases would be shared simultaneously with all companies that need it, eliminating the bullwhip effect and enabling the retail store and its suppliers throughout the network to greatly reduce inventory. For example, a clothing store that sells jeans, teeshirts, and sweaters would install advanced technology such as smart tags in its point of sales system to track purchases as soon as they are made, and immediately send this information to all relevant participants.

Pervasive software would record, for example, that 20 pairs of size 8 women's stonewashed, boot-cut jeans sold at Store 123 within the past hour, and would send this information to the jeans manufacturer and at the same time send it to the fabric manufacturer that supplies the jeans maker. The resulting ability to obtain information about customer purchases as frequently as necessary would ensure that clothing manufacturers produce clothes in the colors, styles, and sizes that are actually selling. This ability can greatly reduce inventory for all participants in the network, along with the cost of working capital that goes with it. It would also increase the return on assets for the clothing store by enabling it to sell more clothes at full price while holding fewer sales to rid itself of clothes that are no longer in style or in season.

The clothing store could also form a network to proactively anticipate changes in fashion and create the perception that the clothing it carries is setting—rather than responding to—these trends. For example, the clothing store could enter into a network with its clothing manufacturers, fashion designers, and a consulting firm that analyzes fashion trends to anticipate new fashions as soon as they arise and get these fashions into their stores within days after they first appear. If paisley prints emerged as the latest fashion show trends in Milan and Paris, fabric manufacturers in the network would know to immediately incorporate these patterns into their fabrics, which would then be used to make clothing that's delivered to the clothing store. Similarly, if teenagers start showing up wearing suede coats and Peruvian ponchos on MTV, these clothing styles would appear in the clothing store just a few days later.

The network also offers retail companies the opportunity to form creative partnerships that attract more customers. For example, an electronics retailer could form a partnership with a car dealer to sell more stereo systems, while offering car buyers more choices regarding the type of stereo that comes with their new car. In this agreement, the electronics shop could install any of the stereo systems it carries into any base model car purchased through the car dealer (Figure 10.2).

FIGURE 10.2 PARTNERSHIP OPPORTUNITIES WITHIN AN ABN

ADAPTIVE BUSINESS NETWORKS WILL GENERATE NEW PARTNER-SHIPS THAT ALLOW EACH PARTICIPANT TO FOCUS ON ITS CORE COMPETENCY WHILE CAPITALIZING ON THE STRENGTHS OF ITS PARTNERS TO PROVIDE BETTER SERVICE TO CUSTOMERS. IN THE EXAMPLE ABOVE, A NATIONAL ELECTRONICS RETAILER HAS JOINED WITH A MAJOR AUTOMAKER TO CO-LOCATE FACILITIES AT A LOCAL CAR DEALERSHIP. THIS PARTNERSHIP ENABLES CAR BUYERS TO SELECT FROM A WIDER RANGE OF STEREOS AND HAVE THEM IN-STALLED QUICKLY WHEN PURCHASING THEIR CARS. AT THE SAME TIME, THE ELECTRONICS RETAILER GAINS ACCESS TO A NEW MAR-KET, WHILE BOTH COMPANIES DISTINGUISH THEMSELVES FROM THEIR COMPETITORS BY ASSOCIATING THEMSELVES WITH EACH OTHER'S WELL-KNOWN BRANDS.

Pervasive software installed at the car dealership would communicate with the electronics retailer and its suppliers every time a customer orders a new car. For instance, car dealers could authorize their customers to choose any stereo system up to a value of $1,000, and install it free of charge along with the purchase of the car. Car buyers would have the option of paying the difference if they want a more expensive stereo system. Receiving these orders instantaneously through technology such as software agents would enable the electronics retailer to respond quickly, and order and install the stereo system by the time the customer picks up the car.

Partnerships within an adaptive business network also offer retail companies the opportunity to save costs. For example, a sandwich shop could locate next to several other fast-food restaurants to attract a greater number of customers, just like Togo's Eateries, the sandwich shop chain, does with Baskin Robbins ice cream shops and Dunkin' Donuts today in the United States. However, rather than simply setting up shop next to the other stores, the sandwich shop could save money by using the same food distributors as the other fast-food restaurants and by pooling resources such as transportation and employees.

SERVICE COMPANIES

Challenges

There are two types of service companies. Professional service firms such as accounting firms, marketing firms, and advertising companies are in business because of their "soft assets"—the employees that work for them, along with their patents, and their reputations. Other service companies such as hotels, airlines, and car rental agencies are in business because of their "hard assets"—the rooms, planes, and cars that they turn into a service for customers. However, for both types of service companies, the challenges are basically the same—maximizing profits by attracting a wide range of customers, keeping the cost of business low, and capturing the greatest return on their assets.

Soft Asset Service Companies

Every professional services firm offers a set of disciplines within the geographical areas it serves. Regardless of the disciplines it offers, the goal is to attract and retain the greatest number of clients for its services. The more opportunities a professional services firm can create by tailoring its existing services to meet the needs of new clients, the greater its profit margin. There's nothing like conducting a study for one client, and then offering small variations of the study to a second and third client at the same price to maximize a professional service company's profits, or perfecting one service and then offering it to as many clients as possible to capture the greatest return on the investment.

Hard Asset Service Companies

As with professional service firms, success for hard asset service companies depends on the number of customers they can attract for their service. For most hard asset companies, the supply is fixed. A hotel has 500 rooms. A rental car company has 2,000 cars to lease. The aircraft has 350 seats. The focus of the company is on attracting enough customers to meet this supply.

Like service companies with soft assets, success in matching demand to supply depends on the quality of customer service and the ability to differentiate this service from that offered by competitors. The service customers receive while staying at the hotel, renting a car, or flying across the country will determine whether they choose that company the next time. The more customers that are willing to pay for this service at full price, the fewer discounts are needed. More customers at full price increases the return on assets.

Hard asset service companies are often required to hold large amounts of standard inventory to run their service effectively, and are faced with all the challenges that go with it. Inventory can take the shape of spare parts for the car rental agency or the airline or food, drinks, and toiletries for the hotel. Like manufacturing companies, hard asset service companies must often pay warehouse costs to store inventory and borrow working capital to pay for it.

BENEFITS OF THE ADAPTIVE BUSINESS NETWORK

Benefits for Soft Asset Service Companies

Rather than acting as a primary partner in their own service-oriented networks, service companies with soft assets will likely participate in multiple manufacturing and retail networks. The benefit for them is greater

visibility into the activity of an entire network, which creates more demand for their service and helps them respond to changes more quickly.
For example, a consumer-products adaptive network could link its advertising company to retail stores via agents so that the ad agency can quickly
create local ad campaigns to promote products of the network that aren't
selling quickly enough. Similarly, the network could link its market research firm to retail stores so that it can rapidly perform an analysis to determine how to increase the appeal of slow-selling products to customers.

By serving an entire network, a consulting firm could significantly
broaden the market for its services while helping those companies adopt
uniform business processes and gain greater visibility into key information of interest to the entire network. For example, by working with several companies within an adaptive business network, a financial services
firm could help those companies adopt standard billing or payment
processes that enable them to work together more efficiently as a network. A market research firm could analyze market segmentation or
brand effectiveness, enabling the entire network to take advantage of
the results. By serving as the consulting firm for the entire network, soft
asset service companies create more demand for their service while helping the network quickly resolve problems and respond rapidly to changing market conditions.

Benefits for Hard Asset Service Companies

Like professional service firms, service companies with hard assets may
also want to participate in multiple retail and manufacturing networks.
By analyzing a network's current shipping and warehouse arrangements,
for example, a warehouse company may discover that the network is not
storing its inventory in the most optimal locations. By proposing that the
network combine its inventory at key locations, the warehouse company
could increase the market for its service while reducing warehouse costs
for the entire network. Likewise, a freight company could ship product
parts for the entire network, thus broadening the reach for its service
while at the same time generating cost savings for the entire network by
streamlining the delivery routes.

In addition to participating in other networks, service companies with
hard assets may find it beneficial to link partners and suppliers into their
own network. For example, an airline company could significantly reduce
costs by forming a network that links together its suppliers, aircraft me-
chanics, and different divisions within the company. By forming a network

with these participants, the airline could streamline its routine aircraft maintenance checks and reduce the downtime for "service intervals," or the time when the aircraft is on the ground for scheduled maintenance.

Today, airline companies typically hold hundreds of maintenance checks on a daily basis. These maintenance checks come in three categories—Class A, Class B, and Class C—each with an increasing amount of downtime and increasing complexity of service. As soon as an aircraft has been in service for its allotted term, it must immediately be brought in for maintenance.

To hold these maintenance checks, airlines must route the aircraft to maintenance facilities as soon as they reach these service intervals, while substituting each aircraft with another one to keep passenger flights on schedule. Scheduling service intervals is no small matter, because each plane's service time must be tracked individually, including the time each plane spends at the gate, stuck on the runway, circling the airport due to inclement weather, and other delays. Airlines must also keep on hand millions of dollars in spare parts so they can get each aircraft back into service as quickly as possible.

By forming an adaptive business network, airline companies could equip each aircraft with advanced technology that tracks the number of hours the aircraft is in service, allowing airlines to manage each aircraft individually through effective scheduling to maximize its use within the limits of the service interval. The software agent in the aircraft would be linked to the airline's maintenance system to enable the airline to more efficiently schedule its maintenance crews as well as the spare parts needed for each type of maintenance check.

By scheduling these performance checks in advance, the airline could save millions of dollars in inventory. Rather than store three-month's worth of spare parts in maintenance facility warehouses, the airline could better coordinate its maintenance checks with its suppliers, requiring them to deliver spare parts only when needed. The spare parts and the maintenance crew could even be timed to fly in and meet the out-of-service aircraft as it arrives at the maintenance facility.

The agent embedded in the aircraft could also be linked to the airline's capacity management system to enable the airline to more efficiently plan when to switch out the aircraft and how to route the aircraft so that it will be close to a maintenance facility as soon as it is due for maintenance. By more efficiently routing planes for maintenance checks, the airline could optimize each plane's service interval, significantly reducing the costs associated with downtime.

FIGURE 10.3 TRAVEL OF TOMORROW

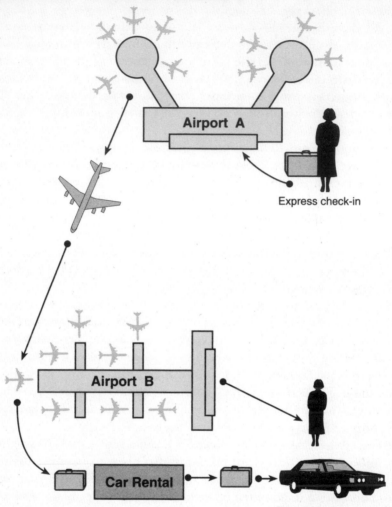

Express check-in

Express rental car pickup
with suitcase in trunk

WITH THE HELP OF ADVANCED TECHNOLOGY AND THE BROAD PART-
NERSHIPS SPAWNED BY ADAPTIVE BUSINESS NETWORKS, MANY
NEW SERVICES WILL EMERGE. IN THE EXAMPLE, A MAJOR AIRLINE
HAS FORMED A PARTNERSHIP WITH A RENTAL CAR COMPANY, A FI-
NANCIAL SERVICES COMPANY, A SUITCASE MANUFACTURER, AND
GOVERNMENT SECURITY AGENCIES TO ELECTRONICALLY TRACK
PASSENGER LUGGAGE THROUGH THE AIRPORT AND LOAD IT INTO
THE TRUNKS OF PASSENGERS' WAITING RENTAL CARS.

In addition to reducing costs, the adaptive business network offers airline companies creative ways to improve customer service. For example, imagine the competitive edge it would give airlines if passengers could choose from a variety of meals rather than the standard two choices. By installing airport kiosks that are linked via agents to the airline's food service company, the airline could offer customized meals to its passengers. As part of getting their electronic ticket, passengers could select their meal order, which would then be filled by the food service company before the plane takes off.

Similarly, adaptive networks and advanced technology may provide even greater service and convenience for travelers in the future. An airline company could join in a network with a car rental company, a financial services company, a suitcase manufacturer, and government security agencies to improve its baggage service for customers. Imagine the convenience for incoming air travelers if their rental cars were parked outside the terminal, with their luggage already stowed in the trunk. No more waiting at the baggage carousel to pick up luggage. No more boarding a shuttle bus to travel to a separate building in order to sign contracts and pick up cars (Figure 10.3).

Within this network, the suitcase manufacturer would manufacture luggage with preinstalled baggage ID units, which the airline would match to passenger tickets upon check-in at the airport. The financial services company that charged the flight and rental car to a credit card would log in the baggage ID number and then share this information with the rental car agency. This would also allow government security personnel to identify each bag before it's loaded on the plane.

When the plane arrives at the airport, the rental car agency would scan luggage on the incoming plane for bags belonging to its customers. Instead of heading to the baggage carousel to pick up luggage, rental car customers would walk empty handed to the curb outside the airport, where a representative from the rental agency would drive up in the customer's car—with the luggage already in the trunk.

The adaptive business network promises many opportunities for manufacturing, retail and service companies alike. It enables companies to create innovative products and services of value to customers, while providing companies in all industry sectors ongoing ways to reduce costs. Chapter 11 explores how adaptive business networks may evolve in the future, and what companies can do today to start moving in this direction.

CHAPTER ELEVEN

Future Implications of Adaptive Business Networks

Genius is 1 percent inspiration, 99 percent perspiration.

—Thomas A. Edison

I t's a typical day, several years in the future: You're driving home from work. As usual, you're thinking about dinner. What are the options for tonight's meal? You speak to your in-car personal electronic organizer, asking it what's on your grocery list. The automotive information system provides you with options for dinner based on your list.

You accept one of the computer's recommendations that requires a stop at the store for fennel root and sea bass. The car asks you whether you prefer to stop at the nearest grocery store or the one that you regularly shop at. With a voice command, you are prompted with directions to your favorite supermarket. Because your personal system—which links your car and home—and the grocery store network know your preferences, you are sent an alert that fresh local strawberries are available and that there's a special on your favorite French goat cheese.

You drive to the grocery store, which looks quite unlike today's big-box supermarket: It's an open-air style market with a produce section, a fish market, a bakery, an old-fashioned meat shop with a knowledgeable butcher ready to carve steaks just for you, and a dairy case with cheeses from around the world. You make your perishable selections, then stop by and pick up the remaining items from your shopping list—hand soap, razors, and salt—already boxed and ready to go. Behind-the-scenes systems automatically ready consumers' nonperishable products from their grocery list, filling the order from backroom supplies or a nearby warehouse (Figure 11.1). Why devote retail floor space to cereal, pasta, laundry soap, and toothpaste when consumers always buy the same brands? Why not have this shopping done for you behind the scenes? This allows you to hand select your avocados, lamb chops, and Gorgonzola cheese without having to push a cart through warehouse-like aisles simply to buy the same brand and quantity of toilet paper that you routinely purchase.

Now that your cart is loaded with fresh produce and other groceries, you walk out the door to your car without passing through the checkout line. This isn't shoplifting: Sensors by the exit doors scan the radio frequency identification (RFID) tags on the groceries and tally the prices as you walk by. Electronic agents in your portable electronic device, whether it be your cell phone, personal digital assistant (PDA), wrist watch, ID tag in your wallet, or a store "club card," notify the store of your banking or credit information, and the total is automatically deducted from your account.

BEHIND THE SCENES, IT'S NOT BUSINESS AS USUAL

This vision of the shopping future sure seems like heaven for the consumer: Your personal devices and systems will keep track of replenishing your groceries. In addition, you'll get to hand select your produce and perishable products while brand-name packaged goods are automatically boxed and delivered to your car or to your door.

This vision of the future also has distinct advantages to the networks that operate businesses such as grocery stores. If the consumer finds it convenient to always know that favorite brands will be in stock—courtesy of agents that relay these preferences to the grocery network—think how valuable this same information is to the retailer. The grocery network will have detailed consumer information about all the households and individuals in its service area. The store management will know who lives there, what their preferences are, and what their shopping habits are. It will be able to precisely target its audience with the products that consumers want. While average shoppers will be delighted to always find exactly what they are anticipating on the shelves, stores will be equally delighted to focus inventory on what sells.

Because the grocery store has access to your shopping profile, it knows exactly what to stock, what brands you prefer, the kinds of fish you

FIGURE 11.1 GROCERY STORE OF THE FUTURE

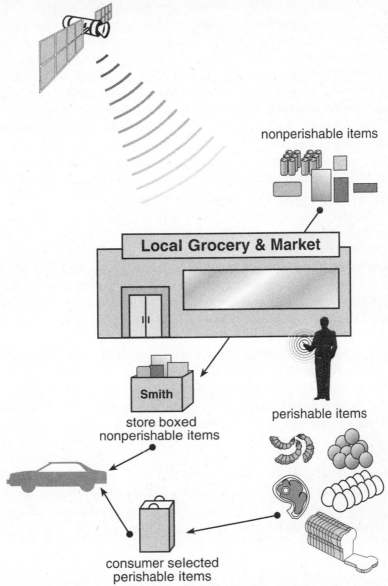

IN THE GROCERY STORE OF THE FUTURE, SHOPPERS MAY ACCESS
THEIR GROCERY LIST VIA A MOBILE PHONE OR OTHER PERSONAL DE-
VICE. CONSUMERS WILL BE ABLE TO AUTOMATICALLY TRANSMIT
THEIR GROCERY LISTS TO THE GROCERY STORE WHERE NONPER-
ISHABLE ITEMS WILL BE AUTOMATICALLY BOXED FOR DELIVERY TO
THEIR CAR OR HOME, WHILE THEY CONTINUE TO HAND SELECT PER-
ISHABLE PRODUCTS SUCH AS PRODUCE, BAKED GOODS, AND MEATS.

are likely to buy. The store will stock what the community profile requires. In so doing, the store will be able to remove hundreds of brands and products that sell very little, such as those cans of spinach and boxes of dried lima beans that gather dust on the bottom shelf. Not only will the retailer be able to reduce inventory, it will also have higher turns on its inventory dollars. It will also have a smaller footprint than modern big box grocery stores, making it more convenient and appealing to most shoppers. This also means lower real estate and overhead costs, and more opportunities for locating stores closer to where people live: If grocery stores focus more on produce, baked goods, and meats, and package and deliver nonperishable products out of a different facility, then these smaller stores can again be located in traditional neighborhoods. Fewer employees will also be required to staff these stores, especially as checkout becomes increasingly automated.

The potential for cost savings doesn't end with the storefront. Because buying patterns can be localized and individualized, manufacturers will be able to focus production much more precisely. A regional baker, for instance, would be able to look at precise sales information of cookies by household, by store, by variety, and flavor. With that level of information, it would know how much flour, sugar, chocolate, and nuts to order months in advance. It would know how many cookies—and which flavors—to bake to meet anticipated demand. If there was surplus production capacity at one cookie bakery, it could be sold to a partner or used to develop new brands or flavors of baked confections.

In response to information about customer demand, the cookie baker could also create special promotional packages designed to appeal to regional tastes, making a one-of-a-kind offering that mixes popular pecan shortbread cookies with new products, such as whole-meal English-style biscuits, to appeal to consumers in the United Kingdom. What's truly appealing about this vision is that consumers will perceive these changes as heightened customer service and access to the goods they truly want, while businesses realize greater profits.

MORE NETWORKED THAN EVER

In the future, each of us as consumers will become increasingly reliant on the technology around us, especially the technologies that will inhabit our possessions and our environment. These technologies will be able to communicate seamlessly with each other, linking our environments to provide us with constant access to our information systems no matter where we are. In the previous example, agents and devices interact to represent you to an array of adaptive business networks. You were visible to the banking network through one set of agents, to the grocery store through another, and to your automobile and appliance systems through yet a different set of agents. The adaptive business networks of the future will interact with each other to provide consumers with increasingly individualized products and services. All of these agents and devices will be seamlessly integrated to provide you with the products and services you expect.

The example also shows how cultural institutions—such as the grocery store—will change as adaptive business networks and advanced technology take hold. The agents that offer service to the consumer will also provide information to the commercial networks that manage them. This more interconnected, technology-driven economic model of the future offers major benefits to these networks. As agents personalize service to the point where the individual feels uniquely addressed, the companies behind these economic transactions will use information gathered by agents to greatly enhance their profits.

YOUR ELECTRONIC DEFENDER

One of the greatest concerns in a fully networked economy will be the preservation of privacy and security. Agents will keep tabs on what we want, what we do, where we go. Today, consumers have very few tools for protecting their identity and personal information. In the future, you will have an electronic defender to protect you, and consumers will have more say over how their information is revealed and to whom.

It's not just marketers that you need to be concerned about. Your agents and systems will know so much about you that other cultural forces will want a piece of the action. It's already clear that your Internet provider knows exactly what Web sites you visit—and so does your employer, if you explore the Web from your office computer. Your electronic shadow grows longer—and more interesting to others—the more connected you become. The agents that report your needs and activities might be helpful if they keep you stocked in your favorite brand of beer. However, they may be a hindrance if they report your comings and goings to your ex-spouse or to the police.

The way to handle privacy issues is through individual control. The devices that link you to the networks, providing them with information about your activities and preferences, can also act as your electronic defender. Your personal devices will include programmable decision agents—one of many examples of this new technology—that will act on your behalf, filtering information flowing in from the networks. You will be able to set up the decision agent in your personal mobile assistant to block all incoming promotions, or if you are grocery shopping, you could authorize it to present only information about specials and offers at your corner store. If you are in an unfamiliar city, you may authorize your decision agent to search guidebook databases for restaurant selections, and then to check for two-for-one meal offers within this selection.

In the adaptive business network, consumers will have control over their information, receiving a certain level of service for the amount of information revealed. In the future, security will not be attained by limiting access to information, rather by authenticating those who attempt to access it. This is a significant shift from the way security is handled today. Powerful industry-standard security encryption technologies will bolster the sanctity of data. Kerberos, a security system that authenticates users when they log in and renews their key at each new session, will be used with many of the coming agent applications. Together with unique ID systems that authenticate users and routes for data, Kerberos security systems will allow consumers and businesses to control access to their information.

THE ELECTRONIC SHADOW

The grocery store example also illustrates a future in which our possessions begin to track us within the larger network. Through your agents, your information will always be with you, accessible to you, and truly mobile. Whether you are in your house, your car, your office, or taking a walk, you will have access to your systems. You will be able to access this information through any number of devices whether it is the chip on your frequent flyer card, your PDA, your cell phone, or your automobile. Your electronic shadow will also protect you from unwanted information. Through the same set of agents and technology devices, the networks will know only as much about you as you let them—where you are, what you want to buy, what you are doing.

Personal Devices

Most of us are familiar with cell phones, and many of us already carry PDAs, which help keep track of our calendars and address books electronically. These two tools have already merged into a single hand-held device that is capable of wirelessly connecting to the phone, e-mail, and Internet networks while providing the features of small pocket-sized computers. In the future, these devices will become increasingly versa-tile—linking us to entertainment and commerce in addition to telephony, electronic communication, and computing. These gadgets will also be-come our primary method of participating in the interlinked networks that will increasingly surround all of us.

These handheld devices already possess the technological heft to function as our representatives in electronic networks. They can serve as our electronic wallets: Point your device toward the infrared reader on the gas pump to charge your gasoline purchase to your charge card. Your personal device could as easily become your primary source of identity in a variety of networks: Use it to check out books from the library, access medical files from your doctor and insurance company, or identify your-self to a security system. These are useful tasks for a piece of technology that many of us already carry.

In addition, your device will track what you do and buy, directing you toward products and services that match your preferences. Infor-mation about your activities can be made available to the networks, which will chart your choices and buying patterns. In turn, they provide you with services and products to address your interests and habits. Personal devices already have the capacity to power global positioning system (GPS) receivers, which track movement and location geographi-cally. At any moment, your position anywhere on the face of the earth can be determined within a few meters by roving satellites and made available to information gathering systems. It's easy to imagine walking the streets of Paris and receiving an alert on your mobile phone or other device: It's a nearby store that knows your interest in rare wine vintages. The shop has a bottle of a hard-to-find French Bordeaux that you've searched for in your travels and on the Internet. You check the display on your mobile personal assistant device for a map to the shop door, and make your purchase.

This technology, like any other, can be abused or taken to the ludicrous. The technology is being used poorly and abusively if it merely collects information about consumers without providing a valuable service. Information will be pervasive, yet access to this information will be very much at the control of the consumer, who can determine how much information to reveal based on the level of service guaran-teed in return.

Automobiles

Your car will also increasingly be your representative in the network system—no small wonder given the amount of time many of us spend commuting. It may take a while to get used to thinking of your car as a moving computer. However, it will quickly become your portable terminal, your mobile interface to the network.

Cars are already being produced with highly sophisticated computing and satellite guidance systems. OnStar, an in-vehicle computing platform with links to GPS, is offered in some General Motors, Acura, Saab, and Saturn automobiles. The system comes with a number of safety, communication, diagnostic, and guidance systems, including emergency service notification in times of distress. For instance, if your airbags deploy, OnStar contacts the ambulance, police, and insurance company. Systems like OnStar will soon allow you to listen to and respond to e-mails while driving, as well as receive personalized stock quotes, Internet news, and sports scores.

Your car will also be a source of information about you for the network. In these cases, the car and its sensors become part of the network. These networks seek information about you from the agents embedded in the car.

Like the cell phone and PDA, the car will be a place where networks overlap. One day, you will be driving down the freeway and notice that your gas tank is low. Your in-vehicle computer service will alert you that the best price for gasoline is at the Shell station, or that the next Exxon-Mobil station is another five miles away. Perhaps McDonald's and Texaco are offering a combined special coupon that involves a free car wash with every Big Mac. Your car becomes a receiver of network deals and offers from the gasoline company—at the same time, it connects to a food network (McDonalds) and remains linked to a GPS and satellite communication system (Figure 11.2).

Home, Sweet Home

Another interface with the network will be your home itself. Consumers, if they desire, will be able to link different devices within their homes to the network to provide a wide range of advanced services to help them manage daily tasks more easily.

Today, companies are already moving in the direction of making the home the centerpiece of a connected environment. For example, General Electric SMART offers a SMARTONE system that connects to household

FIGURE 11.2   GAS STATION OF THE FUTURE

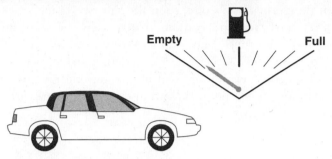

**The in-car navigation
and information system**
Points out gas is low
Provides directions to the gas station
you prefer
Automatically deducts your fill-up
from your credit card as you drive away

FUELED BY PARTNERSHIPS FORMED VIA ADAPTIVE BUSINESS NET-
WORKS, MULTIPLE TECHNOLOGY SYSTEMS WILL BE LINKED TO DE-
LIVER NEW SERVICES AND CONVENIENCES FOR CUSTOMERS. IN THIS
EXAMPLE, ELECTRONICS AND SATELLITE SYSTEMS INSTALLED IN CARS
DIRECT DRIVERS TO THE NEAREST GASOLINE STATION TO REFUEL
USING MAPS ON A MULTIFUNCTION DISPLAY SCREEN ON THE CAR
DASHBOARD. THE GASOLINE PUMP IS READIED FOR THE CUSTOMER'S
PREFERRED QUALITY OF FUEL AND AUTOMATICALLY CHARGES THE
GAS TO THE DRIVER'S BANK ACCOUNT OR CREDIT CARD.

structures to enable your home to automatically open windows and sky-lights when dangerous levels of carbon dioxide are reached, close win-dows when it's dark, feed pets automatically, view the front door from your TV when the doorbell rings, plus a host of other features. The com-pany, formed by Smart LLC, General Electric Industrial Systems, and Mi-crosoft, focuses on developing consumer automation systems that combine hardware, home network, and operating systems with state-of-the-art automation software.

THE ELECTRONIC YOU

It may already seem like technology is everywhere, but for this vision of the future to take effect, devices and technology will need to be even more omnipresent. Computing will need to be pervasive. This may con-jure up frightening images from sci-fi thrillers, but the truth is that the more agents and technology are embedded in the environments we live in, the more services they can provide. These services will seem frag-mentary and easy to dismiss until they are seamless. A talking refrigera-tor, a smart cell phone, and a car with an on-board computer are each fascinating in their own right. However, it's only when these devices are linked together into an expanding series of networks and services that we will see the full potential of agents and other advanced technology. At that point, this technology will seem no more unusual than electricity, a now-pervasive wonder from another generation.

In the future, pervasive technology agents will be everywhere. They will be present in the tools we use to transact business and access enter-tainment, in the products we buy and consume, and in the environment that we live in. We will use them for our convenience and pleasure. Based on the permission we give them, they will constantly gather information about us—our preferences and our needs. The networks will use the in-formation to better provide us with the services and products that we will come to expect.

How will the networks gather all this information? Accompanying the evolution of the adaptive business network will be a highly sophisticated technology concept called Extended Relationship Management (XRM). The next evolution of customer relationship management (CRM), this new technology will chart the relationships between buyers and sellers and adaptive business networks. Through agents, XRM will track your electronic identity across multiple networks. This system will know about you, your direct family and your extended family. It will also know about your "influencers," another network of friends and compatriots identified by e-mail and phone patterns. XRM will also know where you go—again through phone calls, sales patterns, and GPS readings. XRM will also know what you buy and what you like: It will know your buying habits and preferences, the hotels you like, the food you like to eat. This information will be available to the networks as a kind of discipline, a deep science to prognosticate your future needs. XRM doesn't exist yet. However, pattern-based learning is a concept and practice that has existed for years and is a predecessor to XRM. Only consumers will have more control over access to these patterns tomorrow than they've had previously.

Through XRM, no matter where you go, an electronic specter precedes you. Your preferences and habits will be known, and predictions will be made about your future choices. Through the information gathered by agents and other technologies, the network systems will be able to create an electronic representation of you. Using your past behavior, the networks will attempt to foresee your next most likely actions. Within the network infrastructure—using knowledge of your past purchases, your present geographic location, and dozens of other traits that are deduced from your previous actions—your electronic shadow will act. This electronic version of you knows what you like to eat, what you like to buy. Through your devices, your shadow can provide you with suggestions based on what you like, inviting you to repeat your patterns.

A Constant Flow of Information

As with consumers, businesses will have a much larger scope of information constantly available to them. The adaptive business network of the future will provide businesses with instantaneous visibility into important information, allowing them to precisely understand and manage their inventory, as well as customers' exact response to their products and services. This visibility will dramatically change the way companies operate.

Inventory Visibility

Companies will have precise information about their inventory throughout the supply chain, and this information will be extremely accurate and always available. As a result, companies will no longer have to go through the costly and time-consuming exercise of physically counting their inventory. All products will have RFID locator tags, meaning they can be found instantaneously, whether they are in a warehouse, en route to a customer, at the store, or located elsewhere within the network. Companies will be able to track inventory at whatever level they desire, whether by pallet or even by individual unit, if necessary. Having information available by unit means that companies no longer need to worry about loss, theft, or counterfeit products. In the future, companies will know exactly how much inventory they have, where it is, whether it's selling, whether it's aging, whether it has been tampered with, and whether someone has created an unauthorized clone.

Customer Visibility

Not only will companies have access to precise information about inventory; they'll also know exactly what customers are buying, and this information will be available to them instantaneously. Companies will be able to track each "moment of truth"—the moment at which a consumer purchases its product. They will know the exact location at which each product and service sells, the time it was purchased, and even the exact customer who purchased the product. This level of information will enable companies to target their products and services to the consumer far more precisely than is possible today. It will also give them the ability to manage their brands and sales channels at a micro-cosmic level, and develop promotions targeted at each individual consumer. Imagine knowing that a first-time customer has just picked up a bottle of your company's shampoo off the shelf to read the label, and being able to offer that customer a 50 percent first-time purchase discount on the spot. These are the types of promotional opportunities companies in an adaptive business network will be able to take advantage of in the future.

TIME AS A VARIABLE

In today's business world, time is thought of as fixed. Most companies work in a small number of time zones, and draw their primary production materials from a limited geographical area. In the future, time will become a variable within the workplace. Tasks like delivering materials to the customer, designing products, and managing product brands become follow-the-sun activities. Once a company shuts down for the day, it can pass tasks like these to a company division across the world, making it possible for work on the project to continue around the clock. As company operations become increasingly globalized and connected with their partners via advanced technology, companies will work 24 hours a day to design, produce, and deliver products and services to their customers. As a result, companies will be able to create new products and services and get them to the customer far more quickly, while responding to changing market conditions much faster than is feasible today.

SERVICE TO THE UNIT OF ONE

Once this level of pervasive computing is reached, the adaptive business network can add more participants, link companies together more tightly, and sense and respond to information more quickly. As a result, networks will be able to deal with you as an actual individual rather than an individual in a certain category. When the networks are integrated and we as consumers can interact nearly instantaneously with them through a variety of constantly connected devices, we will reach the serviceability of one. The networks will have so much information about your tastes, your habits, and your history that they can deliver to you what will seem a level of unique personalization and customization. The products and services that are offered to you will be so individualized that it will seem as if all the power and resources of the networks are focusing on you and you alone.

Let's say you are flying to Europe. Connected to a larger network, the airline will know your seat preference and provide you that seat. In the seat flap in front of you are the magazines you prefer. Because the network is aware of your interests, specialty promotions and information sheets are also provided. If you love classical music, you may discover reading material about the London Philharmonic. You may find a two-for-the-price-of-one coupon for classical music recordings at your favorite music shop. At mealtime, you will be served the food and drink that the networks know you prefer. Once you arrive, your hotel will already know that you prefer rooms with a separate bath and shower, and that you want a U.S. standard bed. On the night table are offers for tours that focus on your interest in gardening. Room service knows to bring you a glass of sherry as you begin planning your next day's well-coordinated adventure in London.

Do the networks that provide you these services actually have you uniquely targeted? Not exactly. The networks will have so much information about you—your activities, your preferences and information about outside factors such as the weather and cancelled flights—that they will appear to know everything about you. The networks will appear aware. In reality, they will simply be parsing your information into ever-smaller categories. The service to the unit of one may feel like it's all about you, but in truth the service is to you and all the other people who fit your description, have similar interests, and who occupy the same geographic location.

A larger audience increasingly will know your personal tastes and needs. This information will lead to more and better-focused advertising and promotions. This will be an inevitable by-product of a more fully and pervasively networked life. As networks move toward truly individualized service, the delivery of promotions and advertising will seem less onerous. We will receive unparalleled levels of service created seemingly for our own uniquely personal delectation. It will become gratifying, because it's all about you.

For companies, the ability to precisely target promotions means more sales. Category management systems will track information with a greater degree of granularity and precision, and will provide information to companies about true patterns in customer demand down to the individual consumer. No longer will companies lose potential sales because of general patterns that don't fit a specific customer. Just because a customer is 65 years old, for example, doesn't mean she doesn't like to play computer games on her Sony Play Station. Today, companies base their promotions on broad purchase patterns. Targeting promotions to the unit of one will enable companies to promote their products and services to customers with far more precision, enabling them to dramatically increase sales.

WHEN NETWORKS OVERLAP

In five to eight years from now, as adaptive business networks become the norm for globalized companies, what will business be like? When business competition is no longer between companies but between networks of companies, how will the business world be different?

As networks grow, they will form alliances with each other. They will overlap. At a minimum, these inter-network partnerships will reduce the inefficiencies that exist between companies and even between networks. Duplicate functions, such as processing orders, will be reduced, and costs for items such as transportation and financial services will decrease as companies increasingly pool resources. You'll also see shared adaptive business networks taking on the power to radically reduce the time it takes to serve customers. The more this time is compressed, the less inventory there is in the system. The resultant cost reductions can be used as a competitive tool against other nonnetworked companies and can be passed on to consumers as lower costs.

THE IMPORTANCE OF BRANDS

The creation of strong product brands will be even more important in the future than it is now. People like brands because they associate them with a certain taste, value, texture, and feeling. They associate them with the qualities that propelled them to buy in the first place. Brands with the highest name recognition and the most perceived value will live on; those with the least will die off.

Strong product brands will be of critical success to the networks. As individual companies continue to form ever-larger networks, their brands will live on. Networks will take consumer's allegiance to particular brands and give them the products they want and expect. However, they will be able to deliver these brands at a fraction of the cost of traditional companies and in new and inventive ways that will simply enhance brand loyalty. You don't care who makes the products and brands you prefer. You just want them to be exactly the same each time you purchase and consume them. How it gets on the shelf, the paper that goes into the packaging, and the ink that goes into the printing—this is where the network can save money and makes profits. All the consumer cares about is that the brand does not change, and that their products and services are consistent.

In adaptive business networks, whoever has the best and most brands wins. For this reason, we will continue to see the global consolidation of companies according to the so-called Rule of Three, popularized by the Harvard Business School, which says that competitive forces in market segments will always end up creating three dominant players.[1] In the future, there will likely be two major dominant companies that each control 30 percent to 40 percent of the market and whose products compete head to head. Think of Twinings and Lipton, tea companies that have dominated the world tea trade for more than a century. There will also likely be a smaller, more innovative third company that will control 10 percent to 20 percent of the market. This company will be able to offer more specialized, more original products than its larger competition because it can move more quickly and deftly. That's exactly what Celestial Seasonings, an alternative herbal tea company based in Boulder, Colorado, did as it introduced flavored herbal teas and expanded globally in the late 1980s.

However grim the Rule of Three may seem to those of us who enjoy broad choice and wide selection, we probably won't even notice—because customers will continue to have a variety of brands from which to choose. As networks merge and grow stronger, their products will have brand cache. For example, German carmaker BMW could have a strong network in the future, focused on the production and distribution of high-end performance automobiles. The association with quality and chic will induce other companies to join the BMW network, to be viewed as part of the BMW brand. A chocolate maker, a clothing manufacturer, or a florist may well see advantage in promoting their products as endorsed by the BMW network. Also, the large brand-driven networks may find it beneficial to join together for strength and market penetration. Imagine the BMW network, the Sainsbury's grocery network, and the Chanel perfume network all joined for mutual promotion and association to provide an image of an upscale lifestyle.

RETURN OF THE GUILD, OR SOMETHING AKIN TO IT

As networks grow larger and more powerful, one fear is that mass commoditization of products will render a gray sameness to the goods they manufacture: a rush to the lowest common denominator. This will not be the case. While the networks will certainly produce commodity products efficiently, they will also deliver opportunities for high-quality, customized products. Every network will require a contingent of people and companies with highly specialized skills that can make customized products for individual customers.

These individuals and companies will also serve as a source of innovation for new products and services for the network. They will function almost as guilds—small groups of experts who band together for greater strength and security. These groups already function at the edges of many industries. In the movie making industry, for example, cadres of costume designers, set designers, and other experienced professionals enhance their value by forming alliances. You see small expert groups in steel making and paper manufacturing forms specialty mills to produce small quantities of expensive, top-quality products. You see it in the computer industry, where expert software and hardware developers work together in ad hoc partnerships to deliver unique, one-of-a-kind products for demanding customers.

Today, these small companies and experts are at a disadvantage because they don't have access to the same distribution channels as larger, better-established companies. The network will need their skills and, in return, these experts will have access to the network's larger market. As consumers, we will see a greater variety of innovative products come on the market quicker and at a lower price than today.

In fact, many networks will attempt to distinguish themselves by the quality and number of guilds and expert craftspeople they can attract. In this way, the adaptive business network has the potential to play a role in the development of economies beyond the first world. Expert craftsmanship will always be a valuable skill and asset for a network. Networks can give craftspeople in emerging economies a worldwide market for their products, boosting their standard of living, and creating local demand for services to fill the needs of these frontline entrepreneurs. By linking these artisans to a globalized network of consumers, adaptive business networks can provide positive, incremental economic change to communities untouched by the traditional engines of today's economy.

THE TIME IS NOW

Although the future may be grand, it will take hard work to make it happen, and the time is now for beginning to change your company. You picked up this book because you know that your company has to change the way it does business. Sticking with the status quo isn't an option. Companies need to confront a business reality in which everything is in motion, and in which they expect the unexpected.

The adaptive business network provides opportunities and benefits for all businesses. It's a model that will help companies prosper in a healthy economic climate, while giving them the tools and resources needed to weather the not-so-good times. In a world where costs are rising and profit margins are constantly squeezed, the adaptive business network provides businesses with a road map toward sustainable cost savings and ongoing new revenue opportunities.

Companies don't need new technology to get ready for the adaptive business network. They don't need agents. The key is to start now. There are very simple and inexpensive actions to take today that will prepare companies for the adaptive business network. Start the small stuff now. You can't jump to adaptability without passing through the early steps outlined in this book, or without verifying that your company has implemented the business processes necessary to move toward the network model. The adaptive business network is a discipline. Because the network is propelled by the dynamics of change and flexibility, building a network is an ongoing process of reinvention and ingenuity. There's no time like the present to begin this journey.

The business world has already seen large-scale changes occur, and their impacts are being felt today. Globalization is radically changing the way businesses operate. The ability to add production capacity is outpacing customer demand for products. Access to working capital is becoming more limited. Consumers increasingly expect customized products delivered when and where they need them.

The question is which companies can adapt quickest to these changing economic conditions. Companies that are the first to move to the adaptive business network will be the winners because they will quickly gain a competitive advantage over other companies. If you want to be a winner, start now. Use the tools and technologies outlined in this book. If not, you will risk extinction.

It's your choice: Adapt or die.

GLOSSARY

A

acquisition Act of acquiring a company, typically in a cash or stock purchase transaction. (See also *merger.*)

adaptability Capability to adapt or be flexible amid changing conditions.

adaptive business network A new business model that flexibly links companies to loose consortia that collectively work together and adapt to meet the needs of customers.

Advanced Planning System (APS) Technology that enables companies to coordinate materials and resources, sequencing their arrival and deployment to best serve customer demands and corporate needs.

agents Small, pervasive software applications that perform single tasks such as counting, monitoring, or scheduling. Agents operate cooperatively with other agents, legacy applications, and other standard software applications. Agents typically operate at the edge of the network in nontraditional computing devices. Examples include point of sale systems, automated gasoline pumps, and manufacturing cell process controllers. Agents enable local operations on unstructured data, and have varying degrees of capability depending on their role. (See also *pervasive technology.*)

automation The removal of manual steps in a process, enabling tasks or functions to operate on their own without human interaction.

Sources: The American Heritage® *Dictionary of the English Language, Fourth Edition* © 2000 by Houghton Mifflin Company. *Merriam-Webster's Collegiate® Dictionary* © 2002 by Merriam-Webster, Incorporated. Computer Desktop Encyclopedia © 2001 Computer Language Company Inc. *Merriam-Webster's Dictionary of Law* © 1996, Merriam-Webster, Incorporated. *Strategic Supply Chain Alignment* © 1998 by editor John L. Gattorna; Gower Publishing Limited. *Wall Street Words* by David L. Scott © 1997, 1988 by Houghton Mifflin Company.

B

bar codes   Patterns of lines, spaces, numbers, and alphabetical characters read by electro-optical systems. Since their invention in the early 1950s, bar codes have greatly improved the flow of products and information in business and commerce.

bow-tie effect   Bottlenecks in the flow of information and decision making that occur as a result of the fact that the purchasing and sales departments or customer service departments form the only point of contact between two companies.

brand management   The process of creating, improving, and protecting the perceived customer value of a specific product. The main purpose of brand management is to create increased customer sales via customer/brand identification.

bullwhip effect   The principle that the farther away a company is in a supply chain from the consumer, the more exaggerated its product orders and inventory accumulation become. The bullwhip effect is similar to the childhood telephone game, in which a phrase whispered ear-to-ear becomes increasingly distorted the farther it gets from the originator. This supply chain concept has come to be known as the bullwhip effect for the analogous way in which the tip of a whip travels faster than the part near the handle when in motion.

bundling   Combining several products and/or services into a single salable unit with greater perceived value than the sum of the parts.

business excellence initiative   A program, system, or concept designed to increase the efficiency of company processes.

Business Process Reengineering (BPR)   A concept that calls for corporations to continually revamp core business processes to increase efficiency and better reflect current business realities. (See also *business excellence initiative.*)

buyer-seller relationship   Roles and interactions between companies in a linear supply chain that are limited to buying and selling specific products. These interactions are typically short-term, individual transactions.

C

cash-to-cash cycle   The period of time, usually measured in days, between when a company turns liquid cash into product inventory, sells the product to a customer, and collects payment.

channel management   The process of coordinating supplies, production, and distribution with a specific sales channel.

collaboration   The process of jointly working together in a cooperative fashion.

Collaborative Planning, Forecasting, and Replenishment (CPFR)   A business concept in which multiple partner companies reduce inventory and decrease costs by working together to plan total inventory, forecast demand for their products, schedule shipments, develop production schedules, and perform other tasks of importance to all participants.

commoditization   The process by which a common product, which is widely standardized in form, size, or other specification, progressively declines in value due to excess supply or pricing pressures caused by multiple companies producing the product with little differentiation.

community   A group with similar interests or goals. In an adaptive business network, the group of companies that exists in the early stages, prior to the emergence of a coordinating partner.

compliance to plan   The measurable ability to adhere to business plans, particularly production plans.

conglomerate   A legal corporate entity comprised of several smaller companies or business divisions.

consumer-supplier relationship   A one-to-one relationship between two companies in a supply chain that includes the traditional buyer-seller relationship properties as well as the sharing of consumption, planning, scheduling, and forecasting data.

consumption   The act of consuming or using a product, materials, or services. In *Adapt or Die,* consumption refers only to usage by a next-in-line company in a linear supply chain.

controls   The limits, regulations, or thresholds set by management or another authority, within which decisions may be made by companies or employees.

coordinating partner   The lead company in an adaptive business network. Typically, this company is responsible for managing the product or service brands and sales channels within a linear supply chain. Or it is the company—often a retailer—that has commercial relationships with the customers who purchase the finished product or service.

core competency   A company's primary business objective, best skill, or strength. The brand or sales channel with which a company has the most success, often responsible for the majority of revenue.

creative destruction   A concept, spawned by economist Joseph Schumpeter in the 1930s and rekindled by more recent books, which suggests that businesses have greater success when they constantly reinvent themselves by shutting down failed business units, ending slumping initiatives, or halting underperforming products in favor of new ideas. More recent concepts include a company rapidly making its own existing products obsolete by replacing them with new products.

Customer Relationship Management (CRM)   Computer software applications or other technologies that manage the various points of contact between the elements of a company and its customers to provide better service.

D

decisions   To decide, come to a conclusion, or commit to an action. In *Adapt or Die,* decisions refer to choices based on information received within preestablished controls or parameters set by the network.

delayed differentiation   The practice of postponing the elements of a product that make it unique until closer to the time the customer makes the purchase. By delaying differentiation, companies broaden the market for their base products while offering customers a variety of post-production options and choices.

E

Earnings Per Share (EPS)   A common financial measurement based on a company's net income or loss, divided by the number of outstanding common stock shares for a given period of time. In the United States, this is typically a three-month-long calendar quarter.

Electronic Data Interchange (EDI)   Internationally standardized electronic communications technology enabling companies to send orders, notifications, and other messages to linked partner companies.

electronic defender   A concept calling for consumers to control access to their personal and private data via aggressively protective technology that acts on their behalf.

electronic shadow   A concept in which people's personal and private data and preferences have omnipresence via portable electronic devices, electronic cards, or other mobile means.

end customer   The company or consumer at the end of the supply chain that purchases the final product or service.

Enterprise Resource Planning (ERP)   Computer software applications or other technology designed to integrate and manage companies' internal resources, such as employees, assets, business units, or functions including marketing, sales, finance, accounts payable/receivable, and human resources, among others. (See also *business excellence initiative.*)

exchange   A computerized clearinghouse for the purchase and sale of goods and services, where an electronic mediator collects bids and routes responses. Exchanges are typically characterized as public and open to any willing participant, or as private and closed, open to only selected participants.

execute   To perform or carry out a decision. One of the key characteristics of the adaptive business network.

Extended Relationship Management (XRM)   A proposed evolution of Customer Relationship Management (CRM) technology that will predict personal preferences and purchases based on complex patterns. XRM is expected to be capable of tracking consumers across multiple business networks. (See also *Customer Relationship Management.*)

Extensible Markup Language (XML)   A technology standard for exchanging data via the Internet.

G

Global Available-to-Promise (ATP)   Technology that allows companies to earmark product inventory and planned production for specific customers and suggests reallocation schemes whereby materials in short supply are distributed to customers based on order value or customer importance. The technology checks stock in multiple locations, and searches against planned production and inventory receipts, suggesting substitute products if the requested finished product or component is not available.

Global Positioning System (GPS)   A satellite system used for military and commercial purposes to pinpoint the location of objects anywhere on earth. To be traced using these satellite systems, objects must have chips embedded in them.

guild A group of workers with a similar skill, trade, or profession who band together for mutual benefit.

H

hard assets Tangible assets such as real estate, vehicles, or other real property. (See also *soft assets*.)

hard demand Demand emanating from the customer at the end of the supply chain that purchases the finished product or service, as opposed to from a supplier's next-in-line customer. (See also *consumption*.)

hard-pegged Product inventory earmarked or allocated for a specific customer that cannot be reallocated or altered based on predetermined factors. (See also *soft-pegged*.)

I

information A collection of facts, data, or knowledge. In *Adapt or Die,* information fuels decisions within the controls set by managers of the network.

inventory A list or survey of items, materials, or products currently in a company's possession or ownership. (See also *Key Performance Indicator*.)

inventory accuracy The ability to precisely tally inventory.

inventory track and trace Technology capable of tracking the quantity and location of inventory from production to storage to shipment.

J

joint venture The resultant new company formed by a partnership of two corporations to jointly target a new market or mitigate risk.

Just in Time (JIT) A business logistics concept under which materials, supplies, or other inventories necessary for production are synchronized to be shipped and available at the last possible moment prior to consumption by the customer.

K

Key Performance Indicators (KPIs) A set of business measurements of efficiency, profitability, or other factors critical to a company's success. These measurements are directly quantifiable.

L

linear supply chain   A cascading and interdependent set of suppliers, each reliant on the next-in-line supplier to manufacture a specific product.

liquid crystal display (LCD)   A specific type of visual display screen used in many electronic devices.

loose consortium   An associated group of companies or business entities combined in cooperation for mutual benefit.

M

management   The authoritative or governing body within a group or corporation. In *Adapt or Die,* management defines the relationships between adaptive network elements. This relationship dictates the controls within which decisions are made by employees or technology.

master agreement   A standing contract that establishes certain procedures, requirements, quality standards, and base minimums, costs, specifications, shipment dates, times, and locations or other factors between companies. Within the adaptive business network, companies create master agreements to define terms for working together and to avoid perpetual paperwork for frequent and routine transactions.

Material Requirements Planning (MRP)   Technology that enables manufacturers and suppliers to determine necessary materials for production and to appropriately sequence production, delivery, and consumption to meet certain goals. (See also *business excellence initiative.*)

mechanization   The use of machines or technology to directly replace manual steps without change in a process, while still requiring human interaction to oversee and validate the completion of these tasks and functions. (See also *automation.*)

merger   The combination or union of two previously independent companies. (See also *acquisition.*)

min-max threshold   The minimum and maximum limits for orders, inventory, and so on. As companies move to an adaptive business network, they mechanize orders that fall within the min-max threshold, while manually negotiating orders that fall outside these thresholds. (See also *controls.*)

N

next-in-line customer   The company immediately succeeding another in sequence in a linear supply chain.

niche player   A company generally small in size and with focused core competencies. Rather than providing a wide range of products or services, niche players commonly develop a tightly focused set of products or services, often dominate their markets, and closely control quality.

O

one-to-many relationship   Relationship in which one participant interacts or communicates with multiple participants simultaneously, as in a broadcast.

order   Formal requisition of goods or services for purchase. An order represents a financial commitment between two legal entities.

order position   Status of an order during the fulfillment process. This includes the state of the materials, their location, order fulfillment time, and the shipment and arrival dates.

order-to-cash cycle   Period of time, usually measured in days, between when an order is placed and when payment is received.

P

peer-to-peer   Direct, unmediated one-to-one relationship between two entities. (See also *point-to-point relationship*.)

Personal Digital Assistant (PDA)   Electronic device, typically portable and enabled with wireless communications connections, designed for personal computing needs such as calendar, contact information, to-do lists, note taking, e-mail communication, and other tasks.

pervasive technology   Technology that when implemented broadly and uniformly enables access to new ephemeral information and visibility into business operations and personal activities, and is capable of automating tasks and functions 24 hours per day, seven days per week. This technology is "always on" and "always there." (See also *agents* and *Web services*.)

plan   Proposed course of action based on prior knowledge and future prediction. The ability to plan is one of the key characteristics of the adaptive business network.

point-to-point relationship   Direct link or association between two entities. (See also *peer-to-peer*.)

portal   Opening or entrance; an access point. Specific to the technology industry, a vast collection of information or resources on a single Web site.

production waste   Unusable material and lost worker productivity that results from the production process. Two types of production waste exist—controllable waste, which results from faulty production, mistakes, and other errors, and uncontrollable waste, which cannot be entirely prevented as in small scraps of leftover material. (See also *Key Performance Indicators*.)

profit   Excess monetary gain resulting from and calculated by the subtraction of total costs and expenditures from revenue of sales.

R

radio frequency identification (RFID)   Wireless technology capable of instantly tallying, tracking, and tracing inventory and data—among other tasks—via electronic identification tags and scanners, or readers, based on electromagnetic frequencies. (See also *inventory track and trace*.)

real-time   Technology industry lexicon describing the ability of computer systems to nearly instantaneously update information as it is generated or received.

respond   To reply, answer, or act. One of the key characteristics of the adaptive business network.

Return on Assets (ROA)   The measurement resulting from and calculated by subtracting the value of certain assets from revenue or profit generated by those assets. (See also *Key Performance Indicators*.)

Return on Investment (ROI)   The measurement resulting from and calculated by subtracting the investment in certain initiatives from the revenue or profit generated by those initiatives.

revenue   The total monetary income produced by a company or a subset.

Rule of Three   A business concept frequently attributed to the Harvard Business School and popularized more recently by authors and professors Jagdish Sheth and Rajendra Sisodia, suggesting that three primary companies will dominate most industries over time. Although theories vary, most estimate that two large competitors will dominate 70 percent to 90 percent of a market, with one primary challenger that is smaller and potentially more innovative, and possibly other niche players operating on the fringe.

S

Sales, General, and Administrative (SG&A)   Financial term and catchall for common generic costs of doing business, frequently referred to as overhead.

sense To perceive. One of the key characteristics of the adaptive business network.

sequencing Systematic arrangement of business processes, such as production, packaging, and shipping to increase manufacturing efficiency and best coincide with the needs of customers.

service to the unit of one Marketing concept in which companies know so much about customer buying habits that it appears to the customer that companies are marketing to them as single entities with unique needs and preferences, rather than as part of a larger demographic group with similar backgrounds and interests.

soft assets Assets that are intangible or difficult to measure such as patents, processes, or the collective knowledge and experience of a workforce. (See also *hard assets*.)

soft-pegged Product inventory earmarked or allocated for a specific customer that can be reallocated to accommodate other orders due to incoming inventory available prior to shipment of the original order or the availability of alternative products. (See also *hard-pegged*.)

stock-out Situation in which a company has run out of available inventory for a specific product or material.

suboptimization Practice of operating individual business divisions within a company as stand-alone units, each with the goal of independent profitability, which can lead to poor customer service and undermine the profitability of the overall corporation. (See also *transfer pricing*.)

T

Theory of Constraints (TOC) Business excellence initiative that seeks to improve efficiency by limiting the bottlenecks or restraints on processes within a company. The theory suggests that, like the weakest link in a chain, the speed of the system is dictated by the slowest part of the process. (See also *business excellence initiative*.)

time compression Reducing the time needed to complete a task. By participating in adaptive business networks, companies can reduce the time required to complete several different types of tasks. (See also *Key Performance Indicators*.)

time to supply The time required to fulfill an order. This is measured from the time a product is ordered to the time it is received. (See also *time compression*.)

Total Quality Management (TQM)   A business excellence initiative designed to increase product quality. (See also *business excellence initiative.*)

transfer pricing   The practice of individual business divisions within a company, which are operated as stand-alone units each with the goal of independent profitability, transferring money and paying each other for goods or services rendered so as to better track profitability per division. (See also *suboptimization.*)

V

Vendor Managed Inventory (VMI)   Inventory replenishment scheme in which the supplier monitors customer inventory levels as well as production plans and demand forecasts and takes responsibility for ensuring products are replenished as needed.

Vendor Replenishment (VR)   Inventory replenishment scheme in which the customer notifies the supplier of its consumption and the supplier determines the appropriate replenishment level and time. The customer retains responsibility for maintaining proper inventory levels.

vertically integrated company   Corporation that controls many, if not most, aspects of its linear supply chain.

visibility   Ability to be viewed or seen. In *Adapt or Die,* visibility means a clear, unobstructed forward-looking view via accurate information and forecasts.

W

Web services   Flexible applications and tools for businesses delivered or accessible via the Internet that can interact with each other based on the exchange of data in standardized protocols, usually XML. (See also *pervasive technology.*)

working capital   Excess assets, measured in liquid currency, beyond debt and other liabilities that a company uses for daily operations. Typically manifested as a revolving line of credit from a bank or other financial institution. (See also *Key Performance Indicators.*)

Notes

Introduction: When Bad Things Happen to Good Companies

1. U.S. Department of Commerce, Bureau of Economic Analysis, "Table 1.16: Gross Product of Corporate Business in Current Dollars and Gross Product of Nonfinancial Corporate Business in Current and Chained Dollars," *National Income and Product Accounts Tables* (Washington, DC, 2002), http://www.bea.doc.gov/bea/dn/nipaweb/index.asp.

2. U.S. Department of Commerce, Bureau of Economic Analysis. "Real Inventories, Sales, and Inventory-Sales Ratios for Manufacturing and Trade: 1997IV–2001II," *Survey of Current Business* (Washington, DC, October 2001), http://www.bea.doc.gov/bea/ARTICLES/2001/10october/1001isr.pdf.

3. Hoisington Investment Management Co., "Quarterly Review and Outlook: First Quarter 2002," (Austin, TX, 2002), http://www.hoisingtonmgt.com/HIM2002Q1NP.pdf.

4. Dan Givoly and Carla Hayn, "Rising Conservatism: Implications for Financial Analysis," *Financial Analysts Journal* 58, no. 1 (January/February 2002).

5. Forbes.com, "The Forbes 500" (May 2002), http://www.forbes.com/2002/03/27/forbes500.html.

Chapter One   In Search of the Holy Grail

1. Stephanie N. Mehta, "Cisco Fractures Its Own Fairy Tale," *Fortune* (May 14, 2001): 104.

2. Weyerhaeuser Co. (March 2002), http://www.weyerhaeuser.com.

CHAPTER TWO   SEEKING PARTNERS FOR GREATER COMPETITIVE ADVANTAGE

1. As cited by Eric Young, "Web Marketplaces That Really Work," *Fortune* special edition (November 19, 2001).

2. Ibid.

3. Ibid.

4. Jupiter Media Metrix, "Online Retailers Will Turn to Drop Shippers As Almost Half Lose Money on Shipping and Handling," press release (February 8, 2001), http://www.jmm.com/xp/jmm/press/2001/pr_020801b.xml and as reported by Eric Young, "Web Marketplaces That Really Work," *Fortune* special edition (November 19, 2001).

CHAPTER THREE   THE ADAPTIVE NETWORK VISION

1. Tony Chien and Dianne Ahrens, "E-procurement: The Future of Purchasing," *Circuits Assembly* (September 1, 2001): 26.

2. John Karolefsky, "Collaborating Across the Supply Chain," *Food Logistics* (September 15, 2001): 24.

CHAPTER FOUR   ROLES AND RESPONSIBILITIES WITHIN THE NETWORK

1. Patagonia Inc., "Defining Quality: A Brief Description of How We Got Here," fall 1998, http://www.patagonia.com/culture/press_room.shtml; revenues as reported in "The 2001 CIO-100 Honorees," *CIO Magazine* (August 15, 2001), http://www.cio.com/archive/081501/honorees_content.html.

CHAPTER FIVE   PREPARING FOR AN ADAPTIVE BUSINESS NETWORK

1. Lawrence Jeff Johnson, "Key Indicators of the Labor Market 2001–2002," United Nations International Labor Organization report, as cited in ILO Focus, Vol. 14 No. 3, fall 2001 issue, at http://us.ilo.org/news/focus/0110/FOCUS-6.HTML.

CHAPTER TEN THE ADAPTABLE BUSINESS NETWORK IN PRACTICE

1. Jim Carbone, "Who Holds the Inventory," *Purchasing* (April 19, 2001): 37; Matthias Holweg and Frits K. Pil, "Successful Build-to-Order Strategies Start with the Customer," *MIT Sloan Management Review* (October 2001): 74; and Gary McWilliams, "Dell Takes the Price War Gambit," *The Wall Street Journal Online* (June 7, 2001), http://zdnet.com.com/2100–11–530007.html?legacy=zdnn.

CHAPTER ELEVEN FUTURE IMPLICATIONS OF ADAPTIVE BUSINESS NETWORKS

1. Jagdish Sheth and Rajendra Sisodia, *The Rule of Three: Surviving and Thriving in Competitive Markets* (New York: Free Press, 2002).

BIBLIOGRAPHY

Ayers, James B., Ed. *Handbook of Supply Chain Management.* Boca Raton, FL: St. Lucie Press, 2001.

Bramel, Julien, and David Simchi-Levi. *The Logic of Logistics: Theory, Algorithms, and Applications for Logistics Management.* New York: Springer Verlag, 1997.

Covey, Stephen R. *The Seven Habits of Highly Effective People: Powerful Lessons in Personal Change.* New York: Simon & Schuster, 1989.

Dobyns, Lloyd, and Clare Crawford-Mason. *Quality or Else: The Revolution in World Business.* Boston: Houghton Mifflin Co., 1991.

Downes, Larry, and Chunka Mui. *Unleashing the Killer App: Digital Strategies for Market Dominance.* Boston: Harvard Business School Press, 1998.

Fine, Charles H. *Clockspeed: Winning Industry Control in the Age of Temporary Advantage.* Cambridge, MA: Perseus Publishing, 1999.

Fingar, Peter, and Ronald Aronica. *The Death of "e" and the Birth of the Real New Economy.* Tampa, FL: Meghan-Kiffer Press, 2001.

Fleisch, Elgar. "The Concept of Networkability—How to Measure and Manage Networked Enterprises." Working paper, Institute of Information Management, University of St. Gallen, 2001.

Fleisch, Elgar, and Hubert Österle. "Lessons Learned From Coordination Theory: Toward a Model of the Networked Enterprise." Working paper, Institute of Information Management, University of St. Gallen, 2001.

Gattorna, John, Ed. *Strategic Supply Chain Alignment: Best Practice in Supply Chain Management.* Hampshire, England: Gower Publishing Ltd., 1998.

Goldratt, Eliyahu M. *Critical Chain.* Great Barrington, MA: North River Press, 1997.

Goldratt, Eliyahu M., and Jeff Cox. *The Goal: A Process of Ongoing Improvement,* 2nd rev. ed. New York: North River Press, 2000.

Goldratt, Eliyahu M. *It's Not Luck.* Great Barrington, MA: North River Press, 1994.

Goldratt, Eliyahu M. *Theory of Constraints.* Great Barrington, MA: North River Press, 1999.

Goldratt, Eliyahu M., Eli Schragenheim, and Carol A. Ptak. *Necessary but not Sufficient: A Theory of Constraints Business Novel.* Great Barrington, MA: North River Press, 2000.

Grove, Andrew S. *Only the Paranoid Survive: How to Exploit the Crisis Points That Challenge Every Company and Career.* New York: Currency Doubleday, 1996.

Hammer, Michael. *The Agenda: What Every Business Must Do to Dominate the Decade.* New York: Crown Business, 2001.

Hammer, Michael, and James Champy. *Reengineering the Corporation: A Manifesto for Business Revolution.* New York: HarperBusiness, 1993.

Heifetz, Ronald A., and Donald L. Laurie. "The Work of Leadership." *Harvard Business Review,* December 1, 2001.

Hughes, Jon, Mark Ralf, and Bill Michels. *Transform Your Supply Chain: Releasing Value in Business.* London: International Thomson Business Press, 1998.

Industry Directions Inc. "Creating Competitive Advantage from Performance Management." Report, summer 2001.

Jiminez, Maria, Lora Cecere, Karen Peterson, and Frank Buytendijk. "Measuring Collaborative Supply Chain Effectiveness." Gartner Inc. report, May 23, 2001.

Kotter, John P. "What Leaders Really Do." *Harvard Business Review,* December 1, 2001.

Kuglin, Fred A., and Barbara A. Rosenbaum. *The Supply Chain Network @ Internet Speed: Preparing Your Company for the Internet Revolution.* New York: AMACOM, 2000.

Maes, Pattie, Ed. *Designing Autonomous Agents: Theory and Practice from Biology to Engineering and Back.* Cambridge, MA: MIT Press, 1990.

Martin, James. *The Great Transition: Using the Seven Disciplines of Enterprise Engineering to Align People, Technology, and Strategy.* New York: AMACOM, 1995.

Peters, Thomas J., and Robert H. Waterman, Jr. *In Search of Excellence: Lessons from America's Best-Run Companies.* Reissue edition. New York: Harper & Row, 1982.

Peters, Thomas J. *Thriving on Chaos: Handbook for a Management Revolution.* New York: Knopf, 1987.

Peters, Thomas J. *The Pursuit of Wow!: Every Person's Guide to Topsy-Turvy Times.* New York: Vintage Books, 1994.

Peters, Thomas J. *The Circle of Innovation: You Can't Shrink Your Way to Greatness.* New York: Knopf, 1997.

Peters, Thomas J. *The Project 50: Fifty Ways to Transform Every "Task" Into a Project That Matters!* New York: Knopf, 1999.

Peterson, Karen, Chad Eschinger, and Ned Frey. "Supply Chain Collaboration: Lessons from the Leading Edge." Gartner Inc. report, August 8, 2001.

Pine, B. Joseph II. *Mass Customization: The New Frontier in Business Competition.* Boston: Harvard Business School Press, 1993.

Radjou, Navi, Laurie M. Orlov, and Taichi Nakashima. "Executive Overview: Adaptive Supply Networks." Forrester Research report, February 22, 2002.

Radjou, Navi, Laurie M. Orlov, and Taichi Nakashima. "Adaptive Agents Boost Supply Network Flexibility." Forrester Research report, March 11, 2002.

Radjou, Navi, Laurie M. Orlov, and Taichi Nakashima. "Adapting to Supply Network Change." Forrester Research report, March 2002.

Senge, Peter M. *The Fifth Discipline: The Art and Practice of the Learning Organization.* New York: Currency Doubleday, 1990.

Shapiro, Jeremy F. *Modeling the Supply Chain.* Pacific Grove, CA: Duxbury, 2001.

Simchi-Levi, David. *Designing and Managing the Supply Chain: Concepts, Strategies, and Cases.* New York: Irwin McGraw-Hill, 2000.

Stone, Peter. *Layered Learning in Multiagent Systems.* Cambridge, MA: MIT Press, 2000.

Valdero Corp. "From Planning to Control: Improving the High-Tech Supply Chain." Report, 2002.

Viewlocity. "The New Extended Supply Chain Concept—Unleash the Potential of Your Supply Network." Report, 2001.

Wisnosky, Dennis E., and Rita C. Feeney. *BPR Wizdom: A Practical Guide to BPR Project Management.* Naperville, IL: Wizdom Systems Inc., 1999.

World Wide Web Consortium (W3C), http://www.w3.org, 2002.

ABOUT THE AUTHOR

Claus E. Heinrich, PhD is a member of the Executive Board of SAP AG, where he is responsible for a range of critical internet supported enterprise software solutions, including my SAP.com applications for supply chain, product lifecycle, and human resources management as well as for finance and accounting. Heinrich serves as vice chairman of SAP's Product and Technology Board and is also responsible for human resources and labor relations at SAP AG.

Heinrich has been a member of the Management Science faculty at the University of Mannheim since 1988 and teaches supply chain management.

Bob Betts has been involved in the information technology field for over 20 years. He has worked on some of the most challenging business and technological problems, including the first and second generation IBM PCs, the World Wide Military Command Control System, on the NASA Hubble Space Telescope, and the NASA Space Station Freedom. Since 1985, Betts has worked globally as a consultant and company employee on supply chain and related business issues.

INDEX